Margaret P. Simkin

四川書简

Letters from Szechwan
1923 – 1944

by
Margaret T. Simkin

Friend in the Orient
Committee,
Pacific Yearly Meeting
of Friends
1978

Printed by Celo Press

Published in 1978 by
the Friend in the Orient Committee of
Pacific Yearly Meeting of the
Religious Society of Friends

Printed by Celo Press
the printing and publishing department of the
Arthur Morgan School
Route 5, Burnsville, North Carolina

ISBN 0-914064-08-8
ISBN 0-914064-09-6

In Memory of Robert Louis Simkin

and

Recorded for Mary, Bob, Arno and Nina

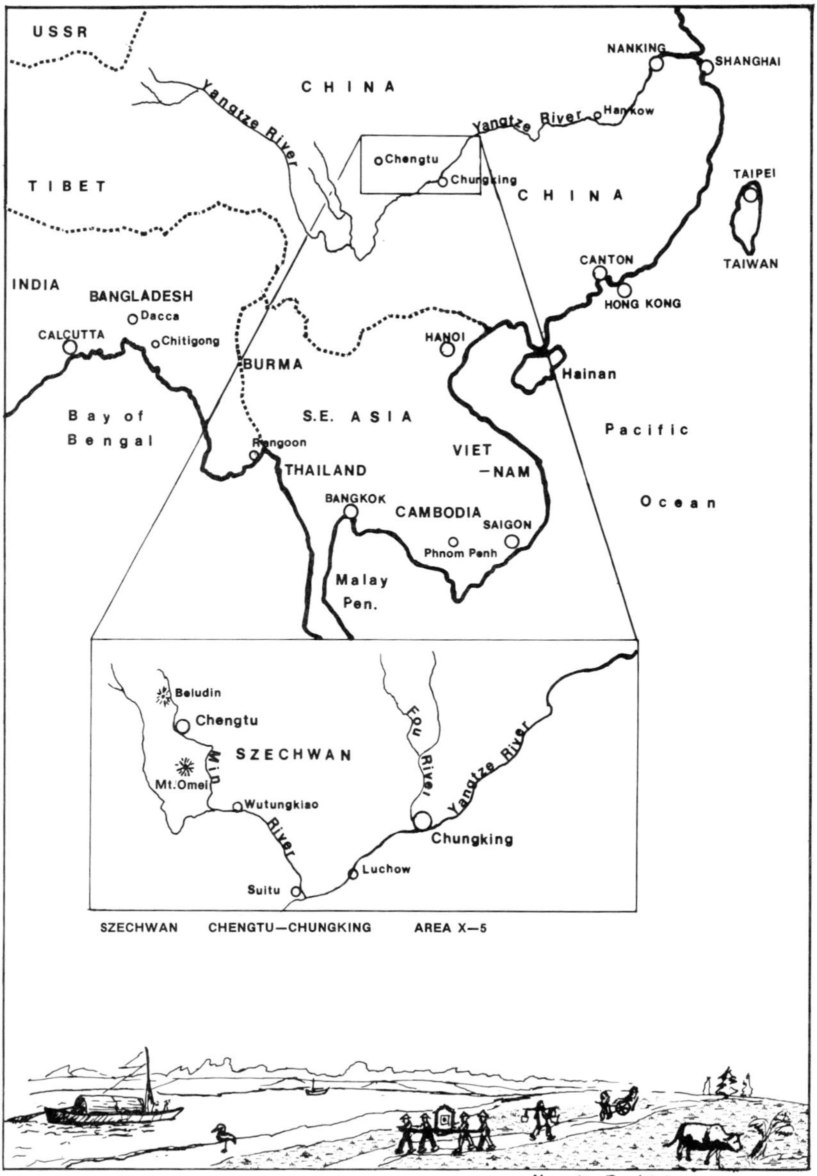

Map by Floyd Schmoe and Jeff Johnson

FOREWORD

Probably the Pacific War (World War II) brought Szechwan, China, to the attention of the American public as nothing had before; it was then that Chungking, Szechwan became known as China's capital. The war mercifully is long since over but it is hoped that the letters included in this book will add a bit of knowledge and interest in this land of the "Four Rivers" (tr. Szechwan).

English Friends (Quakers) entered Szechwan in 1886. Well before 1923 when the writer first went to China there were five Monthly Meetings (Quaker equivalent of local churches) in the province, at Chungking, Tungliang, Suining, Tungchwan and Chengtu. In 1910 English Friends together with Canadian Methodists (later the United Church of Canada), the American Methodists and the American Baptists founded the West China Union University (W.C.U.U.). About 1918 the English (Anglican) Church Missionary Society entered the union. American Friends also shared in the University through the appointment of Robert L. Simkin to the staff. The cooperation in this union was outstanding. The plan was this: Each participating Mission maintained a unit comprising dormitories and athletic field for its students and residences for its staff. These were grouped about a central plot on which were located the main University buildings. In this central section the teachers contributed by each Mission all joined in teaching the students of all Missions. Students were not only Szechwanese but some came from Yunnan and Kweichow provinces as well.

The W.C.U.U. was located about a mile outside the south gate of Chengtu, the capital of the province. Within the walled city of Chengtu the Manchu rulers had built and occupied a walled garrison. After the overthrow of the Manchus in 1911 the Chinese gradually absorbed their conquerors and the wall of the inner city was torn down. That section of Chengtu, however, continued to be called Manchu City.

Chengtu lies in the center of a plain some seventy miles long and forty miles wide. The plain is supplied with water from a river which has its source in the high mountain country west of northwest Szechwan. The river waters are led off at Kwanhsien by means of a marvelous irrigation system initially planned by Li Ping in the third century B.C. The waters fertilize the entire plain, which yields exceptionally heavy crops. Famine has never been known in the immediate area. Although Chengtu is the same latitude as New Orleans (30 degrees) it is colder because of its altitude, about 1750 feet. Excessive humidity adds severity to the summer heat and to the winter cold.

All Szechwan has an area approximately that of France. In 1923 it had an estimated population of sixty million; its two largest cities, Chungking, a treaty port and trading center, a population of 600,000, and Chengtu, administrative center, a population of nearly 500,000.

This book is a collection of excerpts of letters written from and about Szechwan between 1923 and 1944. Many of the letters are offhand notes meant for intimate family members. Others were intended for wider reading and are more thoughtfully and carefully written. Letters of Robert L. Simkin are also included for clarity and continuity.

To the many friends who have encouraged the writer and have given advice in editing the great numbers of letters carefully preserved by Fannie C. Timberlake warm thanks are due; also to the Los Angeles, Claremont, University and Orange Grove Friends Meetings and the Pacific Yearly Meeting's Friend in the Orient Committee, all of whose generous support has made publication possible. Special thanks go to Lois NeSmith who typed the manuscript, to Aimee and Langdon Elsbree for their great help in its final editing, to Martha Dart and Floyd Schmoe who from beginning to end have given counsel and encouragement, and to Robert Vogel and the American Friends Service Committee office in Pasadena for their generous help in launching the completed book. Grateful recognition is due Davis Miller and Danny Liu for the book cover design and its Chinese calligraphy. A special word of thanks goes to Floyd Schmoe for his sketches.

Claremont, California — Margaret Timberlake Simkin
October 29, 1977

Table of Contents

The authors are standing beside their boat after it had been wrecked during their trip to Chengtu, Szechwan, to begin work there in 1923.

四川書简

Land of the Four Rivers 1923 – 1931

A journey of a thousand miles
begins with a single step.

Lao-tze

A Long Journey 1923

Prelude

"Go up on the bridge at once if you hear shots," we were told by the captain as we boarded the *Fuhwo* at Hankow. It was all very exciting and I didn't feel the least bit afraid. I was a bride of a few months and had already heard of the perils of the Yangtse Kiang. Had not Robert, my husband, told me many a tale of shipwreck and brigands? I had the utmost confidence that he with a bit of God's help would be equal to any eventuality! I was a *tsai lai di* (newcomer); he had been well schooled in China's ways since 1906.

We had sailed from Vancouver September 6, 1923, on the *Empress of Russia*, the first ship to leave Canada after Japan's disastrous earthquake on September 1. Sailing had been delayed for several hours so that cargo already in her hold could be removed and food stuffs for Japanese sufferers loaded. This was but one of many delays on our long journey to the West China Union University at Chengtu, Szechwan in western China where we were to make our home in the years ahead. We had orders not to touch at Yokohama and consequently missed seeing Friends from the Mission in Tokyo who were to have come to meet us. But we did have a day at Kobe, which we took to go up to Kyoto, and later a day at Nagasaki. Our Japan visit was not quite what we had planned, but as far as we could learn, the Shiba section of Tokyo had escaped serious damage. Esther Rhoads* and other Friends were safe. The charm and beauty of the island country, in which just about everything from the kimonoed girls to the tiny gardens seemed so very diminutive, were a sheer delight.

Then for us it was on across the rough Yellow Sea to Shanghai where

---

**Earlham College friend teaching at Friends Girls School, Tokyo.*

we were met by Charles Boynton,** a classmate of Robert's at Union Theological Seminary in New York. The great international city of Shanghai with its famous *Bund* and beautiful office and state buildings was impressive; the other Shanghai, the native Chinese city, crowded and sordid, was depressing. Being in Shanghai meant an opportunity to meet with outstanding people such as Henry T. Hodgkin (English Quaker) and prominent Chinese figures including Mr. Chung, secretary of the National Christian Council.

In Shanghai our baggage was loaded on the *Fuhwo*, a name auspiciously meaning "Happiness and Harmony," for the river journey to Chungking while we boarded the train to Nanking to visit the Friends (Ohio Mission) there. Time was short and sightseeing limited to a ricksha ride to see the new buildings at Nanking University and nearby Ginling College in its beautiful setting. Since the *Fuhwo* was not scheduled to stop at Nanking we caught another steamer to Hankow to wait for her there.

Now on October 3, almost a month after our Vancouver sailing, we were aboard the *Fuhwo*, a trig little boat, clean and pretty, with powerful engines to take us through the Yangtze River gorges and rapids. On board we found Dr. and Mrs. Joseph Taylor of the West China Union University in Chengtu and Miss Crawford, a nurse stationed at Suifu, whom I had met the previous summer at Northfield. The three of them were to prove good companions. The captain was a young Welshman and we all liked him even after his warning about brigands. The chief engineer and the first officer were Scotch and talked with a delightful burr. Going up on the bridge we found it well protected. There were iron plates which could be let down over the windows in case we were fired upon! All seemed well.

October 6, 1923 — *On board the* Fuhwo

Dear Ones at Home,

We are anchored in the river at Ichang. We do not know how long we shall be delayed here. We hear bad reports from up river. Chungking is under fire. Yang Sen, a lieutenant of Wu Pei Fu, is trying to hold the city against the Yunnan and Kweichow troops of an opposing faction. Wu Pei Fu is reported to have told Yang Sen that if he fails to hold Chungking he may expect no more aid from Peking, so Yang Sen is not likely to surrender until he is absolutely forced to. The soldiers are

---

***In 1923 Charles Boynton was principal of the new American School in Shanghai.*

seizing food and impressing the coolies.* Two buckets of water sell for a thousand cash,** a sum about equal to a coolie's wages for two days. Our captain is awaiting instructions from Shanghai before proceeding up river.

October 7, 1923]*Confucius' birthday*] *On board the* Fuhwo *at Ichang*

We went ashore this morning for a walk. In one crooked street we met a funeral procession, which was a strange mixture of Christian and non-Christian practices. Our attention was first attracted by the loud explosion of firecrackers. Then we saw coming along the street a large cross decorated with paper flowers. The little girls marching behind looked very neat in their clean blue cotton jackets. Each wore a white paper lotus blossom, symbol of immortality. The boys who followed had bands of rough unbleached cotton cloth around their heads. The most peculiar sight was the "chief mourner," the eldest son dressed in a long robe of sackcloth walking slowly ahead of the coffin (carried by men) with bowed, covered head and supported on either side by a relative or friend. The women of the family rode in chairs which followed the coffin in a long single line. They were dressed in sackcloth or white garments, or at least had bands of unbleached muslin about their heads, and wept audibly and ostentatiously into large pocket handkerchiefs.

We almost had to stoop to get through one street because all along the way, just over our heads, wet clothes were hung out to dry. How convenient a method! Slip a bamboo pole through the sleeves of the jacket and one of the trouser legs and then place the pole across the narrow street so that it rests on the low eaves of the opposite house. Along the edge of a pond women and little girls were beating clothes on flat stones. The pounding of many wooden paddles sounded like house cleaning time at home when the neighbors beat their carpets.

And such miserable dogs! You hear at home of the dog scavengers of the East, but you have no conception of what they are like until you see these wretched curs on the streets of Ichang.

**"Coolie" was a term commonly used for a Chinese laborer. The word is derived from two Chinese characters meaning "bitter strength"--not inappropriate considering the extremely hard labor these people did.*

***Nominally the copper cash bore a fixed ratio of 1,000 to a tael, or silver ingot, later silver dollar, but the ratio naturally varied with the price of copper and silver. In 1923, 1000 cash was probably equivalent to less than 50 cents in U.S. money.*

We five passengers attended the five o'clock meeting at the Church of Scotland chapel, the service being read in English. I have never heard the Bible read more beautifully or reverently than it was by this Scot, Mr. Kearney.

October 8, 1923

News from up river is still far from reassuring. One British steamer has been sent back down by the British gunboat because it had passengers aboard. The *Alice Dollar* is going up soon but only to carry cargo. It does not look as if we should get through soon.

October 10, 1923

Birthday of the Chinese Republic. We still wait for the river to quiet down....Robert and I walked to the old Ichang pagoda and back this afternoon, a fine walk along the river of about five miles.

October 22, 1923 *Chungking, Szechwan*

Dear Ones at Home,

We finally moved back onto the *Fuhwo* for good the evening of the 16th. Before light the next morning we were off. Formerly it took twenty-six days to go by houseboat from Ichang to Chungking. By steamer we made it easily in four days. The beauty and grandeur of the Yangtze gorges delighted and thrilled us. For many miles the river twists and turns through noisy, swirling rapids or through the lonely stillness of deep gorges. Sheer cliffs rise hundreds of feet from the river. At times we were hemmed in on all sides until a sharp turn brought us around a shoulder and opened up a new vista of river, mountain, sky. Along the towering cliffs above the river we saw the footpath used by the trackers who pull the junks through the rapids and also saw the grooves cut in the solid rock by the friction of the heavy bamboo ropes. Although steaming ahead at the equivalent of fourteen knots, the boat barely held its own in the *Yie Tan* (Wild Rapid) which at this time of year is especially hazardous. So steep is the river bed at the *Yie Tan* that the inclination of the river surface is clearly perceptible from the boat. No wonder these rapids with their swift currents were the despair of steam navigators for many years! We saw no houseboats --only a few junks--and these tied up near cities because of the unsettled conditions of the country.

Steamers coming down river informed us by messages written on a blackboard of points where they had been fired upon by brigands. Nothing eventful happened to us, however, until last Saturday when we had a rather exciting day. First we met Yang Sen's retreating army. There must have been several thousand soldiers. They looked like a never ending stream of ants moving in an unbroken line, up hill and down, along the north bank of the river. The entire line stretched for miles. When our boat drew in closer to the shore we could see stretchers and sedan chairs with wounded men being carried by coolies who had been impressed to bear them. Besides all this we saw boatload after boatload of uniformed soldiers going down river. We kept partly under cover behind the iron plates, which had been put up along the deck, but no one threatened to fire on us. It was feared that there might be looting at Ichang when the troops got down that far.... About eleven o'clock the first officer called us foreign passengers up on the bridge. We were nearing a point where brigands had been reported to be hiding and the captain wanted us to be safe. At 11:33 at Lidu the shooting began. The bridge was well protected and all the windows were closed with iron plates except the center one where the pilot stood. The captain and the first and second officers stood with guns pointed through the small openings in each of the three window plates on the south side. I didn't mind being fired upon, for we were quite safe, but I didn't like the officers firing in return. Perhaps they didn't shoot to kill, but their obvious zest in making the men on shore scurry to cover distressed us. Fortunately we were soon past Lidu, but we stayed on the bridge until we had passed another danger point. There was no more firing, however. Later we found that one of the bandits' bullets had hit and slightly dented the iron plate set up outside our cabin.

We arrived in Chungking Sunday morning (October 21). Chungking is a great city of 600,000 "set upon a hill." We climbed a long flight of wet, mucky steps and through the gate into the city. All water, except from wells and cisterns, must be brought up from the river over these steps in buckets slung from a pole carried on men's shoulders. The Yunnan troops still occupy the city. Soldiers are everywhere and they still impress coolies. I saw a soldier beat a poor fellow on the back who was staggering up the steps under a heavy load. We have seen families trying to restore their homes after they had been used to stable horses, and we have heard that parents are taking their engaged daughters to their fiances to be married to relieve themselves of all responsibility. One wonders how long the Szechwanese will endure this military occupation. More than once before the troops of Szechwan and Yunnan have united to drive out the northerners.Then the Szechwanese have had to turn about and oust their recent allies.

We have engaged passage on a small steamer to Suifu and expect to go by native boat from there to Chengtu. I shall be glad to have some mail once more.

October 29, 1923 *On the Yangtze River above Chungking*

Dear Fannie,

Last week at this time we were in the hills opposite Chungking, first with the R.J. Davidsons and then with Miss Cumber, all of the Friends Mission (English). The hills are beautiful--pine woods, vines, and lovely ferns. We enjoyed our walks over the hills immensely. Two nights we heard firing only a few miles away. There was no danger, but it was not pleasant, especially one evening in particular when we had to walk along a lonely path from Huntley Davidson's. To be sure it was almost as light as day because of the moon (the moonlight all three nights up in the hills was simply entrancing), but we were relieved to get back to the Hill School compound. Miss Cumber, small and elderly, is a brave woman. More than once the soldiers have come to her gate and pounded upon it demanding admittance. Alone she has faced a hundred soldiers, called for their officer, explained to him that the place was a girls' school and that she could not let his men come in. She told us how on one occasion the officer apologized and took the men away at once. She says they are afraid of her!

I found Chungking a dreadful city. After coming down from the beautiful hills it seemed worse than before. To step immediately from America into such conditions would be unendurable, but the gradual transition makes it more bearable...the filth is awful and I do not dare attempt to describe the beggars.

We had moved onto the *Shutung* bag and baggage Friday afternoon (October 26). I wish people at home might know what "moving" in China means. Heavy trunks, packing cases, bags, camp beds, pianos--*everything*--must be carried by *men* down the long flights of steps at Chungking to the river bank.

Captain Lupton, the master of the *Shutung*, is a fine young Englishman. He is most courteous and gentlemanly, and is greatly admired along the Yangtze. He has given up his cabin to us ladies. The boat is supposed to carry only Chinese passengers. The men sleep in the Chinese cabins using oiled sheets to protect them from vermin. We are traveling comfortably and so far have had no excitement except for a few shots from bandits yesterday afternoon. They were holding up junks but we steamed on past without stopping

Language study does not progress as I like. I have decided that this business of learning Chinese is like the wandering of the Israelites in the wilderness before entering the promised land. It is the necessary chastening before the raw recruit is fit for service.

We should reach Suifu tomorrow night or the next day. Our journey from there will be by native boat.

November 9, 1923 *On the Min River below Kiating*

Dear Folks at Home,

First it was an ocean liner, then river steamers, and now a small river boat. The first few days were bright and warm and I thoroughly enjoyed this new experience. It is a simple, idle life--endlessly fascinating. We watch the trackers pull and maneuver the boat through the ever changing scene. The country along the river is open with now and then a hamlet and occasionally a walled town. Our cook prepares three meals a day for us on a stove made out of a five gallon oil tin!

Today is a real November day, drizzly and dreary and cold. You would marvel as I do to see the trackers plunge, sometimes waist-deep, into the cold water with never a quiver. Going up stream they walk along shore pulling the boat by means of a bamboo rope, except at places where there is a bad current, or when, for some other reason, they have to wade out, clamber onto the boat, and row to the other side. This is a much nicer way to travel than going across country by sedan chair, getting up before daylight in order to get an early start, and having to rush with meals. It is not without its thrills, however. Day before yesterday at a bad rapid our rope broke twice midway in the torrent. The second time our captain and helmsman jumped onto the Taylors' boat to fasten our rope to its mast so that it might be carried across a wide intervening bay to the trackers who were then far ahead.* The boats drifted apart and here we were going down stream with none of the crew left aboard except the cook, an old woman! Robert, however, managed the boat successfully with the help of the woman** and the shouted directions given by men from the other boat, until the two boats could be brought together long enough for the helmsman to leap aboard. It was an exciting moment! We then rowed out of the current into a little inlet where we waited for the trackers. They put up the sail and rowed furiously across the river. When the trackers, four to seven on a boat, row with all their might for the opposite shore, the strong current carries the boat diagonally down stream for a long distance. This particular instance was one of the few times that the men have used the sail. I heard them whistling and asked what it meant. They were calling for the wind to come to their aid, and surprising to say, the sail did begin to puff out and away we

---

**Sometimes the trackers are over two hundred yards away, and at others but forty or fifty.* [From Robert Simkin's notes.]

***Probably the wife of the pilot-helmsman boat owner and thoroughly familiar with maneuvering a boat.*

went simply flying across the river. If it works as successfully every time I do not wonder they whistle with such a serious, earnest air.

We walk when we can get ashore. We can easily keep up with the boat. In China roads are paths, and such a path will never cease to have a charm for me. These "roads" are not laid out in any studied fashion. I do not mean they are not *built*; indeed stones and steps are laid, but they seem to go where the tramp of feet has already packed the earth or worn the way. It is fun to follow one and let it take you where it will: along the top of a narrow dike which separates the irregular-shaped rice fields, or over the brow of a hill, or under the hill beside the steep bank covered with ferns and vines and growing things, then over a quaint little stone bridge--almost *anywhere*, winding and turning in a most fascinating way. I love the clumps of feathery bamboo and the grand old banyan trees (*whang-go*)* with their wide spreading branches and gnarled roots. Under the *whang-go*, in its inviting shade, there is almost sure to be a wayside shrine with images and half burned incense sticks.

We left the Yangtze at Suifu having followed its course for 1,700 miles. It was a joy to see the clear, green waters of the Min after that long journey over the mighty but muddy Yangtze. It was interesting to see the waters of the two streams mingling as they swirled around in whirlpools.

It was great fun getting into Suifu that evening. There are eighteen adult foreigners in the place and practically all of them were at the river to meet the Taylors, Miss Crawford, and ourselves. We stayed with the Cossums, who live across the main river from the city at the Baptist Middle School for boys. I never felt more accepted anywhere. These people living far inland do appreciate the sight of home folks. The Baptist Mission people at Suifu are a splendid, congenial group with a fine spirit.

You may be interested to know more about how we are living on our *bantou* (native boat). We have our two camp cots at one end of our quarters in the center of the boat; a box of stores on top of the steamer trunk makes a washstand, separated by a curtain from another big box which serves as our dining table. In this section our cook is already asleep on his *pu kai*. This much of the boat is permanently covered with bamboo mats which keep out the rain fairly well. The crew members sleep on the stern and bow on the *pu kais* (wadded quilts). At night

---

**Actually the Chinese* whang-go, *although a tree of the same genus, is not a banyan.*

they pull mat strips over these parts of the boat also. Four times a day they eat their rice and vegetables prepared in a shallow iron pan over an open fire built in the front of the boat. There at the bow they sit on their haunches and, holding rice bowls close to their mouths, they shove the food in with their chopsticks with great relish. Under the floor is our baggage. The boat leaks some and has to be bailed frequently, so we keep close watch on our boxes to be sure they do not get wet. I practice my meagre Chinese on our cook. You should hear me hesitate and stammer and then listen to him say the thing to me in English! We have just about the same things to eat that we would in our own home.

Saturday morning

We are getting into Kiating (pronounced jah-din'). It is still cool, but I am comfortable wearing several wraps. As soon as the river goes down after the summer floods crops are planted along the banks which makes the landscape with its fresh green growing things look more like our New England May than our November.

November 20, 1923 *The Last Lap of Our Journey*

Dear Friends at Home,

Yes, we are on the last lap of our long river journey into the heart of China. To really know the perils and thrills of this mighty water system one must travel on a native boat as we have these last two hundred miles since leaving Suifu. I have thoroughly enjoyed the simple outdoor life, especially before I became personally acquainted with its dangers. Let me tell you what happened to us at Kiating.

We had just crossed the river and were pulling up alongside a raft of logs when another boat, also crossing the swift current, crashed into ours, crushing in one side and driving the cross partition through the other side. I could hear the water pouring in, and we quickly began to sink. We picked up our typewriters and Robert helped me across the raft. By the time he could get back to the boat everything was under water and he had to stoop down to reach under the mat roof to pull things out. For several minutes it looked as if the boat must go to the bottom. And on that boat were our wedding presents, clothes and supplies to last for years!

By this time some of the foreigners who had seen the boat flying an American flag were on the shore to help us. A crowd of Chinese had also gathered but most of them looked upon the accident as an entertaining spectacle rather than as an opportunity to lend a helping hand. After considerable shouting and bickering about price, a few small boats were brought alongside the wreck and men began to pull up our boxes and trunks with long hooked poles. Naked divers brought up more of our possessions. It is not a pleasant sight to see your trunks being hoisted out of the river with streams of water pouring out of them, but that is much better than having them sink to the depths below or be swept away by the current. As it was, our suitcases, my traveling bag, some tinned goods, and a box belonging to the Sawdons* were tipped out or washed away and were never seen again. We believe now that our twenty cases of kerosene oil which filled the bottom of the boat kept our other cargo from sinking. After filling, the boat had tipped until the mast was nearly level with the water surface. With a rope fastened to this mast, the men finally succeeded in pulling the boat around the raft toward shore and into shallower water. Here men in small boats on either side raised the hulk so the remaining boxes could be recovered.

As soon as the baggage and packing cases were brought to shore coolies began carrying them, dripping wet as they were, to the Baptist Mission compound. There Mrs. Adams and Mrs. Clark (Baptist missionaries) and I began at once to unpack. We soon were standing in pools of water. It stood inches deep in the trunks and had worked its way everywhere into everything. Pasteboard boxes were soggy and when we took the covers off to get at the contents the water streamed out. Had we been longer in getting things out colors would have run much worse than they did. Before many hours most of the foreigners of Kiating, kind hearted people that they are, were at work helping us and we had clothes strung on lines all over the compound and papers and books laid out to dry. A number of those who helped had a sympathetic feeling because they had had similar experiences.

We were favored with a good bit of sunny weather, unusual in Szechwan, and were fairly well dried out and repacked seven days after the accident. Some things will need further attention when we reach Chengtu.

We engaged another boat, loaded on our goods, and here we are on the way once again.

Yesterday I saw, for the first time, men riding on wheelbarrows. This means we are on the Chengtu plain. We hope to arrive in Chengtu on the 23rd, in plenty of time for our Thanksgiving Day dinner.

**English Quaker family in Chengtu.*

November 24, 1923 *Home of the Sawdons [English Friends]*
Chengtu, Szechwan

We arrived yesterday in time for dinner with the Sawdons (with whom we are to live). We walked the last three miles. *It is simply great to be here* and quite worth all the trouble of the trip. I am most enthusiastic about the campus and the buildings with their Chinese style architecture. People are giving us a wonderful welcome. It was good to have some mail. It has been nearly three months since I have had any word from home!

November 30, 1923 *Chengtu*

Sometimes here in China I feel as if we are living in the Middle Ages! The cities are walled. There is no regard for sanitation, and there are no public water systems. The streets are usually narrow and crooked. Factories are uncommon, at least in West China, and spinning, weaving and other industries are carried on in the home. There is no strong or real central state in China; faction contends against faction, and those who are allies one day may be enemies the next. Interests are local and provincial rather than national. Officials work for their own private gain and the entire system is so rotten that the few who are upright are powerless. The hope is that enough of the people will become educated to the point of realizing their civic responsibilities in order to make their influence felt.

Here on the campus (outside the city wall and to the south across the Min River) it is a different world--tree-lined roads, comfortable looking homes, fine brick university buildings all interspersed with wide, green spaces.

December 10, 1923

My only business now is learning the language. I started language school a week ago today. It is hard but interesting work.

We are excited now about the prospects of having a house. We have decided to build for ourselves and already have a lot on the Middle School row. By scraping together all savings, we can manage.

December 27, 1923

It begins to look as if we should have a house sometime. They are putting in the foundation for the compound wall now, and men are still bringing brick, lime, and poles for scaffolding. Perhaps you will realize that great logs will be brought later, all of which will have to be sawed by hand into lumber on the site. These logs are floated in the river to the university gate. Then it takes at least sixteen men to carry one log to the desired spot. It is hard to appreciate, until you see it, what all this man-labor means. All loads, except those on wheelbarrows, bear down on the flesh of men. The pushing of a wheelbarrow on Chinese roads is no easy task either. I wish you could see them carting pigs along the street that borders the campus. The squeals of the animals blend with the squeaks of the barrows!

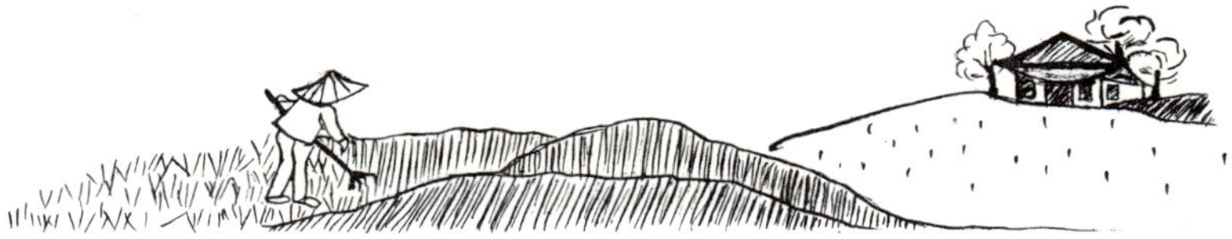

A New Life in an Ancient Land 1924

January 3, 1924 *Chengtu*
Late afternoon

Dear Folks at Home,

The students are out playing soccer, tennis, or volley ball on their respective athletic fields. The Chinese are not great athletes but I certainly am glad to see them making a try at it. As I write I can hear the boys out on theFriends field. It looked strange at first to see the boys (men, I should say--the university students object to being called "boys") running about with their long gowns flying but I am becoming accustomed to it. To be sure many of them take off these cumbersome outer garments while at play.

Tuesday (New Year's Day) was a holiday for all of us. Chinese New Year, which falls this year on February 5, is a time of great festivity. Bills are collected and accounts settled. Then everybody, except the very poor, plays. Sometimes this celebration lasts two weeks, sometimes a month. When you consider that during the remainder of the year shops are open and people work seven days a week, week in and week out, do you wonder that they are ready for a gala time? But to return to *our* New Year.

Since the students had some leisure time they anticipated what would come later by having a lantern procession with "dragon" performers. In the evening we heard a great din, a Chinese attempt at a band (their music at best is monotonous and strange sounding), and looking out our windows we saw pretty red lanterns coming along the Friends campus. We ran for our coats and got out to the gate in time to fall in line with the procession. We went on to the American Methodist section, which adjoins Friends, and there the funmakers formed a great ring, the red lanterns furnishing the light. Then the boys let off great strings of firecrackers which they had on a stick with fuses connected. Several fellows appeared in the center of the ring, the one in front wearing a huge "dragon" head,* the others covered with a long decorated drapery which floated out behind. Another fellow wore a mask, an oversized human head, and carried a fan flitting it about before the dragon's face and mouth. The dragon was big enough to swallow him whole, but he dodged it successfully, and so on and so on. They love this sort of play. You see quantities of these great grotesque masks in the shops now.

A number of weeks ago Robert and I were in the city one morning when we saw three such masked performers in their make-up walking on stilts. A laughing crowd followed them along the street. They came right for us, the big dragon and all, and blocked the way for Robert. Of course he laughed and after giving them a few coppers cash, they were satisfied and let him by.

Perhaps you will be interested in the political, or shall I say military, situation here in Chengtu. After we left Chungking, Yang Sen did finally succeed in taking the city. Report now has it that he is marching toward Chengtu. Whether this will mean trouble here or not we don't know. The city will very possibly be turned over to him without resistance. In any case, as far as we are concerned, there is nothing to fear. Soldiers are flocking to the city. However, since they offer paper notes which are either greatly depreciated in value, or worthless, the shop-keepers are closing their shops in self defense. This means suffering, for the common people who always live from hand to mouth can neither buy nor sell their rice. A farmer brought in a pig to market the other day for which he hoped to get $20.00 (Mex.).* On the way a soldier requisitioned the pig and gave the farmer some paper notes worth hardly a quarter of the proper price. The farmer was helpless. Yet the soldiers are not entirely to blame; they are paid in these paper notes. Meanwhile some official lines his pocket.

January 17, 1924 — *Chengtu*

Dear Folks at Home,

About a week ago I had an interesting experience. One of the teachers at the Language School offered to take any of us who cared to

**Traditionally "the dragon with wide open jaws, red lolling tongue, swinging head is supposed to devour evil influences." Robert Simkin's notes.*

**Two Chinese silver dollars were worth approximately one U.S. "gold" dollar.*

go to one of the Buddhist temples to see the annual ceremony of initiating the new priests. The ceremony consists largely of burning the nine small spots on each man's shaven head. Robert had seen this ceremony a number of years ago and had told me about it, so of course I wanted to go. The temple where the ceremony was to take place is near the North Gate. This meant a long walk across the city or securing a sedan chair. I chose the latter, sharing the chair in turn with Mrs. Blanchard. Along the way the carriers missed a turn and fell well behind the others. Consequently I was late in arriving. When I got out of the chair and stepped over the high threshold into the court of the temple (thresholds a foot or two in height are common) no foreigner was in sight. I nosed around, exploring the different courts and peering into various rooms. I couldn't find anyone observing the burning ceremony and went back to my chair to ask the chair men if it were really the right place. One of them went with me when we were met by a young priest in robes who bowed and bowed and escorted me across several courts to an area in the rear. I supposed that one of our party had sent him to find me.

Somebody opened two immense, heavy doors into a large room with a raised wing at either end. The priest stepped in and bowed for me to follow, which I did. I expected to find my friends inside and when I discovered that they were not there nor a single foreigner in sight I must confess I felt rather disturbed. Cautiously I bowed, smiled and proceeded to step back out over the high threshold into the court before those massive doors should close behind me and shut me in! The priest looked terribly troubled and the crowd of probably twenty-five children, men, and women at my heels gazed in wonder.

I stood there feeling very foolish and wondering what I should do when Miss Loree, a kindergarten teacher in the city, appeared from behind somewhere and called to me. "It is alright! Come in." I felt decidedly relieved. Behind her were my own crowd from the Language School. They had all been too late for the burning cermony, which came off at one o'clock but were enjoying a Chinese feast at the invitation of some important layman. Of course, I need not have been the least bit afraid even if no foreigner had been there but you do feel ill at ease and helpless in a place like that when you don't know the language.

I learned that one hundred and thirty-nine priests had taken the rites that day and I don't know how many hundreds had feasted there. It was evidently the one big day of the year. While peering around by myself I had seen a great dining hall with line after line of narrow tables on which were rice bowls placed in neat rows. I wondered if the place was a sort of monastery and this the room where the priests ate.

Next year I shall try again to see the priests take their rites.

January 20, 1924

This evening comes the opening session of our Quaker Yearly Meeting. A few Chinese have already arrived in Chengtu. I wonder how many Friends in America would go on a ten-day journey for the sake of attending Yearly Meeting and run the risk of encountering an army on the march, or of being taken by brigands in the bargain. Here there are "wars and rumors of war." For the past two days the city gates have been open only for a few hours each day because the enemy is reported to be approaching. Many men of the coolie class have been impressed for service by the local soldiery. The "boy" who works for us dares not go into the city alone for fear of being forced to become such a burden bearer for the soldiers. We foreigners can rest in security. But think of those poor Chinese who live in constant dread and terror....

February 16, 1924

Dear Folks at Home,

Our house is coming along nicely. They now have the bricks up to the first floor level and are putting in the floor joists.

Because of New Year we had a vacation at Language School last week. Robert is having a much longer vacation at the university, but he has kept exceedingly busy with the house and Yearly Meeting affairs. Imagine the disappointment (to put it mildly) of the Chinese to have their city beseiged at this holiday time! I have written before that Yang Sen, after his capture of Chungking, was expected to come on to Chengtu. His army arrived just before New Year's. With the news of his proximity the city gates were locked. A few foreigners were permitted to scale the wall, being pulled up or down by ropes, but no Chinese were allowed either to enter or leave the city. Food was hoisted up over the wall. Every morning we could hear the marketers shouting from across the river as they bartered with one another from the ground outside and from the wall. The city was closed about one week.

There was nothing that could be called heavy fighting except on Thursday night when a sudden fusillade of shots seemed to come from both sides of the house. We quickly pulled the mattress from the bed to a sheltered corner and managed to get a fair amount of sleep. We were fortunate to have the protection of brick walls. Those living in lath and plaster houses had a bad night.

It seems so peaceful now that it is hard to realize that anything unusual ever happens here. We have had quite a social whirl this week--out to dinner three nights in succession and an invitation for Sunday night dinner. One evening we were with the Silcocks, English Friends. A curious thing about the Friends families here is that each has a Margaret S.--Margaret Silcock,* Margaret Sawdon, Margaret Stubbs, and myself.

March 25, 1924

Yesterday Yang Sen, the general who drove out Hsiung Ke-wu, a robber chief, was given a reception here at the University. I stood in the hall long enough to see him and his bodyguard come in. He is small of stature but perhaps has more than average ability. On Thursday the British consul is giving a buffet luncheon in his honor to which the men of our community are invited. That same afternoon there will be a farewell tea at the Administration building here on campus for those who are leaving us to go on furlough. This includes the Sawdons and Margaret Stubbs who is returning to England with her little John who is very poorly.

Easter Sunday

Dear Folks at Home,

The Sawdons got away last Tuesday morning at 6:30 with the usual din of many firecrackers. In China whether you are welcoming an important guest or saying goodbye, celebrating a birthday anniversary or having a wedding or funeral, there must be plenty of noise. It has been a sight to see the different families start off on their furloughs. I feel badly to have them go but am glad for their sakes that they are going home. It is a lot of work packing one's household goods and preparing for a long overland journey. Baggage and journey equipment must be divided into loads of proper weight for the men to carry. Equipment includes camp beds, bedding, cooking utensils, food, lanterns, etc. This means twenty-four carriers or more. Can you picture a family as they start off?--several sedan chairs, then carriers by pairs bearing loads slung between bamboo poles, and all this amid the smoke and din of firecrackers!

Since the Sawdons have left we have become master and mistress of this house, and I am having my first taste of what housekeeping in China means. By using the Chinese that I know and with much shaking

---

**Wife of Arnold Silcock, architect for the Friends College, younger brother of Harry T. Silcock.*

and nodding of the head and *much* pointing I am able to make most of my wants known! We are fortunate in having a good cook. But simply the giving out of supplies, coal, kerosene, oil, soap, sugar, and what not, and keeping the wheels running takes a good bit of time so that with my language study I shall be busy enough.

This evening we had our first guest, one of the students of the Friends College, a delightful and interesting young man. He had come in when we first arrived to show us a picture of his fiancee. He told us this evening that he hopes she will enter the women's college which is to be opened this fall. (Hurrah!) While we were eating he said, "We respect women in China now." He is certainly modern in his thinking as are many of the college students.

April 21, 1924

This has been a holiday because of a big track meet in the city in which all the schools have been participating. I took this opportunity to go into the city to do some errands. I do not go into the city often enough--although we are a little less than a mile from the South Gate--nor have I lived in China long enough, to fail to find the commonplace sights interesting. Don't imagine as I did that foot-binding is entirely a thing of the past. Here in West China I seldom see any women, except the young school girls, who do not have bound feet. How they get about as spryly as they do is a marvel to me. I wish you could see my sewing woman, the cook's wife. She gets up and down stairs as quickly as anybody, but I must say that this practice of foot-binding makes the ankles very stiff and the gait ungainly. The women appear to be walking about on stumpy sticks. The head-dress of the Szechuanese women is interesting. They comb their hair back straight and wear it in a low knot or twist at the neck. A silver or jade (real or imitation) pin holds it in place. Then just above their foreheads and around back to the knot of hair they wear a band of black cloth. The working men also wear cloths twisted about their heads.

I often wonder as I ride along the street in my chair if the average American sees in his entire lifetime as much misery as one may often see in a half hour passing along a Chinese thoroughfare. Do these people accept their misery because it is the only sort of existence they have ever experienced? There is practically no privacy for the common people. Their houses, which usually consist of but one or two small rooms, are crowded together upon the narrow streets. Fortunately there is ventilation because the fronts of the houses and shops are entirely open to the street. Such an arrangement gives the passerby the opportunity to see all that is going on inside, except when a bamboo mat or cloth curtain is hung in the open space. As a matter of fact, the women do their washing (placing the clothes flat on a board and scrubbing them with a brush), their mending, their nursing of babies, and many other household duties right on the street.

Children and dogs are everywhere. Many of the streets are greatly congested. The chair carriers are continually calling out to clear the way. Pedestrians, chairs, wheelbarrows, pack mules, men with heavy water buckets hung from either end of their shoulder poles, men carrying great pieces of furniture or loads of lumber on their backs, tradesmen with their wares displayed on portable stands, load carriers with all sorts and conditions of burdens jostle one another with much shouting and great confusion. At first the newcomer is inclined to be somewhat terrified by the jostling crowd and the meaningless shouting, but this feeling is supplanted by a sense of security when one comes to know a bit of the language and to understand the people. Except at times of civil war when one might be hit by a stray bullet, a foreign woman is quite as safe in the streets of a Chinese city as on the streets of an American city.

May 10 [Robert's Birthday], 1924
Dear Ones at Home,

April 24th was a big day for us here. It was University Day celebrating the fourteenth anniversary of its founding and of special significance because of the dedication of the new science building. Guests, alumni, students, faculty and officers in full academic dress assembled at the Administration Building and marched to the new Atherton Biology and Preventive Medicine Building for the formal program. General Yang Sen was presented with the key and formally opened the building. Inspection of the building was interesting; students were at work actually dissecting or at microscopes in the various laboratories.

Yang Sen is very favorable to education, in fact is modern and progressive in many ways. A rather delicate situation has arisen, however. He is eager to have one of his concubines enter the Woman's College this fall. With the Woman's College just opening and in an experimental stage it will hardly do to have a concubine as a student, neither will it do to offend Yang Sen!*

**When the Woman's College actually opened the question of enrolling Yang Sen's concubine did not again arise.*

May 11 [Sunday Evening], 1924

Robert and I took a long walk this morning out into the country. The rape (mustard) is now dry and is being thrashed and the bean stalks (*fu deo*, a large flat bean) are being stacked in the fields for further drying. The leaves are first stripped from the stalks for fodder. We walked past fields of young rice seedlings of a fresh, beautiful green and saw fields of barley now a beautiful pink. The ripe wheat still standing is a lovely pale yellow. We visited two small temples, dingy, tawdry, run-down places. In one, chickens and dogs were wandering about picking up what they could from the earth floor. At one end of the room in which was a large image of Gautama Buddha, silk spinning was being carried on....

Crowds of people were out along the river today to observe *fang sen*--releasing of life, a religious observance. People purchase birds, rabbits, eels, fish, and other living things and set them loose. Of course it does not matter if small boys or men recapture these "released" creatures and resell them!...

Have I written of seeing the mountains? Occasionally the snow mountains, lofty peaks 10,000 feet or more high to the northwest of us, are visible. I have seen them once this spring. Often these last weeks I have seen the lower mountains to the southeast. They look good to me for this Chengtu plain is very, very flat....Our house is coming along splendidly. They have begun plastering.

May 18, 1924

Dear Fannie,

Robert and I had planned to remain on the plain this summer and watch progress on the house. Some have felt that it wasn't very wise my first summer not to go to the mountains and so we have been very much pleased with a new development. Mrs. Homer Brown (Muriel) of the Canadian Mission, a perfectly splendid person, has invited me to go with her and her children to Behludin (White Deer Summit) while Robert stays with her husband down here. Both men will teach in the summer school. This will mean a great hustle but I am sure it will be worth it. We are leaving on the twentieth.

Marguerite Brown, (another Canadian Mrs. Brown), who is also in the Language School, and I are getting to be pals, especially since we have another bond in common. She, too, is expecting a baby, a few months later than ours. The very day before Marguerite confided in me, Margaret Silcock told me the same thing about herself. It is thrilling!

May 20, 1924

A few weeks ago the whole landscape was a brilliant yellow from the cultivated rape or mustard. The oil extracted from the rape seed is used for cooking and illumination. Oil is poured into a saucer-like dish and a slender wick is placed in the oil, which when ignited provides all the lighting most Chinese can afford. Now the fields are flooded and rice seedlings are being set out. Men take bundles of these seedlings and throw them into the fields, then, separating the bundles, they walk backwards, dabbing the plants down into the soft mud and setting out five rows at a time. The flooded fields will soon become lush with the growing rice.

June 9, 1924

Commencement Day is June 16th. The city gates will be kept open until eleven o'clock that night. Strange in this age to think of a city closing its gates at sundown or even of a city *having* a wall and great gates! But as I sit here and write and look through the open French door, there just across the river is the city wall* in plain sight (except for the foliage of the trees which partly hides it). Do you remember Robert's picture of the great water wheels on the river (a part of the Chengtu public water system)? We hear their rhythmic creaking day and night except for some weeks in the winter when the river is too low to turn them. We hear, too, the beating of the gongs and the bell-ringing at the temple nearby. Late at night and every morning very early the drum is sounded and the bells ring. Otherwise while on this campus one can easily think himself in the homeland.

June 23, 1924 — *Behludin [White Deer Summit]*

Dear Folks at Home,

Here I am in the mountains, 6,000 feet above sea level. Tier upon tier of wonderful mountains rise above us. It certainly is a glorious spot....The Browns and I left Chengtu Wednesday soon after noon. We meant to get off at 10:30 but then our troubles began. Sometimes overland journeys are made without such difficulties as we had but from what I have heard Robert say they seldom proceed smoothly from start to finish.

I had four men on my chair because a chair rides easier with four men than with three and besides I wanted my bedding (rolled in oil sheet) along with me. In addition to these four men there were three

---

**The massive wall was not only imposing for its height but for its width of about forty-four feet.*

carriers to take my loads, each man carrying two baskets hung from shoulder poles. The Brown family, of course, required many more men than I had. I wonder if anyone can appreciate the wonders of "civilization" until they are obliged to travel under such primitive conditions. Can you see the men jogging along with their swinging loads suspended from their poles, brown bodies glistening with perspiration? In the heat of summer they wear usually nothing but a pair of short trousers, an enormous sun hat and grass sandals.

We got to the North Gate of Chengtu (an hour's ride through the city) and there the men stopped at a teashop. They usually stop every hour or so for rest and the inevitable tea. Here our troubles really began. Seven men ran off but since the *fu teo* (head man from whom the carriers are hired) was along he got us straightened out after a time. This practice of men disappearing continued, however, until I should have thought Mr. Brown,who took full responsibility for us, would have been completely worn out. He is naturally of a very mild disposition and bore it well, although he remarked more than once that he was quite disgusted with China's method of transportation.*

We stopped the first night at a little Canadian Methodist School in a small village. The three young Chinese women teachers were most hospitable. I had my camp bed put up in the schoolroom, unrolled my *pu kai* (comforter), spread sheet, put white cover on my small pillow which I kept for comfort in my chair during the day, and with mosquito net up was ready for the night. This was heaven compared to a Chinese inn, an experience I have been spared so far. The second night we got to Penghsien and were the guests of the Walkers at the mission compound....We ate at teashops along the road. The Browns have their tableboy along as cook and I have our laundry-tableboy along as my share of servant help. In addition the Browns have a houseboy and a *da niang* (chamber maid, nursemaid, etc.).

Their cook and my tableboy kept ahead of us on the road (they walked all the way) and would have a cloth on a table in a teashop, the table set and the meal practically ready by the time we arrived. These

---

**Very probably the carriers went off to smoke opium. In an early letter [1908?] Robert Simkin wrote: "A very large percent of carriers are addicted to the opium habit. After a smoke they go rapidly for an hour or more, but if deprived of it, it seems impossible for them to work. Some carriers depend on it more than food. Nearly all their money goes to satisfy the craving; clothing is in tatters. Many of them go down and down. Finally they become beggars."*

teashops are quite open to the street as are all businesses, and we always had a crowd of spectators, often fifty men, women, and children watching us. When the children's chairs were put down people crowded around them also. If one were not afraid of catching some "bug" one could better appreciate the good-natured interest. The Chinese are very fond of children. The foreign dolls were a special curiosity; eyes which opened and shut were a marvel.

It was market day at one town and the street was jammed with people. When we stopped they crowded about the children's chairs like flies. We continually had to ask them to stand back. Mr. Brown in his good natured way could do this kindly though he had to be firm.

You would be surprised to see how fast the chair men can travel. Once they make up their minds to start they proceed with surprisingly good humor. They step along smartly in perfect rhythm. The second day the roads were fearfully muddy due to rain the night before--muddy and slippery. I held my breath sometimes for fear my chair would be precipitated into a stream or rice paddy. "Roads" in China, you know, are merely paths. The third day the roads were stonier and there was less danger of men slipping. That day the country was wilder and the men forded streams and crossed rushing rivulets on narrow planks. You learn to have a lot of faith in these chair-carriers! And on that third day we began to see the mountains!

It took three men to bring me up this great ascent in a mountain chair--a canvas seat slung between two poles. Before we got to the top it began to pour but I had a poncho to wear and did not get wet except for my feet. My! but it was slippery and stiff climbing for those men.

The Browns are very fine and most kind to me. Mr. Brown will be going back to the plain in a week. They have three girls--Isabel, who is perhaps nine or ten; Julia, who is six; and little Muriel, who is two years and three months. Mrs. Brown is trying what seems to me an interesting experiment. She is speaking French almost entirely with little Muriel. In this way the child is growing up in an environment of three languages. Her *da niang*, of course, uses Chinese and she is getting that easily (wish I could get it with as little effort!); she speaks French with her mother and her other contacts are in English....Yesterday we walked over to "Rocky Notch"--the Simkin bungalow rented this summer to an Anglican bishop. The approach is through a natural gateway of woods and rock. Through this opening is a magnificent view. I can hardly wait for next summer when Robert will be here with me in our own bungalow. How I wish you might see it!

July 6, 1924 **Behludin**

Dear Alice, Fannie, and Grace,

I have been enjoying so much the things which came before I left Chengtu; now Robert writes of the other boxes arriving. Alas! The hats you sent are a total wreck, "fit for the junk heap," he says. Of course I feel disappointed, but if you live in West China you have to take chances and expect such things to happen. Some things came through beautifully. Some people seem never to lose a thing; others will have wrecked parcel after wrecked parcel arrive. I am convinced of one thing--there can be no guarantee against disaster.

I can tell you stories of people who have had lots worse trouble coming up the river than we did. The Walkers of Penghsien, with whom we stayed the other night, had a terrible experience. I also know Miss Wilson, a teacher in the Canadian School (school for foreign children in Chengtu) who was in the same party. Their steamer was wrecked. Miss Wilson escaped through her cabin window. At the same time three men of the party were terribly sick with dysentery or cholera, and on Christmas Eve two of them died. Mr. Walker was the third and he managed to recover. It was a sad Christmas for a welcome to West China! Their trunks were in the river three or more months and they had absolutely nothing save the clothes on their backs. Of course they had to send to Canada for more.

I am not writing this to scare you, because in spite of it all, Szechwan is a wonderful place and I would not be anywhere else for anything, but you see it sometimes pays to look at your own troubles and disasters as relative to other people's.

August 10, 1924 **Behludin**

*Dear Girls,**

My time up here is getting limited--only a little more than a week now. The air is good and the place is altogether so fine that I ought to hate to tear myself away but actually I am becoming impatient to get back to Chengtu. I suppose the heat and mosquitoes will seem worse than ever but I want to be with Robert....Dr. T. advised me not to delay too long in getting down the mountain, predicting *The Event* in three weeks!

Robert has had his difficulties with the house and fears it will not be ready when I get down. Fortunately, the Browns have very kindly offered us their house. Robert is there now. While I am in the hospital

---

**Sisters Alice Miller, Fannie Timberlake, Grace Timberlake.*

he also has been invited to live with the Browns. I am sorry the hospital is such a long walk across the city from the campus and there is a city wall in between. However, I ought to be thankful there *is* a hospital to go to.

September 5, 1924

Canadian Mission Hospital for Women and Children

Dear Ones at Home,

Robert has written you all that we lost our baby. I really have gotten along beautifully. This is the seventh day and when we were remarking the fact this morning Miss Campbell, one of the two foreign nurses, said, "Thank Goodness! You are out of danger." I had not realized there was any danger for I have, as I say, gotten along so very well. I believe the doctor thinks my progress has been rather remarkable.

The Chinese nurses are dear. I have quite fallen in love with my little day nurse. She is as sweet and lovely as can be--reminds me of a modest, sweet little wood violet. We can't understand each other well enough to talk except in a very limited way, but we smile at each other and get along famously.

Robert walks in at least every other day to see me. It is a long, long way and he is awfully busy on the house. It rather worries me to have him working so hard with no let-up. The University opens the eleventh and he has a heavy schedule this fall. All summer he has been at it early and late through the heat and all. He says he feels alright but I know he is tired. We can't hope to get everything done and settled inside the house until January at best. Then there will be the outside--the terrace, lawn, and garden to do. But it is going to be lovely when it is finished. Nature is so generous here that it's nothing to make a place a bower of beauty with roses, wisteria, lilies, chrysanthemums, shrubs, and trees, given a little time. As for the present, as soon as I leave the hospital we are going right in and camp out in two or three rooms.

People have been very sympathetic. The Chinese would have been more concerned, Robert says, if the baby had been a boy. The loss ot a *girl* is nothing from the Chinese point of view, so consciously or unconsciously are they steeped in the theory of ancestor worship. My poor little darling! We surely would have loved her.

One day my *da niang* brought me some flowers and ten fresh eggs. I was quite touched.

September 17, 1924
Dear Folks at Home,

In my last letter I wrote how the Chinese feel about girls. You see, only the son of the family can carry on the worship before the ancestral tablets and unless the ancestral spirits are properly worshipped they are unhappy and never know peace. Therefore it is *imperative* that one should have male descendants to assure one's happiness in the future life. This is one reason for China's over-population. When my sewing woman's baby son was born last spring they had it announced at first that a girl had arrived in order to deceive the evil spirits, the thought being that if evil spirits believed there was a girl in the household they would not think it worth while to disturb *her*!

I believe I wrote how much I am enjoying my little Chinese nurse Lo Fu Shin. She is a dear. The other day I was thrilled when her fiance came to see her. He has been in Peking studying and Miss Campbell says he is handsome and likable. I have learned since that this was the first time Lo Fu Shin had seen him and they have been engaged seven years!--one of the usual arranged affairs, you see. My! I hope this will come out alright. There is no display of affection ever, although it must exist in the case of some matches. Some of the educated young people simply rebel against the old system. Miss Campbell told me that the nurses were much impressed down in the operating room by the way Robert kissed me, which goes to show that these girls have feelings just like ours. As for these arranged affairs--you may guess what they mean by this fact. There has been known to have been three brides here in the hospital at the same time, all attempted suicides.

October 16, 1924 *Chengtu*
Dear Folks at Home,

We are now in the new house and are enjoying it hugely. As I write I can hear the workmen pounding downstairs. They are working in the study now, the last room to be finished. Of course, there will still be painting and little odds and ends to attend to. I am anxious to get everything in order for we are going to entertain the Dyes* when they first return from furlough. I suppose they are on the Pacific now.

Have I written that there are eight girls in the university this fall? They are a picked group. It is quite an experiment for West China and the plan is to proceed very carefully. At present the poor things have to be chaperoned everywhere. Two hours a week I act as escort, meeting

**Jane Dye [Quaker] and Daniel Dye of the Baptist Mission.*

them in one building and taking them to another, sitting in class with them.* Last Monday was my first day. It was a class in chemistry, taught by a Chinese teacher and held in a fine big lecture room. It is these Chinese teachers, as much as anybody, who want the girls chaperoned in keeping with old Chinese custom. Young men and women are never left alone in each other's company. But I am sure *these girls* are demure enough. Before class they sit with downcast eyes, their attention apparently glued to their books. When the teacher comes in the entire class rises to its feet, the teacher makes a low bow and the students return it, I standing and bowing with them. At the close of the class the same courtesy is repeated. The teacher and sage have always been the most revered and honored men in China, the soldier being the least honored.

Don't think the girls have no life. Quite the contrary. The remainder of the class hour proceeds exactly as it does at home with good-natured give and take between instructor and student. Outside the girls are as full of fun as can be, laughing and chatting together....I am so glad for this opportunity to get acquainted with them. I am so stupid with the language that I need some special point of contact.

Wish you could all come and see us and the new house.

I have not had a letter from any of you for four weeks. We have heard of a mail being robbed. Either this or the fighting down river may be the cause.

I am quite well now.

November 9, [Sunday Eve], 1924
Dear Ones at Home,

We had a fine walk out in the country this afternoon. We stopped at one farm where they were cleaning rice with a fanning mill. As we turned in, the children ran to cover but their curiosity soon got the better of them. One of the younger men who acted as host was most genial. He came and opened the gates, and an older woman brought a bench for me to sit on. By that time the children had gathered about us and the woman was feeling of my dress and sweater between her fingers and asking questions. They often do this and a common question is, "How much did it cost?" Robert took his turn at turning the wheel much to the amusement and delight of all the spectators and the same man who had opened the gates went to a tree and picked some loose-skinned oranges which he presented to us. Even the simple

The practice of escorting the women students to classes was soon discontinued.

country people are most hospitable and gracious. I wondered how generations were represented in the group. A farm house is built around an open square, just low, one-story mud buildings usually with thatched roofs. Trees or bamboo are planted around the outside border. The rooms have no windows, the doors of each open onto the inner court.

December 9 [*Evening*]. *1924*

I am just back from Hart College having walked there with Robert* to his office. He is giving examinations these days. He examines each student orally. It takes a long while but no longer I suppose than grading papers, although the examinations are spread over a very much longer period. The students like his method because they feel that they are getting individual attention and he believes that it is the best way of determining a student's knowledge. Anyway it relieves him of looking over page after page of Chinese characters. That must be *awful*! Robert has the reputation of being one of the very best Chinese speakers in Chengtu. (Wifely pride!) What a brutal language this is, if after studying it seventeen years and having as good a command of it as Robert has, one cannot understand a native lecturer (to get *all* that he says) or read fluently the literature of the country or even a letter written in the flowery style which Chinese love. It is because there are thousands and thousands and thousands of characters, all different, and the meaning is often so hidden.

I walk into the city to the Green Dragon Street Meeting every Sunday now. I always find the sights on the street interesting. Usually at the hour we go we meet carrier after carrier with his buckets of "liquid gold" (human excrement which is used universally for fertilizing) so the air is pretty "rosy." On either side of the long bridge which we must cross before coming to the South Gate vendors always have their wares spread before them. They sit or squat on the rough stone and have their little bunches of peanuts, ten or a dozen in a bunch, on a tray before them. Sometimes it is persimmons which they are selling. Frequently I have seen old garments patched beyond all possibility of recognizing the original cloth spread out on the stone. You cannot imagine what rags and what patches these poor people wear!

**Robert Simkin was associated with the School of Religion, teaching Old Testament History and Church History. In teaching he used the Chinese language.*

December, 1924 *Chengtu, West China*

Dear Home Friends,

I have just had a long walk out in the country. It is the kind of weather for a brisk walk--crisp air and not too bright sunshine. This afternoon we visited the *Wu Heo Shi*, one of the best kept and most popular of the Taoist temples in this locality. The numerous mud and plaster gods looked quite respectable in their gayly colored and freshly painted robes. Sometimes these gods are very much out at the elbows! We saw one devout worshipper going the rounds and stopping before each idol to make three profound bows. Two other young men were kneeling before a shrine where incense was burning while a priest beat a large gong close by to attract the attention of the gods. Before them on the floor were bunches of bamboo sticks held in cylindrical containers. Each picked up one of the containers and tipping it to a horizontal position continued to gently shake it until one bamboo stick tumbled out. On each stick was a number written in Chinese character. Then we watched to see what they would do next. At a room on the further side of the open court they presented their sticks to a priest who gave them slips of paper numbered to correspond with the numbers on the sticks. On these papers were written certain fortunes in the obscure language of Chinese classical diction.

Last Sunday was a full day. We attended Bible School and the morning meeting at *Chin Lung Kai* (Green Dragon Street) Friends meeting house which is about three miles from the University, had a hurried dinner with John and Dorothy Rodwell, and went back to the meeting house for a funeral service. We hoped that the service would be thoroughly Christian as the son himself is a Christian, although no other members of his family are. I shall describe the setting as I saw it and let you judge its character. There are, of course, customs pertaining to funerals in America which might be questioned.

The mourners were dressed in coarse white cotton garments--long white coats and white turbans with streamers falling down the back and two queer little tufts of cotton on the end of strings dangling down one over each ear. They wore real sackcloth, too. At least the chief mourner, the eldest son, did, and he is the one who counts in China. He wore a short jacket of it over his long white coat and also had a sort of sackcloth visor over his eyes. All over the walls at the front of the church were scrolls, scores and scores of pairs of them, bearing inscriptions honoring the deceased. The body lay in a black lacquered coffin which was sealed and unadorned. There was not a single flower to soften its grimness. Lashed along either side with rough hemp ropes were two long heavy poles by which it was carried.

At the close of the simple service admirably conducted by S.C. Yang (a Friend and principal of the Middle School allied with the University) the carriers--coolies hired for the purpose--bore the coffin out to the street where it was covered with a canopy, an elaborate affair wound and festooned with strips of white cotton. The procession started with drums and bells and horns ahead announcing the coming. (Usually firecrackers also are used). The sons of the family walked abreast a few feet in front of the coffin and held white cotton cloth streamers which were passed from the bier over their shoulders to their hands. This made it appear as if they were drawing the bier after them. Actually, the sixteen bearers were doing all the carrying. Just outside the city gate the canopy was removed and the coffin was covered with a rich, brightly embroidered cloth. The procession, minus the band and half the carriers (the music and other display, which are for the purpose of honoring the dead, may, for reasons of economy, be dispensed with where there are fewer people to see and hear) then proceeded about a mile and a half into the country.

It is customary in this part of China to bury very shallowly and to heap the earth over the coffin into a high mound. Grave land dotted all over in hit-or-miss fashion with these high mounds is to be found everywhere. To such a plot our procession wended its way and stopped before a freshly dug grave. When the grave digger saw us coming he shouted across to a nearby farm demanding an armful of straw, which after considerable wrangling was finally brought, dropped into the open grave and set on fire. When the blaze was over the ashes were raked out and the coolies lowered the coffin into the ground. Now, as you know, the *position* of the coffin is of tremendous importance in China. This is because of the old idea that each spot of ground has its own spiritual influences which may be friendly to one person and unfriendly to another, and on no account whatsoever must the *feng shui** be disturbed. Whether or not geomancers had been consulted, it was quite evident that the overseer of ceremonies, corresponding to our undertaker, and the eldest son were using every care to have the coffin placed in exactly the right position. They were not satisfied until it was absolutely in line with a string strung between two stakes driven into the ground at either end of the grave.

During the reading of the Scripture and the prayer there were sharp words between two of the carriers who were quarreling about their

**Translated: wind [feng] water [shui]: elements which must be kept in balance.*

pay. I felt sorry for the bereaved family, not only because of the noisy quarreling but because the burial arrangements were extremely crude. The undertaker sprinkled a reddish powder over the coffin, then took great mouthfuls of tea, or water, from the spout of a teapot and sprayed it over the powder! Beginning with the eldest, the sons put the first clods of earth upon the coffin. Pulling off their mourning garments they tossed the sackcloth and head-dresses into the grave but put the long white coats in a neat pile at one side. The ceremony ended with the eldest son taking from his sister's chair a new melon hat which had a white button on the top of it, the mark of mourning, and placing it on his head.

Rising Nationalism 1925 & 1926

January 2, 1925
Dear Home Folks,

The Dyes arrived on the Saturday night before Christmas. We sat down to supper that night at 10:30! They had come in much earlier but they were afraid their boat was leaking and they had to get it unloaded. We enjoyed having the Dyes here very much and we would have liked them to stay longer but they left the day before Christmas. They are now living on "Baptist Row."

On Christmas Eve we had a party for the servants and their children, ten in all. That evening was the first time we have used the living room. We have been using our dining room nearly three weeks now.

January 24, 1925
Dear Ones at Home,

The big General Conference (Christian conference of all denominations united in the work in western China) opened the thirteenth of January and we did some hustling to get the house in a semblance of order ready for guests who arrived the twelfth. I had seven guests in the house counting the little Lee boy. Miss Cumber of Chungking was the only Friend with us. We have had ten different guests who have slept in the house during the past two weeks and thirty-five different people--Chinese and foreigners--at meals, not counting a special little tea I had one afternoon. There have not been more than eight at the table at one time, however. I couldn't have done all this so easily a year ago. Now that I know more of the language I can direct the servants with less difficulty.

The General Conference is generally considered a success. There were two hundred and fifty Chinese delegates and one hundred and fifty foreign. Visitors brought the total attendance to seven hundred. The leadership was in the hands of young Chinese, mostly our Union University graduates. It was impressive that women, who customarily have little to say, were ready to stand up and take part--all this a product of a little over forty years of Christian effort. Friends first entered Szechwan in 1886 and other missions probably somewhat earlier.The University was opened only as far back as 1910.

Following the big conference have come the denominational conferences. Our Friends Yearly Meeting has just closed and now we are in the midst of the meetings of the C.O.M. (Committee of Missionaries).

I am going to Tungchwan for two months. I thought last summer I never would go away again and leave Robert for so long a time and here I am off once more! Here in Chengtu there is such a large foreign community that I have too little contact with the Chinese. I want to know what real mission life is, rough it a bit, and find out what I am good for. At Tungchwan, Friends have schools and a hospital. I shall live with the three ladies there (Edith Brittle, Rose Tebbutt and Miss Riley, a nurse), study with a private teacher and seek contact with the school girls. I need to go to some place where I shall just *have* to speak Chinese. I spoke of the plan to the C.O.M. last evening and they all seem to approve heartily. So I am off next Friday with the Wighams, Miss Cumber and Miss Brittle. We shall be travelling by chair and it will be my first experience with inns. Everybody says they are simply *frightful*. It is not easy to leave our comfortable, lovely home now that we are a bit settled and are enjoying it so much, but I have made up my mind to do it. I hope Robert can make some arrangement to eat with the Browns or the Dyes while I am gone. He agrees that I should have this experience.

This has been Chinese New Year--their big day. It is like our Christmas. Last evening many people had beautiful lanterns and were walking about. The Yangs had their little girl pulling a gay rabbit lantern on wheels and Mrs. Yang* had a fish lantern in her hand. The lanterns are made of a thin paper painted in bright colors and fastened to light bamboo frames. This is the time when many Chinese make gifts. A fine Chinese gentleman came to call yesterday and brought us several pounds of loose-skinned oranges and a slab of native-cured bacon which the Chinese consider a great delicacy. Today people have

---

* *Wife of S.C. Yang, principal of our Union Middle School and a leading Quaker.*

been appearing in fresh new garments. It is very noticeable for many people in this poverty stricken land usually dress in shabby old clothes.

February 1925 *Tungchwan, Szechwan*

Dear Girls,

It is Sunday morning and I still have some time before we go to the *Fu Yin Tang* (Happy News Hall), viz. the Meeting House. While I am writing I will relate something about my trip to Tungchwan.

A big party of over fifty of us, counting chair carriers, load coolies, and servants, left Chengtu a week ago yesterday morning (January 31st). I came with the people returning from the General Conference and Yearly Meeting. It was indeed a caravan. Of course we could not keep together but each went at his own (or chair-carriers') pace. The paths always wind and turn so very many times that one may not see a particular member of the party until the next stop at a teashop.

Now I do not know what comes to your mind when I say "inn" but let me tell you that a *Chinese* inn is more like a very dirty stable than anything I know. We got in before dark the first night so I could really see a typical inn. At the front there is the teashop where we eat, entirely open to the street. In the center is a sort of court open to the sky and used as a passageway and a storage place for fuel, sedan chairs, and what-not. There also is the open drain into which the dirty water, tea leaves, and slops are thrown. Around this court and in the rear are the rooms which are let by the night. No one could possibly want to stay more than one night! Miss Brittle and I took a room together. In it were three beds, no other furniture. Chinese inn beds are rather crude affairs of wood covered with straw over which a piece of straw matting is laid. The Chinese rolls himself up in his *pu kai* (comforter) and sleeps like a top. Our arrangements are hardly as simple. First, on one of the beds we place an oiled sheet on which to lay our wraps, rugs, and bags. This also serves as our dressing table. Then our "boys" set up camp beds on the other two, first covering the Chinese beds with oiled sheets for protection against vermin. Underneath the cot is space for laying one's clothes. The bed is the one clean spot in the midst of all the dirt and we always go to bed as soon as we can after supper.

The rooms usually have no windows, but if there are any they are covered with paper through which the people poke their fingers, then glue their eyes and calmly watch all proceedings. There are no floors, only the hard earth, and the walls are festooned with dusty cobwebs. If there is any straw or litter on the floor we never disturb it. It is just as well to let the bedbugs and fleas lie low! As for food--in cold weather especially we can take a good bit with us all prepared. The cook, a personal servant of some member of the party, warms up the vegetables, cooks porridge, et cetera, over the inn fire, and spreading a clean cloth over one of the not too clean inn tables we dine happily, balancing ourselves on the Chinese benches (*ban den*). The crowd which immediately gathers is not as annoying as I found it last summer. One does not mind having the air cut off in cold weather. The people stand quietly, now and then grinning broadly at one another in amusement at the foreigner's strange ways.

On the second day we crossed the mountains. As we started out that morning at daybreak we were advised to keep together as we might see bandits. As a matter of fact we saw no bandits at all but we did run into an army while passing through a small city. There must have been some 2,000 soldiers equipped for the march heading for battle (?). Do you think the populace was thronging the streets to send them forth with cheers and flag-waving? Not a bit of it! The town was closed tight as a drum. There were a few women, *no men*, standing along the streets but nothing could be bought. Our carriers could get no rice for their breakfast until the bugling had all died away and the last company had left the town. All that day we followed that army, overtaking their lame and ill, stragglers who were left by the roadside to take care of themselves.

We frequently hear of how the soldiers *la fu* (impress for service) the poor people and that day I saw one poor farmer being dragged off to carry some load. The soldier had him by the shoulder. He was moaning pitifully but he did not dare resist. At his heels was a little tad of six or eight screaming in terror and rage. I, too, was indignant but I could do nothing.

The remainder of our trip was uneventful. We got into Tungchwan on the fourth day in time for a late dinner. I walked the last five miles. The remainder of the party went on to Chungking by boat the following Friday and we are gradually settling into the routine of life here.

February 22, 1925 *Tungchwan, Szechwan*
Dear Home Folks,

Without any responsibility here whatever, I have all the time I want for study. I put in seven or eight hours every day. The teacher is here five hours, a kindly gentleman of about sixty. He has the typical Chinese moustache with the long drooping ends. I hope I am making progress. I surely know more than I did a year ago but that is not saying much! I feel quite at home here.

Rose and I are starting for Suining (pronounced sway-lin') on Wednesday. Mr. Fung, my teacher, is going with us to teach us both and I am taking my boy, Pen San Hsin, to look out for us en route, to cook, etc. Why are we going? At this time of year the great Buddhist pilgrimage comes to the Goddess of Mercy temple in Suining. With so many people there the Missions find it an opportune time to make friendly contacts. Rose is going on that account; I am going to learn more about the pilgrimage and to see the Friends in Suining.

Later

Here in Tungchwan English Friends have a hospital, girls' school, and boys' school. The school girls are lots of fun. You should have seen them this noon. They had one of the Chinese girl teachers in my sedan chair and were carrying her about the garden. They must be strong to be able to do it. The chair itself is heavy. Last evening they had an impromptu play, a favorite pastime among students. The group chooses some plot then the actors improvise as they go along. The middle school (high school) boys at the University love to dress up as women and girls. I noticed that the girls last night chose men's parts largely. They had lovely painted moustaches! They are bubbling over with life.

We shall probably be three days on the boat going to Suining, remain there perhaps two weeks and be a week or more on the boat returning. It takes longer returning than going. If the river is too low at that time we shall have to come back by chair.

I am having my share of chilblains along with the rest. Miss Riley, the nurse, says that they are especially bad this year. People have great sores on their ears, fingers, toes. Mine are on my fingers but they are not bad. Robert has terrible ones on his feet which have broken; his feet are very sore. "It is cold enough to slow up the blood," Miss Riley says. Yet in spite of the cold we get green stuff from the gardens. And winter time, too, is the season for the beautiful pink and fragrant *mei hwa*.

March 8, 1925 *Suining, Szechwan*

Dear Home Folks,

Going down river to Suining the men rowed. Eight or ten rowers stood on the front of the boat and pushed the oars. You should see and hear them at the rapids. The song they sing is a thing to be remembered. They are most apt to sing when they are rowing the hardest and how I love to hear the call coming over the water from a distant boat and then, perhaps, our men taking up the chant. Then suddenly, at just the right second, they drop the oars, rush to the huge sweep which projects from the front of the boat and with all their might swing it this way or that and we are over the rapid in safety. You hold your breath and marvel at their skill!

We were three and one-half days on the boat, arriving here in time for dinner on Saturday, February 28th. Dr. Henry Davidson and his brother, Alfred, are the hosts. Both men have families in England. Irene Hutchinson also arrived from Chengtu on Saturday, so there are five of us foreigners altogether. The Davidsons are Irish. Dr. D. makes an excellent housekeeper. His servants, tried and true, had everything nicely arranged for us. It is a real British household including tea served in bed each morning. Being the only married lady in the party, I sit at one end of the table and help with the serving, also pouring coffee in the "drawing-room" after dinner each evening, and tea in the afternoon. I am having a good time.

March 10, 1925

Outside Suining, on a hill in a grove of old, old trees, is one of the most famous Buddhist temples in this section of China. Thousands of pilgrims are now coming here for the great Goddess of Mercy festival. Many come because it is a carnival occasion, no doubt, but it is a serious affair for countless others. Great processions come with banners and flags and huge decorated candles to burn before the idols. A great revolving tower at least fifteen feet high has shelves all around it along its full length with some three hundred idols. A person can go inside the tower to revolve it. The idea is to accomplish the worship of all the gods at one full turn. This afternoon the people were throwing their incense sticks up onto the tower until all but the very topmost shelves were well covered.

I have found it worthwhile to go along the road mingling and trying to talk with people. In fact I have been giving away tracts and selling Gospels. I do not have a great deal of faith in the method but I am sure the Gospels may bring some light to the people and it gives me a splendid chance to practice my Chinese. It is rather easy to gather a small crowd. I start by going up to a group of people and asking them if they can read. I almost never find a woman who can recognize characters. The men who read were very scarce this afternoon. Others see a foreigner talking to a group and come to look on. Once I noticed a priest standing on the edge of the crowd. I wondered if he would drive me away but he offered no objection to my attempts to sell my books, although I, of course, openly labeled them as *Christian*.

I wonder how much influence the priests have. Soldiers are on guard at various places on the grounds and some of the idols are actually so hidden by booths where articles are being sold that they can't be seen.

April 3, 1925 *Chengtu, Szechwan*

Dear Home Folks,

I came home from Suining with Irene Hutchinson arriving March 21. We had a good trip and made excellent time. Most people tried to dissuade us from attempting to make the trip from Tungchwan in three days but we did it! This was because we had good men who did not continually stop in opium dens for a smoke. The last day we got up at four o'clock and were on the road well before daybreak. We made 110 *li* (three *li* equal one mile) that day, approximately thirty-seven miles. We walked a good deal, especially the day we crossed the mountains when we made the entire ascent on foot and came down the steepest incline on this side, leaving the men to follow us with the loads and empty chairs.

We had no unusually thrilling adventures except that one night we slept in the *dirtiest* inn I ever hope to see. Pigs were on the other side of a flimsy partition from us! They squealed all night long--at least I heard them whenever I was awake. They took delight in rubbing and scratching their backs on the door which opened from our room into their sty. The door was directly beside my bed and when they came and rubbed and scratched they seemed to shake the very structure until I expected it to tumble about our heads. As for the smell--?!! But all this is part of the fun of chair travel and I would ask no lovelier sight than the Chinese countryside in springtime. As you travel from city to city and from village to village you are in the very midst of beautiful fields. The rape, or mustard, was at its height; it was like looking over a sea of brilliant yellow. The beans and peas were in bloom and the pear, peach, and cherry trees were magnificent.

Robert came out to meet us, several *li* north of the city. And then we crossed the "big capital city" from the North to the South gates. We say that China is slow, but it would be hard to find a city anywhere which has made greater progress outwardly in one short year than has Chengtu. When I arrived here in 1923 we considered the *Wen Miao Hou Kai* to be one of the very best streets. It was a comfort to walk upon it after jumping puddles and balancing oneself on wobbly paving stones (which sometimes sent the water flying into the air like a fountain) or trying to keep one's equilibrium on the crest or in the trough of narrow ruts made by wheel-barrows. Today, the *Wen Miao*

Hou Kai is nothing compared with the fine new wide streets. Our military governor-general, Yang Sen, who certainly has many progressive ideas, has accomplished the impossible.

I was astounded to ride all the way from the North Gate to the South Bridge, more than an hour's ride in a chair, along wide smooth streets. I felt as one does in landing in New York City from the country! Crowds of people were out on the streets and rickshas were flying hither and thither. I felt I should not be surprised to see a trolley-car come around the corner; I could imagine I was in Shanghai! Of course, one might not be so thrilled if just out from home, but to one who has become Chinese-ized it is truly marvelous. Years ago rickshas were used here but were discontinued until this new street improvement was inaugurated. Moreover, the city gates are left open all night now and some of the streets are lighted with electricity!

These are busy times since I am trying to put in full days at the Language School. I am glad to get back to school with the others. I have made a start on the language and I have a "feel" for it. It gets more interesting all the time. I feel happier and more encouraged about my progress than I have for some time.

Sunday, April 26, 1925 *Chengtu, West China*

Dear Folks at Home,

Perhaps I bragged too soon in my previous letter about our modernized city. The other military leaders and political aspirants in Szechwan have combined against Yang Sen in an effort to oust him. There has been fighting a day's journey from Chengtu. We hope it will not come nearer. I believe there is a good deal of popular feeling against Yang Sen in the city, but as far as we foreigners are concerned we should like him to remain in power and continue the improvements. Well, one never knows in China what the next day will bring forth. It will be interesting to see what happens.

Carl* asked if there are any automobiles in Chengtu. At present, no. Yang Sen has some ordered and I expect they are on the way. You will be interested to know that Yang Sen's plan is to fine a man $40 Mex. ($20 gold) for running down and killing a person! He dare not put the sum higher lest people throw themselves in the path of the machines.

There is more or less excitement in the air due to anti-foreign and anti-Christian agitation. It has reached considerable proportions in

---

**My brother, Carl B. Timberlake.*

Chungking and has already manifested itself here in a strike of the student nurses in the women's hospital. Students in the Christian schools are dubbed "foreign dogs" and "foreign slaves." I suppose it is rough on them, but the ultimate results may be good if it will bring out the best in them. At present we as foreigners have nothing to fear. We need to correct our faults and to ignore the slander. The agitation here is only a part of the anti-religious student movement which is expressing itself pretty generally all over China. The Chinese quite justifiably are objecting to imperialism and the invasion of their country by imperialistic powers. It is quite evident that the Chinese are cordially receiving ideas propagated by Bolshevist agencies.

May 25, 1925 *Chengtu, West China*

Dear Folks at Home,

Mt. Omei is one of China's "sacred" mountains famous in story and legend for its beauty and renowned as a mecca for Buddhists. During an ordinary summer thousands of pilgrims ascend the "Golden Summit" to worship and win merit for themselves. Omei is a resort for Westerners as well. Robert has never been there and of course I never have, so we are going for self-education as well as vacation. We shall take a boat down to Kiating, which you will remember is the place where we were wrecked. Then we have a day overland and up the mountain. We have rented our Behludin bungalow. I am sure I can never like Omei better than Behludin.

I took my first Language School examination the other day and got a nearly perfect grade (it was the sort of exam on which one should easily get a good score) and I plan to get two or three more examinations out of the way before school closes.

We live on an undeveloped (as yet) part of the campus out in the country and this is an interesting time of year to watch the fields. The beans, rape, and wheat have been harvested and the fields are being flooded, plowed, and harrowed before dabbing in the rice seedlings. In fact, some are already in. This is the time of year, too, when the farmers simply sling the liquid manure all over the country and the air is "rosy." However, it really isn't as bad as it sounds. It is only during the slinging process that you get the smell. The land is never idle here and the extensive irrigation system, 2,100 years old, is both truly marvelous and efficiently used.

...Yang Sen seems to be gaining victories, therefore I doubt if the fighting will reach Chengtu. Of course, that does not mean less distress elsewhere. Although Szechwan is the richest province in China there are sections now in terrible famine. Somehow everything goes on happily here. With the lack of communication and transportation facilities--how *can* the people be one in sympathetic action or one in anything else?

June 28, 1925

Pao Lin Shi
en route Omei San

Dear Folks at Home,

It is no small task getting the house closed up and things ready for the summer trip. We have to take *everything*--food supplies, as sugar, flour, tinned milk, salt, peanut oil; lamps and kerosene; bed and bedding.

In the midst of it all the servants went on strike one day! I expect you have read in the papers of the student demonstrations in Shanghai and elsewhere. They started after one or more Chinese were killed in a Japanese factory in Shanghai. This incited the students to an anti-foreign parade. The police in seeking to keep order in the British concession imprisoned some of the student leaders. Other students who surrounded the prison in an attempt to get them out were fired upon and several were killed. That was enough in this time of anti-foreign agitation to arouse students all over China to action. The Chengtu Student Association issued tracts, propaganda against foreigners, and staged a parade. All servants of foreigners had to parade, under threat of death. So, as I said, a week ago we were without household help.

The students had organized, we are told, in such a way that if news came from Peking of an unfavorable settlement of the down-river troubles, all the servants could be forced to go on a *permanent* strike. The idea is to boycott the foreigner. As a matter of fact, a good many servants would no doubt remain faithful in spite of threats. For one thing, they are too dependent upon the foreigner for their rice. At any rate, our cook and helper came away with us on Wednesday without any hesitation. The gateman-gardener is left in charge of the property and the *amah* took sewing to do at home. I should add that our University and Middle School students, although they participated in the demonstration, have in general remained friendly to us all.

We came by boat to Kiating and had a fine trip. From Kiating to this Buddhist temple where we are now stopping we travelled by chair. Such beautiful country!!...

We did not plan to stop here more than over night but a heavy rain came up and we were afraid to start again lest we get our loads wet.

The men will come back for us tomorrow. Sacred Omei is close at hand, a great peak towering into the clouds....

July 14, 1925 *Mt. Omei, Szechwan*

Dear Friends in the Homeland,

While following the winding paths across the lovely country it is easy to forget the horribly dirty and ill-smelling villages where the poor people live crowded together in such sordidness. It is hard to realize that famine stalks certain sections. Even in this rich fertile Szechwan of ours, the most wretched misery is probably the lot of thousands.

Not long ago we had a letter from a missionary who lives in Pachow, a fourteen days' journey east of Chengtu. He wrote:

> *Pachow has had a very bad time, and though just at present things are easier owing to the good spring crops, yet there will be a very bad time again before long, and it will last until the rice harvest is in....We had a good rain here yesterday and the young rice seems to promise well, though in some places there have been so many deaths in the country, that though there has been water in the fields, there has been nobody to plant out the rice. People have been dying like flies....Brigands are very bad in the near country now and the soldiers do not do anything to put them down.*

We continue to get newspaper reports of the anti-foreign disturbances in Shanghai and other port cities. Experienced missionaries feel that this is indeed a critical time. The Chinese are an exceedingly proud people and the history of the past fifty years rankles in their minds. The student class, especially, have a sufficient knowledge to make them peculiarly sensitive to the humiliations which this country has suffered at the hands of the Great Powers, but on the other hand they may lack the experience which would enable them to realize the pitiable weakness of China. This is a time of rising national consciousness and the students are determined to secure complete sovereignty for China. However strongly we may disapprove their methods we can not but sympathize with their aspirations.

July 29, 1925

The anti-foreign agitation in Szechwan has been directed principally against the British. The Chinese succeeded so well with their boycott against the English and the Canadians in Chungking that the British consul ordered the women and children down river. The British men lived for a time all together down on the shore near the gunboat, subsisting chiefly on tinned goods. Even our two English Friends had to go there, but they of course refused to bear arms. We hear now, however, that the Chungking Chinese servants have returned to work and that the situation there is a bit easier. But for a time we wondered if we should have to help our British friends pack and leave since the consul advised the evacuation of all mountain resorts, but people were loath to leave unless it should become absolutely necessary, because the fearful heat and other conditions of summer travel are apt to seriously endanger the health of young children.

Recent reports state that the situation in Chengtu is fairly satisfactory. Conditions in Chengtu have never been as bad as in Chungking, partly because Chengtu is not an open port and foreign gunboats have not been present. Governor Yang Sen has now suffered serious reverses and the local political situation is therefore far from good. He was badly defeated at Luchow, a city a few days' journey north of Chungking, and it is said he has gone out to personally direct his forces.

In spite of the turmoil and unrest abroad in the country we are enjoying a comfortable and restful summer in the mountains. The climate is very much like that of my New Hampshire home. William and Hilda Sewell, young English Friends, live in the other half of the cottage with us. They are language students too, and when we all are at study in the morning and saying our lessons out loud after the Chinese teachers there is quite a din.

Only a few days ago we four took a trip to Mt. Omei's "Golden Summit." We started off in a pouring rain and were obliged at the outset to wade through several flooded mountain streams. It soon cleared, however, and we had remarkably good weather for most of the ascent. The summit is 11,000 feet. From the edge of the sheer cliff, which some say is itself a mile high, we had a marvelous view of the plain and the mountains nearly encircling us. At sunrise we saw the snow mountains of Tibet. There is one peak which stands out above all the others, an exquisite gleaming white cone, fascinating in its mystery. Probably no person has ever climbed it. Some of our scientists at the University believe it may be higher than Everest!* Another charm of the "Golden Summit" is "Buddha's Glory." With the sun at your back in the late afternoon you see your shadow cast upon the clouds below and encircled by a golden halo. You wave and the figure below answers with a similar wave of the arms.

---

*Minya Konka was found to be 24,900 feet high.

August 20, 1925 *Mt. Omei*

Dear Girls,

The patch-work pattern of rice fields spread out below us is taking on a yellow hue and there is a bit of autumn tang in the air, although I dare say it is still hot enough on the plain. The dry leaves fluttering down and scattered by the wind help to remind us that it is time to get back to Chengtu.

...Rival generals with combined forces have finally succeeded in ousting military governor Yang Sen. At present the province is in a most unsettled state. The game always, it seems, is for each "victor" to grab all he can for himself while he has the chance. There may be a recombination of generals before the spoils are finally divided and yesterday's enemies may become allies tomorrow. Who knows? Meanwhile, the territory between the large centers, which are held by the generals, is a "no man's land" where bandits have free play.

We have been thinking a good deal these past few days of the party of C.M.S. missionaries who are passing through difficult times at the hands of robbers. From a small (English) Church Missionary Society summer colony near Mienchow (three or four days journey from Chengtu) these foreigners, seven or eight in all, including Bishop and Mrs. Mowll, Mr. and Mrs. Donnithorne and their little daughter, all of whom we know, were recently taken off by bandits. The brigands came boldly into their houses at night and forced the missionaries to go with them into the hills. The foreigners were permitted to send a letter to the British consul, and the brigands no doubt helped to dispatch it. They are of course looking for a big ransom. What has happened to these friends of ours has been happening every day for the past several years to numbers of Chinese. How much it all sounds and seems like days in England a few hundred years ago*....

September 6, 1925 *Chengtu, West China*

Dear Fannie,

I am going to let you in on our secret right away. If all goes well we shall have a baby arrive sometime about early May. I have been very well all summer. I had hoped to be able to go to Language School this fall but now I doubt if I can manage it. I hate to have more set-backs in my study.

**The foreigners were finally released, no serious harm coming to any of them.*

Robert has just come in and told me that young Dr. Leslie Kilborn was shot and wounded while in Kiating. The Kilborns, with others, were to follow us from Omei the next day. They have not yet appeared and no word has come until this news today. It appears that Yang Sen's enemies have surrounded him at Kiating and have it in for him. I suppose Dr. Leslie got a stray bullet. We realize more than ever how exceedingly fortunate we were to get through when we did. There is a foreign hospital in Kiating; fortunately Mrs. Kilborn herself is a doctor, too.

With all these stories you will think more than ever that we live in a wild country. However, most of the time we live along just about as you do at home. I wasn't a bit nervous coming up river on our return from Omei. Perhaps I don't know enough to be afraid....

We were ready to start down the mountain the twenty-sixth, but our carriers failed to appear and we were delayed one day. However we arrived at Tang Fang and were on our boat at about six o'clock on the twenty-seventh. We went down the river that evening to Kiating--at considerable risk we were later told. There were two bad rapids to make in the semi-dark, but we got through them without mishap. Besides, as you know, this is wartime in Szechwan and there were sentinels at intervals along the shore who halted us. Robert stood on the front of the boat a good part of the time in readiness to call out to them, "We are foreigners come from Omei." Otherwise we were afraid they might fire on us. No one fired on us that night, but at one place after pulling in to shore at the sentinel's call, one of the soldiers came aboard to inspect our cargo. He came onto the boat with his knife drawn and was generally uncivil but did us no harm.

From Kiating on up the Min River to Chengtu we travelled with others in a flotilla of eight boats. There were two with the American flag, two of Canadian ladies with the British flag, a young German selling dye stuffs with the German flag, a boatful of Chinese schoolgirls sailing under the British flag and returning to the school under the auspices of the Canadians in the city, and two boat loads of Chinese teachers and students. The last two boats had no flag. Going down river to Kiating the students who were to teach the language school people travelled on a boat together under a huge American flag.

And all this after the recent anti-foreign agitation! It would be laughable if it were not so pitiable. Think of it, a Chinese does not dare travel in his own country without the protection of the despised foreigner! The students in our schools are, for the most part, still friendly as ever, at least in their individual contacts. However, we are expecting a smaller enrollment in the University than usual.

In passing through the region between the two lines we were fired on at two different places but with no bad results. The soldiers simply got panicky and thought the enemy were coming. After a little negotiating we got through safely.

October 13, 1925 *Chengtu, West China*
[Day before Confucius' birthday]

Dear Home Folks,

...Chengtu is now quiet but conditions throughout the province are not good. They have had a terrible time in Kiating, city under siege, people starving, filth piled in the street, disease, etc. I wrote that Dr. Kilborn was shot through the shoulder while waiting there. He is recovering. In fact all our foreign community is now safely back. The poor Chinese do not get off so well.

The enrollment in the schools so far is not short of last year's, and the students' spirit is good. Three students were in yesterday and had afternoon tea with us. We were interested to hear one of them turn to Robert and say in his studied English, "I hope you and Mrs. Simkin will stay here for a long time." It was his way of expressing his personal good-will toward the foreigners.

We are as quiet and happy here on campus this evening as you are at home, as you begin the day we are ending. It is almost as difficult for us as for you to realize the hard conditions a few miles away from here when all is so peaceful close at hand. To be sure many nights this fall we have heard shots out in the country. The robbers, working in a band, were attacking a nearby farmhouse. The local militia is almost powerless to deal with them.

January 3, 1926 *Chengtu, West China*

Dear Home Folks,

The days are full. We have had a good many guests and it seems sometimes a missionary wife's chief business is entertaining guests, which takes time. We have anywhere from one to four at a meal; some stay all night. Of course we have our Chinese help, but who is going to see that hot water is set outside the doors of the guestrooms at the proper time if not the mistress of the house? Or that the beds have enough bedding on them? Or who is going to order the meals and reckon accounts with the cook? Or unlock the fuel house while the house boy gets out coal and kerosene? For several weeks now Dr. Stubbs has been coming here pretty regularly for lunch and with the beginning of the New Year we have taken in a roomer, Miss Andrews who is Dr. Beech's secretary. We are trying to put our home to good use.

Yesterday the Friends College, a beautiful new building built by English Friends, was formally opened.

Christmas went off as usual. It was a beautiful day, bright, warm, and sunny. We had dinner with the Dyes. On Saturday we went to the school in the Manchu City for their party. We were first invited to dinner with Mr. Wu.* ...We enjoyed watching the children as they went through their program, much as children do at home with proud parents looking on. They were pleased as could be with their small toys. Besides, each child had a package of peanuts and an orange. On Monday after Christmas we were at a belated Christmas dinner party at the Rodwells in the city. We spent the night at Green Dragon Street. The city gates do not remain open these days. However, the construction of fine roads continues since Yang Sen left.

Did I write about the other party I attended at the Rodwells? Dorothy had me in one noon especially to meet four Chinese ladies of the upper class. My contact here on the campus is limited to students, of course, and I was delighted with this opportunity to meet some real "ladies." They were dressed in black figured silk skirts and beautiful light silk jackets, heavily padded with cotton wadding for warmth. They were also rather heavily bejewelled with long earrings, fancy pins, strings of beads, and rings. Mrs. Tsai I liked especially. She is very pretty with that lovely complexion which the Chinese have sometimes, a delicate rose under a bloom like a ripe peach. She was very sweet and very much of a lady. Mrs. Rodwell told me that as a matter of principle Tsai Tai Tai does not have gambling in her home. As a consequence she cuts herself off from the social life which the other ladies enjoy....

April 5, 1926 *Chengtu, West China*

Dear Home Folks,

We have been breaking in a new house woman, one who will be able to help look after the baby. I miss Pen Da Niang but I think the new woman will prove satisfactory after she learns the ropes.

I must tell you about the box of freight. The Johnsons, new people, brought me the remains--a battered pasteboard box about a foot square. I must confess I sat down and bawled when I saw the contents.

**Wu Seo Chin, Quaker principal at school. The Manchu City School was supported by American Friends.*

The things were simply pushed into the box, not wrapped or even decently packed. The box contained among other things a hat much jammed which I first thought I could not wear, but which I since have pulled into shape and now am wearing with great satisfaction. There was no sign of the wool skirt nor the nice sweater (which I need so badly) and of the baby's layette, only a little soiled dress. To think of your putting all the time and effort and love into making those little things and then for them never to get here!

...Some days ago we saw a very interesting Confucian service at five o'clock in the morning. No idols but the offering of a huge ox as sacrifice.*

May 6, 1926 *Canadian Women's Missionary Society Hospital*
Chengtu, Szechwan

Dear Home Folks,

Robert has already written you about our little May Day gift of Dorothy Ellen, nine pounds one ounce, but I must add my bit. I wish you all could see her this minute as she lies waving her arms happily in her crib. I guess there never were parents more daffy over a youngster than we are. I surely did not imagine how wonderful it all would be.

I have the same room here at the hospital as before. The Chinese nurses are nice as can be and are very much delighted with the wee foreign baby.

Friends have been kind in sending notes and flowers. You couldn't imagine a nicer community to live in than ours here. My good Pen Da Niang brought me flowers and ten eggs today. Four of the college boys sent flowers, eggs (characteristic Chinese gift) and firecrackers to the

---

**In a Confucian temple there are no idols, but only tablets to Confucius and to his disciples. Twice each year--in April and October--the carcasses of cattle and hogs are set up on racks before these tablets. About three or four in the morning the temple court is illumined by fires of kindling wood which cast a lurid light over all. The official of highest rank in the country or in the province, together with subordinate officials and gentry, prostrates himself in worship in the center of the temple court. The following day the flesh of the animals which have been sacrificed is divided among those who have contributed, for the Chinese are always practical and never waste anything.*

[*From notes of Robert L. Simkin*]

house. The house servants all seem much pleased, Robert says, "even at the arrival of a girl."

June 6, 1926
Dear Home Folk,

Dorothy has not gained well but otherwise is fine. Fortunately we have a very good baby doctor right here on the campus, Dr. Janet Kilborn, who has Dorothy in charge. Without her help I might be worried....In less than three weeks we expect to start for Behludin....

June 10, 1926

I expect it may get into the papers at home so I may as well write you the facts as far as we can know them. A tragic thing happened here on Monday. The details are almost too horrendous to tell. Mrs. Sibley, a Canadian missionary, in from Junghsien for medical and dental attention at the capital (Chengtu is the provincial capital), was brutally murdered while walking on the street. The murderer is believed to have been a madman. He had a sword with which he beheaded her, leaving her body in the street and carrying the head some little distance and then throwing it into a cesspit. The body lay in the street some time before a foreigner chanced along and discovered it. The murderer was followed by police and shot.

On the very next day Grace Manly of the Methodist Mission, our neighbor, was attacked on the street while riding in a ricksha. A well-dressed Chinese came up behind her, seized her by the throat and pulled her out of her ricksha onto the street. She got away and was attacked by him a second time. Again she escaped and, telling the ricksha coolie to run as fast as he could, she got away from her assailant altogether. The people on the street, especially the other students, helped her as best they could. She had a servant with her who was responsible for having the man arrested, getting some bites on the knee in the scramble. Grace is alright now except for some prints on her neck where the skin was broken. Of course people here are much agitated.

This has come after getting past May 30th, the anniversary of the Shanghai incident, peacefully. We don't believe it to be part of any widespread movement. Putting it in the best possible light, it all is a result of the anti-foreign propaganda which has, for these past months, been preached on the streets. It was fuel for the madman and in the second case, suggestion created an impulse which wasn't inhibited. No doubt the fellow had been turning over and over in his mind the incident of the day before. He saw a foreign woman and the impulse to strangle her came over him.

At present foreigners are not going out on the street much, but I presume matters will quiet down in a few days. You need not worry. If anything dreadful happens you will know of it before this letter can reach you. Hearing nothing until you read this you may rest assured all is quiet again in Chengtu.

July 25, 1926 *"Rockynotch"*
Behludin

Dear Home Folks,

A glorious summer day in the mountains! How we wish you were all here to enjoy the beauty with us. I suppose we are at an elevation equal to that of Mt. Washington (New Hampshire) and the views are magnificent. Of course being farther south than Mt. Washington it is warmer, but even here the air is cool and bracing. From our front piazza I can see the great Chengtu plain with the river meandering across it. In the near foreground is a rocky pinnacle, somewhat overgrown but on one side a sheer precipice. This we call the "Tiger's Tooth." On the top is a tiny shrine--most picturesque. About six feet in front of the porch the mountain drops off and standing on the edge I can look down into the little valley some hundreds of feet below. To the west and northwest are higher peaks, some snow covered. They are lovely with the morning sun glistening on them.

Normally we are a two days' trip from Chengtu--some fifty miles. But this time it took us three days. It is not easy to travel in China with a baby. The first night we made Penghsien where there are foreigners and I could get fresh cow's milk for Dorothy. The second day we only got as far as Kwankeo. There a plank bridge was out and our men would not carry us further lest we could not complete the next stage....I had no fresh milk for Dorothy on the third day and had to use evaporated milk which did not work at all well....

Robert's letter of August 5 gives details of our trip.

Dear Friends,

Early on July 7th, we started for the mountain, Margaret with baby Dorothy in a four bearer sedan chair, Chiang Da Niang, the *amah*, in a two bearer chair, and I on a wheel. It was so difficult to secure carriers that we had to leave most of our baggage to follow two or three days later. I dispatched the chairs first and then remained to close the house and attend to items of business at the Friends College. It was eleven o'clock before I reached the west gate of Chengtu. Imagine my surprise to find there the *amah*. Her carriers had set down her chair outside the gate and disappeared, and there she had sat for over two hours! As no bearers were in sight and it was manifestly impossible for that chair to reach Penghsien that night I told the woman if no better plan could be found to call local men to carry her back to the University and make a fresh start in a day or two in company with others who were coming to Behludin. I then rode on and overtook Margaret's chair just before it stopped for dinner.

...At one point on a narrow road I attempted to pass Margaret's chair. Just then the carriers stopped to shift the weight to the other shoulder, leaving me so little room that the handle bar touched the chair and threw me off my balance. The first thing Margaret saw was her husband taking a header, bicycle and all, into an irrigation stream and out of sight. Fortunately the water was only about four feet deep, so I soon fished the wheel and myself out. I wasn't hurt at all, and my watch didn't stop! The same watch was under water at our wreck at Kiating. The bicycle rode alright at first but gradually developed a weak handle bar stem which broke off six or seven miles before we reached Penghsien.

We were most hospitably entertained by the missionaries at Penghsien and spent a comfortable night. The next morning it rained so hard that we did not leave until after dinner. I cleaned and reset the handlebar stem further down so that I hope it will be possible to ride the bicycle back to Chengtu on our return trip. As the roads were presumably deep mud and it would have had to be carried up the mountain in any case, I left it at Penghsien for the summer and walked the rest of the way. We found the newly constructed road far better than we expected and followed it about ten miles to its end. At several places considerable detours had to be made on the narrow dykes between rice fields and a four bearer chair is an awkward thing to get over sharp angled turns. Two or three times one of the carriers fell on the slippery banks of irrigation streams. Once the forward men on Margaret's chair were crossing a narrow plank over an irrigation stream at the same time as the rear two men were on a similar bridge over a second stream, where neither pair could have helped the other in case of a misstep. However, at no time did they actually drop the family into the water.

West of Kwankeo the river is crossed by a long suspension bridge of bamboo cables; at other places heavy planks carry the traveller from pier to pier over rushing water. These planks are carried away after heavy rains, but are tethered by bamboo cables fastened to one end so that they shall not be entirely lost and can be replaced when the water recedes. One of these plank bridges was thus submerged before we arrived, so we spent a night at Kwankeo, a village where the river emerges from the mountains. Imagine our surprise as Margaret handed me the baby from the sedan chair to see a Chinese woman who was standing among the crowd offer to take her. It was our own Chiang Da Niang. She had at last secured carriers and the previous night had slept at Dragon Bridge, fourteen miles from Chengtu. She had pressed on all the second day, and because of our delay at Penghsien had just overtaken us.

There was no decent inn in the place so I scouted around to find a place for the night. A schoolroom in a temple offered the best prospects and the teacher very kindly permitted us to sleep there. For lack of carriers our camp beds had been left behind, but on one of the loads was a couch which had fortunately arrived. Although it was narrow for two I spent a comfortable night. Margaret might well have wished for a husband less tall than six feet three plus!! The schoolroom consisted of several small buildings in the form of a rectangle about a "heavenly well," a small paved area open to the sky, which provided air and light. In rainy weather the pupils move back from the centre to the sides where the rain cannot reach them. Of course there is no provision for heating in winter, except that the teacher and perhaps a few of the pupils carry a small charcoal handstove. The room proper had no floor except mother earth, but the place was very clean and satisfactory. The teacher was cordial and much interested in chatting about school affairs and American customs.

Anti-foreign feeling? Yes, of course it does exist but the great majority of the people are as friendly as ever. We heard one oath directed at us as we entered Kwankeo, but it was the only instance when we encountered any treatment which was other than courteous. The people were very much interested in the baby, women and children especially crowding around whenever we stopped.

On the third day, the bridge having been replaced, we proceeded six or seven miles to Si Wen Tsang, a village at the foot of the mountain. Here we stored Margaret's four bearer chair in a temple and secured a two bearer mountain chair for the ascent. Being high on the shoulders and shorter than a four bearer sedan these mountain chairs do not drag and catch so badly on rocks and bushes in turning sharp zigzags of the narrow path. Margaret had two splendid mountain men, and although it rained hard and the road was very slippery they pushed on up the mountain at a rapid pace, reaching the top at five o'clock.

Robert L. Simkin
Chengtu, West China

September 8, 1926 *Chengtu, West China*

Dear Folks,

I have just seen Dr. Janet Kilborn and she advises a milk nurse for Dorothy. It isn't that she is not gaining at all but the doctor maintains that a baby should have mother's milk to withstand the rigors of this climate. It will take a lot of time and trouble to manage such an arrangement, but perhaps no more time than I have to spend at present boiling bottles and milk. Don't get the idea that Dorothy is pining away. She is a strong, happy youngster in spite of failure to get sufficient and proper nourishment.

Robert's letter ot September 29th will give added understanding of our serious political situation.

September 29, 1926 *Chengtu, West China*

Dear Friends,

Reports are so contradictory that it is difficult to know exactly what is happening. The following, however, seems to be true: Yang Sen, who until August 1925 was governor at Chengtu, now controls the Yangtse territory for a large part of the distance between Ichang and Chungking. His headquarters are at Wanhsien. Some of his soldiers attempted to commandeer a British merchant vessel below Wanhsien. A few boarded the steamer and tried to rush the bridge and the engine room, but the officers shut themselves in, and the soldiers could not gain admittance. Seeing other soldiers coming in small boats, the captain gave the signal, "Full steam ahead," and got away from them, but the waves from the steamer capsized one or more boats and some of the soldiers drowned.

News of this was telegraphed to Wanhsien, and Yang Sen attempted to intercept the steamer there. The steamer, however, did not make the usual stop at Wanhsien and passed on up the river. Very angry at this, Yang Sen seized the two British merchant steamers which next arrived at Wanhsien, confined their officers on board, and threatened their lives if the British gunboats attempted their release. The British disguised a steamer, loaded marines on her, and drew in between the captive steamers. They landed a party upon one of these steamers and released her officers, but they seem to have been unable to board the second steamer. During the melee her officers made a dash for liberty and jumped into the water to swim to the rescuing ship. In the fight at least nine British marines were killed or fatally wounded, this number including two or three officers. At the close of the engagement the British ship shelled Wanhsien, striking Yang Sen's headquarters and killing some soldiers and some civilians.

All this has greatly aroused the Chinese, especially in Chungking, and to a lesser degree here. In Chungking a boycott was organized to sell no food to British. British subjects concentrated at one point for protection, and now most of them have gone down river. As the agitation is thus far chiefly against the British, few if any Americans felt it necessary to go. Alfred Davidson and Irene Hutchinson, who were the only British Friends in Chungking, left about a week ago. The most serious element in the situation there was that the local militia on the hills opposite the city became hostile and insisted that the Friends High School for boys must be closed. This hostility is blamed, whether rightly or wrongly I cannot say, to Bolshevist propaganda. F.L. Yang* was badly maltreated. Full details have not yet been received. It seems probable that this will break up the school at least for this term.

Here in Chengtu we have had several rather anxious days, but the outlook has never been so serious as in Chungking, and it is now improving. On Sunday morning I was twice called a dog by some students, and one occasionally hears curses as one passes along the street. So long as it amounts only to this it does not really matter. There is to be a big parade day after tomorrow, the purpose of which is to arouse public sentiment against the British, and it is reported that an extensive boycott is being organized to cut off supplies of food from the British, and to induce their servants to leave their employ. We have laid in a considerable supply of food against such a contingency.

In some quarters it is believed that the educational institutions in Chengtu are honeycombed with "Red" Communistic propaganda and that at any moment the generals who are in power may throw in their lot with the South and inaugurate a Communist regime here which will be distinctly anti-foreign. This is a possibility--indeed, one may never say in China that a thing cannot or will not happen--but I do not look for this to take place for a considerable time yet, if at all. The general who is at the moment strongest in power has assured foreigners that he will protect them and has expressed the hope that they will not leave. More

---

**Principal of Friends High School and a leading Chungking Quaker.*

important, our most trusted Chinese workers take a hopeful view of the situation. They assure us that we have a great many friends among the gentry and substantial citizens. Last spring when Mrs. Sibley was murdered on the street, a cultured and educated man who is a trusted adviser of the government visited every foreign family in that part of the city and expressed his personal regret and sorrow.

Chengtu has an advantage over down river ports. Here there are no British or American gunboats to stir up trouble.

Robert L. Simkin

October 4, 1926 *Chengtu, West China*

Dear Home Folks,

You will be interested to hear what is happening in this part of the world. Such an upset world it does seem sometimes.

Just as I was starting this letter I was called to the door. A young fellow stood there with a circular notice in his hand. He said, addressing me in Chinese, "*Si mu*, you are an Englishwoman?" When I told him that I was an American he said something about its not being important and went off. I did not see his circular notice but I can easily guess that it had to do with arrangements for the parade tomorrow for we are told that the Chinese helpers of English people are to march in protest of the Wanhsien affair. (I refer to the bombardment of Wanhsien by the British.) The students are the prime agitators. A boycott of all Britishers seems very likely. Since a large number of the workers here at the University are British (Canadian or English) we shall be pretty hard hit if the agitation becomes acute.

Later

This evening the situation looks rather bad to us but one never can tell. Sometimes everything seems to be closing in about us to make an almost intolerable situation but after a few days matters clear and we wonder how we could have had such a fancy. This campus on which we live is a beautiful and peaceful spot. Whatever does happen we *do* hope we shall not have to run away down river. If people can only stay quietly and calmly at their work and take what may come with a Christlike spirit it will be a greater victory for Christianity in this land than anything else which has happened for a long while. The Sibley tragedy of last June has helped many Chinese to better understand the missionary's motive for being here. The fact that the church and Christians did not seek to retaliate but remained kindly disposed toward the Chinese was an eye opener for them.

The next evening

The day has brought some unexpected events. Our cook announced at breakfast that he and the other servants must go out onto the street to participate in the demonstration. They dared not do otherwise. It did not matter so much to have the men go, but when the baby's milk nurse announced that she must go too or the students "would kill her," my heart sank--not that I thought the students would really harm her but because the baby is so dependent upon her. She thought that she would have to be away all day but as a matter of fact she came back to feed Dorothy in the middle of the day.

Of far more importance is that the students here at the University have struck. The trouble started by the students publishing and distributing a "declaration" vilifying the British. Now the students this year have been unusually courteous and thoughtful in their relationships with foreigners on the campus and their manifesto was only a way of saving their faces in the eyes of the students in the city. They doubtless did not intend that anyone should believe what they wrote or believe that they believed what they wrote. However, some of the authorities here at the University did not think it could be overlooked. So, figuratively speaking, they picked up their cudgels and further inflamed the students!

Sunday, October 10, 1926

Well, the student strike is over and we are glad indeed. It has been a time of strain for students and foreigners alike. There is too much dynamite lying about these days to make it safe to play with fire! It is hard for the Chinese student, for *any* Chinese, to stand out for the right against the crowd. Perhaps we can hardly understand the amount of moral courage which is demanded. No doubt some of the more thoughtful students will have been helped by this difficult experience to know that they must mean what they say and say what they mean. And the foreigner has learned, I hope, that this is a time when he needs to be especially forbearing.

October 19, 1926

Dear Fannie,

We are expecting that all our servants will walk out tomorrow. The student agitators from the city, aided and abetted no doubt by the dissatisfied faction of students here following our student strike, are directing this thrust against the University with the hope of crippling it. The servants really **don't** want to strike but dare not stand out against the threats. I feel awfully troubled about the baby's wet nurse leaving, but if the strike does not last long perhaps it will not matter seriously. The baby is getting a good start now and is dear and cunning. She is a happy little thing and a real comfort.

Sunday we took her to the Friends Meeting at *Chin Lung Gai* (Green Dragon Street) and had a little dedicatory service for her. Robert and I stood up, Robert holding her in his arms, and I said a few words (in Chinese), as did Robert. Then there was a prayer. Dorothy was as good as could be and smiled at people so that the Chinese were quite delighted with her.

October 20, 1926, 10 p.m.

We have had one day of it! The servants all left this morning. They did as much of the work as they could before they were called out. The baby's nurse came back just as we were eating dinner to get her *pu kai* and fed Dorothy. The rest of the time Dorothy has been having cow's milk. I have kept busy all day long but it has been rather fun--for one day. I guess I'll find out what it means to be a *real* missionary if this keeps up. These are exciting times to be living through. One has a chance to take close notes on mob psychology. Crowds of middle school (high school) students go by howling like hoodlums, "Strike the foreigner!" "Kill the foreign slaves!" etc., etc. It is making men out of some of the students and demons out of others. Many do not dare stand out for what is right; some of great moral caliber are enduring real persecution. The poor ignorant woman who works for us was terribly agitated this morning, simply scared stiff by the threats.

We do not expect any serious difficulty but are preparing ourselves for whatever may come.

November 19, 1926

The boycott and servant strike made strenuous days, primarily because we lack conveniences such as running water, plumbing, electricity, and have no ice or grocery store. I do not care to repeat the experience, but we may have to.

Robert's and my joint report for 1926 sums up some of the outstanding events of the year:

The intense nationalism which burst into flame as a result of the Shanghai incident of May 30, 1925, has during 1926 steadily grown in intensity. It is the result of the meeting of two cultures, a protest against a too servile surrender to the Occident. Its anti-Christian aspect is itself a witness to the inroads which Christianity has already made into the conservatisms of this ancient civilization.

Young China is seething with new ideas of liberty, equality, Communism, Bolshevism, and a hundred other "isms." In common with the rest of the world she is in revolt against authority. Standards of thought and conduct which have been considered forever fixed are being re-examined. Everything is thrown into the melting pot. China has passed the stage where her most characteristic response was, "As you wish, teacher." Now she wants to work things out for herself, not to acquiesce in plans ready made and forced on her from without, but to reach conclusions in accord with her own genius and past history.

Such a situation calls for patience and sympathy with the fundamental aspirations of the Chinese people, no matter how unwise and futile may be the particular means employed to attain these ends. So, too, it is in the light of these conditions that the following events of the year should be viewed.

Last June the whole community was shocked by the murder on the streets of Chengtu of Mrs. Sibley, a Canadian missionary, by a madman or fanatic. His mind must have been unbalanced by the agitation against foreigners. The following day Miss Manly, an American missionary, was attacked while riding in a ricksha by a young man similarly unbalanced mentally. Being very agile, she escaped serious injury. These events and an anonymous warning of a plot to massacre the missionaries at the various summer rest places kept most of the Chengtu community in the city for the early part of the summer. A few bolder ones ventured to the hills and others followed. In a valley perhaps ten miles from the hilltop where we, with about twenty other families, were spending the summer, the Red Lantern Society gathered a group of fanatics who believed themselves to be invulnerable, and started out to kill and destroy. They offered sacrifice and consulted their god whether they should proceed to the hilltop or in another direction. Fortunately for us the lot did not indicate our mountain! At White Water River their passage was contested by the local militia. These militia were well armed, but they were so unnerved by superstitious fears of the magic powers supposed to be possessed by the enemy that they fired only a few shots and fled. The Red Lantern people burned the town and proceeded down the valley. They were lured into a temple for a meal and their leaders were captured and beheaded. The movement then collapsed.

The autumn term opened auspiciously with a good enrollment, but the seizure by the General Yang Sen of two British merchant ships at

Wanhsien and an attempt by British marines to recapture them and free their imprisoned crew caused in Chengtu a fifteen day boycott and strike of the servants of practially all British and American missionaries and mission institutions. During this period the University suspended classes temporarily. It should be stated that the servants were the tools of agitators whom they dared not disobey and that in many instances they smuggled in food and in other ways assisted the missionaries as much as they dared. Our baby's nurse left, but by bootlegging methods we were able to secure fresh cow's milk. None suffered seriously for lack of food.

In Chengtu the anti-foreign feeling has all along been less extreme than in Chungking where the local militia looted the Friends High School and beat the Chinese principal. Doubtless the presence in Chungking of foreign gunboats for many years has intensified the feeling against foreigners. At Tungliang, another Friends station, the meeting house and the dwelling house were looted. Leonard Walker left for Suining and later went to Tungchwan.

The Exodus 1927

January 6, 1927 *Chengtu, West China*

Dear Folks at Home,

...Rather bad news has come from Hankow. You'll probably hear the details sooner than we. It is reported that the foreign concessions in Hankow were surrounded by mobs and that foreigners have been forced to evacuate. It is also said there are British and American boats in Chungking waiting to take us down river! Does this mean the Powers are planning intervention? If only they would keep hands off poor China!

Here in Szechwan there have been reverberations of the revolutionary blows struck down river and our province has had her own dissensions. Yesterday we witnessed the turn-over of the province to the Nationalist party. All shops were ordered to fly the new flag and lo, the streets *blossomed* with the red flag with the blue and white star of the Kuomintang! It was as simple as that--the display of the new flag. In reality, I doubt if the governing military officials cared a whit whether the province affected an allegiance to the rainbow flag (five stripes of the Chinese Republic) or to the star flag, except as it meant their own personal advantage. And certainly the average man of the street had nothing to say about it and cared less.

January 22, 1927 *Chengtu, West China*

Dear Home Folks,

The reports from down river are disquieting. It looks as if Great Britain means intervention. How deplorable such a move would be! I don't know what international law would have to say regarding the seizure of the foreign concessions, custom houses, etc. by the

Southerners, but by all that's right and true under God's law, the Chinese surely are entitled to possess the land of their own country. Of course certain recompense should be made to the foreign powers, but for Great Britain, or any other nation, to demand the return of the concessions at the point of the bayonet--well, it seems as if the world has advanced too far for that. We hope and pray that the United States keeps hands off. There are, according to reports, too many American gunboats and men-of-war in Chinese waters to let us feel easy.

It is impossible to predict what would follow a declaration of war by any of the Powers, but judging from the reaction to the bombardment of Wanhsien we can make certain surmises. The local British consul has urgently and persistently advised the evacuation of all British, and he himself left Chengtu yesterday. The American consul in Chungking has also been urging Americans to leave the province and go to the coast. The situation is no doubt serious. Living as we do about eighteen hundred miles from the coast, one must almost decide to leave when there is still no need to leave, otherwise it may be too late to escape. To those with impaired health, those with a number of children, or those whose furloughs are nearly due the issue is fairly clear. During the last ten days since the close of the semester's work there has been a general exodus of British especially. I suppose that hardly one-third of our missionary group remain. Will it be possible to re-open the University next term with the pitifully small group of workers left? It is difficult to say, but we are going to "carry on" as long as we can. So far it is clear to Robert and me that our place is here.

Robert is tremendously busy with all sorts of accounts and details pertaining to the Friends College and the general work of the F.F.M.A. (English Friends). Dorothy Ellen is content to spend her waking hours laughing and cooing and bringing happiness to all of us. As for myself, I am trying to bend my energies to acquiring a bit more of this difficult and interesting old Chinese language.

January 24, 1927

This afternoon I went to the *ma teo* to see a third big party off. There were nine boat loads. It makes one weep to see the break-up of families, sending the mother and children off down river. The Sewells, too, went today and we are the only foreign Friends left in Chengtu except Jane B. Dye. There is still quite a good company of foreigners left however.

February 16, 1927

Dear Friends,

In my letter of January 22-24 I spoke of the exodus of foreigners and of the depletion of our missionary ranks. For a short period following the exodus we settled down for a bit--or tried to--but telegrams and letters kept coming in, bringing more and more pressure to bear on those of us left. As a consequence of these and especially of messages sent back by President Beech, who had just left for furlough with Mrs. Beech and their four children, a number of families began a hasty packing and they, too, have started off down river this past week. Today there are only five Canadian men left in Chengtu, three of whom are on the campus, and sixteen Americans including Dorothy, twelve of whom are living here at the University. There are no English now in Chengtu. All the English Friends have left their stations with the possible exception of Alfred Davidson who may still be in Chungking. Dorothy is the only foreign child in town and I believe in all Szechwan. Normally there are enough foreign children in the province for the Canadians to run a fair sized boarding school. The situation no doubt is harder on the British than on us Americans, at least up to now. I fear the "Red" army is no respecter of persons, however, when it once gets started!

What does it all mean? It is less than six weeks since it was first reported to us that the "Reds" had seized the British concession at Hankow. In some respects it seems as if months have elapsed since that day. We can get no satisfactory news of what is happening down river; we simply know that people believe the situation to be exceedingly critical and fraught with danger. If negotiations fail, as now seems likely, resentment and hatred of the foreigner will, it is feared, sweep over all of China. Our native friends will be powerless to help us for any attempt on their part to aid us will imperil their own lives.

A week ago Sunday was one of the darkest days I ever spent. Telegram after telegram had come urging us to leave at once. I should say at this point that Robert has not wavered for a moment. He feels that it is his duty to stay by the Chinese and help as long as possible. But what should I do? There is little Dorothy's life for which I am responsible. The trip to Shanghai was a gloomy prospect--crowded refugee conditions of travel, running the gauntlet between opposing armies, having a naval escort and arriving in Shanghai to nobody knew what conditions, to say nothing of the usual dangers from the rapids of the upper river and the possibility of encountering robbers. Yet I felt that if Dorothy and I remained here we should be imperiling Robert's life for we should certainly be a handicap if he had to flee. On the other hand, I could not go away and leave him here with the likelihood of being cut off from all communication with him. We asked for guidance and help; we tried to think the problem through carefully together. That night I went to bed with a struggle going on in my mind and heart.

The next morning I woke with the conflict gone. I felt that I was ready to follow either course; I was willing to go or I was willing to stay, and the thing that really mattered was God's will for us. As the day wore on it became more and more clear to both of us, and we arrived at our decisions independently, that it was right for Dorothy and me to stay on. Personally, I discovered that I was ashamed to tell our Chinese friends that I was thinking of running away. Moreover, neither of us liked the thought of going down river with a naval escort. As I say this I want it clearly understood that I do not mean in any way to pronounce judgment upon those who find themselves forced to accept armed protection. The issue is too involved to label arbitrarily one course right and another wrong. But we do feel that for us this is an opportunity as a united family to bear our little testimony against armed force.

So here we are. At odd moments I am packing some of our smaller possessions into trunks which we may be able to hide somewhere in the city out of the way of looters. I am also arranging a few loads of necessities (in split bamboo boxes to be hung from carrying poles) to be taken with us in case the family has to run. How much we shall be able to take depends upon how many men are willing to carry for us and how long a time we have in which to make our escape.

Perhaps all this preparation will be proved unnecessary. We hope so, but it seems wise to provide for emergencies. Yesterday afternoon we walked out into the country and located a number of places where we might hide temporarily. The country people are very friendly. People on the street generally are courteous. The soldiers who always have been inclined to be rude are perhaps more free with their curses than formerly and with extravagant threats to cut off our heads, etc. Chinese friends and acquaintances take particular pains these days to come to see us. Mr. L..., a very fine Chinese gentleman and a man who because of his integrity is sought after as an advisor by the officials, has called twice at our home. You can plainly see that we are in no difficulty so far.

February 17, 1927

Mail is rather irregular, I suppose because of the trouble down river. Perhaps later mail will not get through, but we'll keep writing.

The servants here can hardly understand what this exodus of foreigners means. My *da niang* begs me to stay and is nearly in tears.

I should have written before, but time has slipped by fast. Last week I was trying to help some of the people get off--played nursemaid two days and had folks in for meals.

I did hate to see Dr. Janet Kilborn go. She is Dorothy's doctor. Poor Dr. Janet; we were so troubled about her, but it is alright now. Her little daughter was born on the boat the second night out. I don't suppose you can imagine these crude boats and, what is more, imagine having to start off on one facing such an experience. Her husband and mother-in-law were with her and they are both doctors. It is a family of doctors, you see. The father was also a doctor and did valiant service here in the Canadian Mission.

The American consul has asked to have names of all those who refuse to leave. He may threaten to refuse us passports next time, but we are doing the right thing as far as we can see and are not worrying.

March 8, 1927 *Chengtu, West China*

Dear Home Folks,

The American consul has admitted to some people going through Chungking that he wants to get everybody out so that the U.S.A. may wade in "if she wants to!"

I have let the baby's nurse go and am breaking in a general woman helper new to us but tried and true. Dorothy is happy and good as gold.

We have to keep jumping these days to get everything necessary done in the twenty-four hours.

April 2, 1927 *Chengtu, Szechwan*

Dear Home People,

I fear you may be anxious about us. I wish I could assure you that there is no cause for worry. We realize that there may be danger for us ahead, but we refuse to be anything but optimistic about the situation and we are taking each day as it comes. Some predict that the recent Nanking affair* will be a turning point for the better. Here in Chengtu

**After the brutality in Nanking the revolutionary armies of the Kuomintang with Chiang Kai Shek as commander-in-chief pushed on to Shanghai where a general strike paralyzed the native city. Later in*

the anti-foreign feeling appears to be no worse. And our University schools are going on well. The most fearful thing is that the soldiers may get out of hand. In spite of all the University authorities' protests they come here on the campus day after day to drill. Some days there are twelve or fifteen hundred of them marching, counter-marching, doing the goose-step, and fighting sham battles on our playing grounds. It is only a sign of the times. "Down with Imperialism!" is the cry of the day. "Take back the foreigners' power!"

To the officials of the city, who have announced themselves as loyal to the Southern faction, or the Kuomintang, and to their military commanders, soldiers on foreign property are quite justified and proper. Each day the soldiers seem to get a bit bolder, coming onto our private compounds and sauntering about everywhere at will. Their attitude is most provoking. But we must be exceedingly moderate in our speech. It would take only a tiny spark to start a big conflagration! It is possible, although I cannot bring myself to believe it likely, that we shall be driven from our homes and that the Kuomintang will take over the University and property.*

These surely are interesting days to be living in China. History is being made! We are witnessing a great revolutionary movement which is going to unify this great people. Whatever may be the unfortunate accompaniments of this uprising the net results are certain to be good. Opposition to "foreign aggression" and to "capitalism" may have its source in Soviet Russia, but there is more than "Red" propaganda back of this movement. One who knows at all the student mind of China knows how keenly sensitive it is to China's weakness and disunity, and the white heat passion which drives the student to almost any means in order to realize his aspirations for his beloved country.

---

the spring [1927] the alliance of Communists and the Kuomintang came suddenly to an end. Within a year Communism was "illegal" throughout China. The purging of the Nationalist party of its most extreme Communistic elements resulted in some cases in acts of inhuman cruelty which were almost if not quite equal to the brutalities of the Communists themselves.

Although we were very aware of the undercurrent of revolutionary ferment, daily life for the most part went on in its customary way. We adjusted to the unsettling things which political change brought and usually accepted the unrest as if it were the norm.

April 10, 1927

Dear Folks,

I am frightfully busy. I teach eight hours a week besides correcting English compositions of a class at Chengtu University. One afternoon a week I plan to go to the women's meeting in the Manchu city. Then there are callers and guests besides Dorothy Ellen's food to be prepared. I should not like to keep this up indefinitely but expect to hold out this term. I forgot to mention that I spend all my spare daytime working in the University library.

Now that there are so few foreigners here, duties are piled on thick. The Chinese are unusually kind to us though. We are getting many invitations to their homes for meals and feasts. I spent all of last Sunday afternoon at a ladies' party at Miss Fu's.

It is the Chinese custom to visit first, spend time leisurely eating course after course and then depart. The hostess first entertained us in her bedroom, also a Chinese custom. It indicated that she esteemed us her good friends. Candies, pumpkin seeds, and peanuts were served on arrival and *of course* tea. After a while bowls of *mien* (vermicelli) and soup, along with chopsticks, were brought in to the bedroom but only to "stay" our appetites. Next we were shown all about the lovely garden and roamed about into different rooms. Finally we were invited to sit down in the dining hall which opens to a lovely central court where beautiful peach trees were in bloom. Summer and winter they live quite exposed on the court side. Miss Fu, a Friend educated in Nanking, is the recreational secretary of the Y.W.C.A. here.

Next Saturday we expect to entertain all the Green Dragon Street Meeting people here on our lawn. I hope our roses will be in bloom then. By the way, our place is beginning to look lovely. Our yard was only a pile of sand two years ago! We are going to call in help from a teashop to manage the *dien hsin* (cakes) and tea. Otherwise we could never feed the crowd.

A wedding I attended yesterday was an interesting affair for two reasons. It was a Quaker wedding and it was the first wedding of a graduate of the University to a student in the Woman's College. The bride was dressed in a lovely pink satin gown. (White would never do for a wedding here; it indicates mourning.) She arrived in a decorated automobile instead of the conventional red bridal sedan chair. The wedding was in the new Friends College building and a feast followed. The hour was set at eleven but the bride did not arrive until nearly one o'clock! Brides never come on time in China. It would not do to appear too eager to leave one's parents!

We are busy and happy. It is so beautiful and peaceful that it does not seem as if anything could go wrong. (The soldiers haven't troubled us much lately.) Our home is pretty well fixed up and we are enjoying it thoroughly and our lovely location here in the country. As I look out over the quiet rich fields I wonder how we can dream of things going smash. The consul and gunboats have left Chungking now, so maybe they won't!

April 29, 1927

Our party for the Green Dragon Street people was quite a success. We had nearly a hundred guests and they entered into the games splendidly. Many people had to walk three miles or more to come so it meant considerable effort, especially for the women with their tiny bound feet.

May 31, 1927

Dear Home Folks,

We are beginning to think about plans for the summer. We had hoped right along to be able to go to Behludin, but it seems doubtful now. The tide of favor is for Kwanhsien. At Kwanhsien proper is the head of the famous irrigation system of this part of China, a system 2,100 years old! The resort is outside the city and is considerably lower than Behludin, so there is greater heat, and mosquitoes. We people here at the University feel that since we have so far kept all this property from falling into the hands of the soldiers it would be a pity for all to go away now and let them come in and take possession. Consequently some of the men are planning to remain here all summer and the others to take turns. I shall have to get into a cooler clime for Dorothy's sake. So far she has kept pretty well. Mrs. Wang is awfully good to her and uses judgment and care. We are fortunate to have her when I have to be away from the baby so much. I can leave Dorothy and feel quite easy about her.

Perhaps I have not told you that Mrs. Wang worked for the Rodwells (English Friends) many years. They took her to England with them once. She is faithful and dependable...and a seamstress, too.

There must be tons of mail in Chungking, or *somewhere*. There have been no parcels for months, magazines are fearfully slow getting through. Our *Literary Digest* was six months old when it arrived.

Merchants in Chungking and all up river cities are badly hit. They would even welcome gunboats back for the sake of safe transportation of goods! Stuff to be exported is rotting and of course they can get nothing up from Shanghai to sell.

We may have a hard time if we can't get kerosene. It is very scarce and dear. For several months we have been burning candles a good deal. We happened to have a supply on hand.

July 17, 1927 *In Temple in Kwanhsien Hills*

Dear Home Folks,

I have done little today but rest and go to our little meeting of worship this morning. Chinese and foreigners met together in a little court beside some idols. I turned my back on the idols and looked at the beautiful scenery. Mr. Tang Bo Chen and Earl Cranston* led the meeting. It was partly in Chinese and partly in English, a very satisfactory arrangement.

It is interesting to see my old friends, the mountains, from a new angle....

August 4, 1927 *Kwanhsien Hills*

Dear Home Folks,

I wish you could come and sit on my little porch and enjoy the view of the plain with me. The evening colors of gold and silver are lovely, hanging over the green of the rice fields and the darker green of the trees. Everything looks especially fresh and beautiful after a heavy rain. The river meandering along across the plain reflects the golden and silver light of the evening.

Dorothy is tucked in bed and asleep. The boy is setting the table (here on the porch) for my supper. There is nothing to do but write letters!

Later

The moon is shining now, a pretty golden crescent. Of course I have had to come inside long since. After eating my supper I visited the Manlys** where I have just about lived.

Dr. Marian (M.D.) is a very versatile person. As well as being a doctor she writes, sculpts, and gives readings. Her younger sister, Grace, is unusually sweet and lovely, also talented. Both girls have an artistic bent. "Mother" Manly is certainly good to me, and she takes great interest and pride in Dorothy.

My teacher has come from Chengtu so I am attempting to study each morning from nine to twelve with him.

**Years later Dr. Earl Cranston was Dean of the School of Theology at Claremont, California.*

***W.E. and Florence Manly and their two daughters, Marian and Grace, were close neighbors in Chengtu.*

We manage, busy as we all are, to get in plenty of fun too. We rise early, (I sometimes get up at 5:30) and work till noon. After dinner, naps are in order. Then comes volley ball and tennis and perhaps a picnic supper.

One day a party of us climbed straight up the mountain behind us to the top. It was not as difficult as it looks because niches cut in the rocks provided footholds. I was pretty stiff for two or three days afterward from pullling myself up over the face of the mountain. From the top we could see good old Behludin.

The temple where we are living is called the Strange (or Miraculous) Cliff Temple. There are various interesting little places about the mountain which the people have found worthy of worship, including a fine spring from which we got our water. The people have cut idols in the rocks about the spring and they burn incense before them.

The temple keeper is a funny old man. He still burns incense and makes his little bow before the door of an empty room where there once was an idol. It wouldn't do to offend that idol's spirit! Mrs. Manly says she has seen him going the rounds bowing and sticking in the incense sticks, then while passing from one idol to another, incongruously cursing someone soundly.

August 26, 1927 *Kwanhsien Hills*

Dear Home Folks,

We expect to start back to Chengtu next Monday. We must have time to get settled before the University opens on September 8....

September 13, 1927 *Chengtu, Szechwan*

Dear Ones at Home,

We arrived back in Chengtu two weeks ago. I wish you could have seen us coming along the road. At intervals it was quite under water for several miles due to the recent rains. This is Robert's account of the trip:

We sent to Chengtu for carriers for our goods and planned for Margaret and Mrs. Wang with Dorothy to travel in rickshas. We were unable to use the autobus because it had rained continuously for several days, yet it dried up enough the day we started so that we got the two rickshas and I rode my bicycle. The cows which had been taken up to supply our little community with milk for the summer started down a little earlier than we did and we were able to get milk for Dorothy on the road. We spent the night at a chapel about twenty miles from Chengtu, the womenfolk in the schoolroom and Dr. Manly and I in a straw thatched shed outside. During the night it poured and I had to move my cot but it was already pretty badly wet.

The whole country through which we traveled the following day is as flat as New Jersey and the water couldn't run away fast enough. Since considerable stretches of the newly constructed motor road were under water I took off sandals and stockings, shouldered my bicycle, and waded through. I must have waded about two miles. At one place where it was so deep that I wondered if I could get through, I made a detour which led me clear through a village, and I wish you could have seen that street! To begin with there had scarcely been any attempt to construct a highway. It was simply one long gutter filled with the filthiest "goo" from two to ten inches deep. As soon as I got through I sat down by an irrigation ditch and washed my feet and legs as clean as I could.

At another village a tea shop was flooded nearly a foot deep, the proprietress sitting on benches high above the water--without any customers. Whenever possible I followed other travelers and avoided the places where they fell into holes. At one place where I was feeling my way carefully across a single plank bridge a young fellow coming in the opposite direction was so intent on watching me that he fell in himself, much to the amusement of others who were also wading through. Everybody goodnaturedly helped others as much as they could to avoid pitfalls. We reached home before dark, but our load carriers did not arrive until the following afternoon. How they ever managed to carry ninety pounds each with a carrying pole through those slippery fords without dunking them I hardly know, but they did it. It was worth some extra tea money not to get our clothing and typewriter soaked with that coffee colored soup!

Robert L. Simkin

Margaret writes:

Here is one incident of my return to Chengtu. It is customary on long trips for the ricksha puller to hire a young boy to push from behind. I suddenly found myself tipped over backward, my feet higher than my head, the puller dangling in the air above me and the little chap squirming and yelling bloody murder under the ricksha. It is the funniest feeling! You have to lie there absolutely helpless until somebody rescues you. When we got started on our way again and I found the little fellow behind was not really hurt I just shook with muffled laughter.

September 17, 1927

D.S. and Jane B. Dye, who arrived safely on Wednesday from Shanghai, are the first refugees to return.* That evening the foreign campus community met at the 3-in-1's for supper. (The 3-in-1 is the nickname for the three Canadian men living together.) We had a wonderful feast and were glad to hear the news from the Dyes. It was quite an adventure for them getting up river. Boat crowded and hot (probably 100°); "pidgin" cargo (illicit cargo) piled in their cabin!

On the sixth we learned that "Mother" Manly has to go to Peking for an operation. The doctors fear cancer. We have been busy helping the Manlys to close their house and taking over some of their teaching work. When Dr. and Mrs. Manly get off the two daughters will remain for work in the city.

September 20, 1927

Jane (Dye) has been telling me of her Shanghai experiences and of meeting the Nanking refugees. She said the first refugee she met was a pregnant woman who told in a sweet-spirited, gentle way how she had been kicked by a soldier. I fear there are some bad tales to hear if the whole story were known, but also some accounts of great courage and daring.

I suppose people will not be returning in large numbers to Szechwan for a long while, but I think gradually now the foreigners will return by ones, twos and threes.

October 24, 1927 *Chengtu, West China*

Dear Home Folks,

Robert and I are both sitting at the dining table, he marking papers and I writing, to save kerosene. The Dyes said that when they were coming back from Shanghai they were asked more questions about oil than any other subject. None of the questioners knew that a Chungking general had taken three-quarters of a million dollars worth of kerosene from one company (without paying for it) and then sold it for double the usual price. We also have heard that the Standard Oil Company has sucked all their tanks dry along the Yangtze. One can hardly blame them with such provocation! But we'll get back to a more or less normal state of affairs after a time. We seem very normal in Chengtu

**Since conditions in Chengtu had become reasonably stable, or at least no crisis threatened for the moment, it seemed right for those who had evacuated to the coast to return to Szechwan.*

already! Last year at this time we were in the midst of the strike. I was struggling in the kitchen trying to keep us fed and taking care of Dorothy without any help.

Mail is coming through well now. Letters have come through fairly well all the time, but now we are deluged with papers and magazines. The University library has been fairly swamped with them. All within a week we have received April and September numbers of the same periodical.

I am just as busy this fall as I want to be, but I am much happier doing my share of the work on this campus than I ever was as a mere language student.

November 24, 1927

Dear Folks at Home,

This is Thanksgiving Day in the evening.

Robert is feeling rather "done in" and has gone to bed. It is not due to too big a dinner but to overwork. He is often at it until very late at night and I am afraid he is rather played out.

Dorothy has been poorly for more than two weeks with a cold and general upset. She is listless. How we do miss her usual sunshine! On top of it all, Mrs. Wang fell two weeks ago and hurt her poor bound feet terribly and cannot walk. It has been strenuous for me. I've had to miss two classes and my library work has been quite neglected.

I had never seen a bare bound foot until I saw Mrs. Wang's. The four toes are bent under the big toe and the arch bent up until the big toe is just an extension of the heel. There is a deep crack between. What untold suffering it represents!

...We are hoping that Dr. Stubbs will get here soon. He is on his way up river.

November 25, 1927

Dorothy seems more like herself today.

People coming up river have to run through a nest of brigands. It's plain piracy. One party had to pay $10,000 (Mex.)* to get through. The British consul will not permit women to come up river. The Methodist Episcopal Bishop started up with four ladies and then turned back. All this is discouraging to people waiting in Shanghai.

**Roughly equivalent to $5,000 gold.*

December, 1927

Dear Friends at home,

During all the upheaval of this 1927 revolutionary period the University has been able to keep open with a good enrollment of loyal students. The Woman's College has almost quadrupled its original enrollment and the girls are having a wholesome influence on the University life. Coeducation has proved itself a great success. The administration of the University has been reorganized and the Chinese leaders now have a large share of responsibility. Steps have been taken looking to government registration, but care is being exercised that no act for the sake of political expediency shall compromise the Christian aims of the institution.

I do not fully sympathize with the point of view which says the missionary cannot work in China so long as extraterritoriality* continues. We deplore these "special privileges" and the irritation caused by the presence of gunboats and other expressions of armed force. Let us work for the abolition of these evils, but at the same time while they do continue to exist it seems all the more necessary that there should be some representatives of our countries who come to this people in the spirit of Christian goodwill and helpfulness.

You cannot half guess what an island of peace the campus seems to us in this sea of turmoil, that is when the soldiers are not here drilling. It is popularly known in Chengtu city as the "Western Paradise." Its quiet shaded walks are indeed a delightful and restful contrast to the bustling, noisy streets of a Chinese city. The graceful curving roofs are dignified and beautiful. The students appear like students at home as they move across the campus between classes, especially now that I have become accustomed to seeing the young men dressed in long gowns.

Life in China continues to be interesting!

**Webster: Exemption from the application or jurisdiction of local law and tribunals.*

The Foreigners Return 1928 & 1929

January 6, 1928 *Chengtu, Szechwan*

Dear Home Folks,

Dr. Stubbs, or Clifford as we shall call him, arrived on the nineteenth. He rooms and boards with us. Later he may have a room in the college (Friends) to be with the students, but he'll continue to get his meals here. He is a delightful person and we count it a privilege to have him with us while his family is in England. He plays the piano and is congenial in every way. His specialty is chemistry but he is enough of a mystic to make a first-class Quaker. While at home in England on furlough he did good work for China, presenting the Chinese point of view to members of Parliament in the House of Commons and touring the country to win sympathy and a better understanding of the situation in China.

Mrs. Wang is able to be back with us after her fall, I am glad to say.

On Christmas Eve we had the students of Friends College come in for a Christmas party and to welcome Dr. Stubbs, and we three were invited to the Friends College on Thursday evening for a Chinese *mien* supper and social.

Christmas Day--sunshiny and warm. Just so we might not forget we were living in China the radical agitators were trying to stir things up and had matters at such a pitch that the churches in the city decided to forego elaborate Christmas celebrations and foreigners were advised to stay at home!

February 11, 1928

Dear Home Folks,

We have been more than busy. The Christmas activities were followed by examinations and before examinations were over came

Yearly Meeting and Central Executive, which met here at Chengtu this year. Robert worked under too great a strain trying to attend meetings morning, afternoon, and night, and get accounts written so that he could make the necessary statements to the Yearly Meeting and get a report off to the London F.F.M.A. office. (The Central Executive had most of their meetings here at the house. We were glad to have our home used.) During Yearly Meeting Robert began to be troubled with lumbago. About two weeks ago the pain spread to his right leg and became more acute. He was glad to go to bed where he has been ever since. The doctor calls his trouble sciatic neuritis. I am glad to say that he is on the mend now.

The work is going to be lighter next semester. Quite a number of foreigners have returned during the past weeks, including Dr. and Mrs. Manly.

"Mother" Manly looks very much better, and the fear of cancer is gone. They brought us delicious apples from Shanghai and also gave us a lemon for a lemon pie. We usually have to make lemon pies out of oranges!

February 14, 1928

...School registration begins this week and classes next week. I am not expecting to teach this term but I shall continue the library work.

Yang Sen is either using the steamboats for transporting his troops or there is a pontoon bridge across the river (I have heard both reports) and our mail is having to come overland. Consequently it is a long time since we have had any letters. A paper mail got in a few days ago.

March 25, 1928 *Chengtu, West China*

Dear Home Folks,

Robert--this past week--has begun to go out a bit. Tomorrow he starts classes. He certainly had a long siege of it. It does seem good to have him about again.

William and Nilda Sewell, who have been in Canton these past few months, are likely to get in soon now. I suppose when they arrive Clifford Stubbs will want to board with them as it will be considerably more convenient for him to be at that end of the campus. We shall miss him.

April 14, 1928

Dear Fannie,

The Sewells arrived Sunday (Easter) and are living with us until they can get settled, so I now have a regular adult family of five.

...Clifford Stubbs is still boarding with us although the Sewells are here now. We enjoy him so much. He has been made vice-president of the University. Since Dr. Joseph Beech is in the United States, he shares full responsibility with the Chinese vice-president. It is good to have the Sewells back and another home open to go to. They are both young and full of life. They had great experiences in Canton this past winter. Perhaps they have not invited Clifford to live with them because they are expecting an heir in September. We're glad to have Clifford here; he is a tremendous help in entertaining guests and a happy person to have about all the time. The Sewells have been married six years and this is the first baby so we all are happy. Clifford expects his family, at least part of it, to come out next autumn.

June 25, 1928 *Chengtu, West China*

Dear Home Folks,

After waiting many long weeks (I really lost count and don't know how many) a foreign mail at last brought a letter.

School is now closed; Commencement Day was just a week ago today. I still have quite a bit of work in the Library and Robert has committees and accounts, but we hope to start for Behludin on July 3.

Since there are several other foreign children on the campus now Dorothy has new playmates.

July 21, 1928 *"Rockynotch," Behludin, West China*

Dear People at Home,

...We made the trip from Chengtu to Penghsien by ricksha in about eight hours. We would have come in much less time by autobus if it had not rained hard that morning. The evolution of transportation that I have seen in less than five years in this part of China is interesting. The jump has been made from mule back, wheelbarrow, and sedan chair, *at once* to the motor car. The horse and carriage have been quite left out. But there is much to be desired. When it rains--heaven help us! We arrived at the South Gate of Penghsien to find it closed. Robert quickly guessed the reason. The nearby countryside was suffering from severe drought. Often under such conditions the south gate of a city is closed while the people pray to the gods for rain. We could do nothing but go around the wall to the west gate of the city. There we hoped to get rickshas to carry us to Kwankeo. None were to be had, so we took to wheelbarrows and shank's mare. (Dorothy made the remainder of the journey in a *beh giao*, a small, covered chair strapped to a coolie's back.) A wheelbarrow is the hardest, most uncomfortable vehicle I ever rode on. There is not a spring in it. It goes bump, bump over the rough road. I felt I was being shaken to jelly and was glad to walk a good part of the ten miles to Kwankeo.

We spent the night in a very dirty place, half inn, at Kwankeo. Father's barn would be the Waldorf Astoria in comparison. We climbed to the top the following day helped by mountain chairs borne on the shoulders of sure-footed mountain men.

We're putting a little addition on our mountain house. It was started two years ago. Robert enjoys working with the carpenters out in the open and getting thoroughly tired physically. He thinks he'll be strong as an ox by the time the summer is gone.

September 2, 1928 *Behludin, West China*

Dear Home Folk,

I wish you were here to sit by the open fire with us. We are still at Behludin and there is a fall tang to the air so that a little fire is welcome. Robert and I have been taking some long walks....Tramping about in these wild but beautiful mountains in the summer keeps me sane. Yesterday we went down the east path of the mountain, skirted about the hill, (Behludin is a very sharp peak with sheer precipices on nearly every side) and came up the west path. I saw a magazine photograph of the White Mountains in New Hampshire the other day, and they looked awfully tame. (Don't worry! I shall adore seeing them again.) There is this difference--the White Mountains are gentle, serene and peaceful. The wooded slopes have a lovely charm. These mountains are majestic, grand, awe-inspiring. The jagged peaks seem to tower straight up to heaven. They are only partially wooded. Moonlight nights in the mountains are beautiful. Moonlight in China is lovely anyway. There is no prettier picture than the up-turned roof corners in the moonlight.

October 8, 1928 *Chengtu, West China*

Dear Home Folks,

...All the foreigners in the city were invited to a feast given by one of the generals and two or three other gentlemen last Saturday. I say all the foreigners--at any rate all the Protestant missionaries, the French fathers, the Japanese consul and perhaps others were included. Whatever there is of beauty in a Chinese city is pretty well hidden behind the shop fronts, high walls, and high gateways and gates, which line the thoroughfares. On entering a *kung kwan* (better class private residence) you pass from the street through a gateway, then immediately through a second, the big doors being opened at your coming if you are an important enough guest; otherwise you slip through a small door on one side of the big one. Then you proceed along a series of alleyways, and still other gateways until you arrive at the home itself which often is built around an open court.

This is what happened on Saturday. We passed along a long alleyway lined by high walls on either side. We glimpsed bits of garden through gateways in the walls. The reception room was in a building like a casino (in this respect the place was hardly true to Chinese form) and the tables were set out of doors. Among the delicacies served were pig's spinal cord and *live* shrimps! The latter, which I did not attempt, were brought in on a plate and covered by a bowl lest they should jump away! I must say the Chinese know how to cook a duck or chicken so that it is wonderfully tender and delicious. They have a way of doing a fish here in Szechwan that is very fine, too, if you like the flavor of Chinese seasonings.

October 10, 1928

This is Independence Day and we are having a holiday--in fact, three holidays. Yesterday we went to a wedding but arrived too late for the whole ceremony. One, I gather, is expected to go and make a day of it. Since we could hardly afford the time and did not know the hour of the ceremony we got in a bit too late. The bride and groom were standing in front of the ancestral tablet when we arrived. We saw them kneel and bow before it. On the table before the tablet were plates of food and cups of wine. The bride was nicely arrayed in pink with beaded headgear, the fringe of which hung down and hid her face. The groom also had rosettes and streamers of pink festooned about him and his foreign hat was especially trimmed for the occasion. The whole place was jammed with guests, many of whom were playing *mah jong*, and gambling, I suppose. Every now and then long strings of firecrackers were let off. We remained for the wedding feast. Small tables were set up in the different rooms and food served by a caterer. I fear many of these people go into debt for life to meet the expenses of such big weddings and feasts. You will be interested to know that the groom's father, through whom the invitation came, was once Robert's cook and it was he who was on the road the time Robert was robbed and the robbers threatened his life.* They also had a knife at the cook's throat.

**In 1911 during the Revolution, when the Manchus were*

He proved a faithful servant. The robbers did not find some silver dollars because he had baked them in biscuits!

November 13, 1928

Dear Ones at Home,

Many foreigners are returning from home and Shanghai and we are having "teas" galore.

The last two or three weeks I have been feeling rather wretched. Indications are that the event for which we have been hoping will come off next June. It will be much too hot weather and near furlough, but we are thankful just the same. We don't want Dorothy to be an "only child."

November 16, 1928

I didn't get very far with my letter the other day. I have resigned my library work. Mrs. Lindsay, who has just returned from Canada, will serve. The rest of our term, that is until 1931, I'll devote myself to my family and language study.

Dorothy is chattering away in Chinese with Mrs. Wang. She gets the tones and little enclitics just like Mrs. Wang's.

Margaret Stubbs and young John are returning to China. How good it is to have so many coming back!

February 2, 1929 *Chengtu, West China*

Dear Girls,

This is Grace's* birthday and a cold, dreary day it is. It can't be worse in New England. We do feel the cold dreadfully here as the wind sweeps under the houses and through the cracks. We are wondering if

---

overthrown, Robert Simkin was forced to flee from Chengtu. Travelling with a Chinese worker, his cook, and a carrier, he planned to walk to Tungchwan. Repeatedly warned of robbers ahead, they turned aside and boarded a small boat filled with fleeing Chinese. They were soon hailed by a band of 25 or 30 robbers who forced them to shore and thoroughly searched all the passengers. They took Robert's watch, razor, fountain pen and typewriter, and about sixty dollars hidden in his clothing load. Four of the robbers stood around him with long knives uplifted and a pistol at his head. He thought they meant to kill him, but after about twenty minutes, they left and went to rob another boatload which came along.

**Sister Grace Timberlake.*

the men are out in the wet and cold today on their return from Yearly Meeting.

Robert and Clifford (Stubbs) left Monday morning nearly two weeks ago. They expected to ride their bicycles a good deal, but it was rainy and cold then, too, and the roads were very muddy. They got to Suining in four adventurous days. They rode their wheels, tramped through the worst mud (a good many miles in all), rode some in *hwa gens* (a light bamboo seat swung between two poles and carried by men) and had a short ride in a motor bus. They fell off their wheels sometimes because it was so slippery and got themselves and their cycles well bespattered. Robert wrote that he tied two pieces of oiled paper together which he wore over his shoulders to keep some of the wet off.

But the worst of all was that they did not see their loads until two days after their arrival. The carriers started out a day earlier and were supposed to be with the men each night so that they could have good food and warm, clean bedding. As it was they had only a little lunch in their pockets and were dependent upon rice, sweet potatoes, eggs and oranges which they got along the way. The people in the *fu yin tangs* (literally gospel halls--mission outstations) were most kind. The men slept on blackboards and had a clean *pu kai* (Chinese comforter) between them. They slept in their clothes. Of course they had no shaving material, so they must have been some weary hoboes by the time they reached Suining.

Margaret Stubbs and John are staying with me while the men are away. We have had guests in a few times and have been invited out several evenings, but otherwise have been having a very quiet time. Margaret goes over to the Sewells every day to help them with the baby* who is a great care.

March 4, 1929 *Chengtu, West China*

Dear Girls,

The Stubbs family had hardly left us when Miss Cumber arrived. I wrote you about her after our visit in Chungking in 1923. She has been in China thirty-six years, came the year I was born! She is getting somewhat weak, but is young in spirit and delightful company. She enjoyed Dorothy greatly. She was with us ten days and then went to Jane Dye for the rest of her stay in Chengtu.

Just now Hilda Sewell is staying with us for a rest of two days. Her baby has been such a care and she is nearly worn out. Nellie Riley, a

---

**Erica was born with a defective spine and is immobilized. So sad!*

sort of independent missionary without a mission board behind her, has come from Tungchwan to help care for Erica.

On Saturday the Sewells, Stubbses, Dyes, and Simkins were all invited to the home of Mr. Shi, one of the University instructors, for dinner. In the main reception hall was a striking series of six portraits of his immediate ancestors (male line, of course) for three generations back. The faces were quite individual but the gowns, Manchu official robes, seemed to repeat themselves in all their gorgeousness. The intricacies of the embroidery were beautifully drawn and painted.

March 17, 1929

Dear Girls,

The Archangelskys (Russian couple whom I met in Tungchwan) arrived yesterday with their retinue, servants, and guards. It seems strange to have soldiers on the place but they seem decent and will not be troublesome, I guess.

While we were eating breakfast General Tien, his wife and three daughters arrived to call. This is the general who has been especially troublesome in occupying mission property. He lived for some months in Tungchwan in a residence belonging to English Friends. His cohorts still occupy the place and apparently there is no prying them loose. Now that so many missionaries have returned the house is needed. When Leonard Wigham is not out on the road itinerating he can't have his own house and office but has to live at the boys' school! This is the general who comes to make friendly calls and entertains the foreigner lavishly on occasion. He has invited the Archangelskys and us to his home for dinner on Tuesday night. Personally, I don't feel too happy in accepting his hospitality. Of course the Archangelskys knew the Tiens in Tungchwan and their case is quite different.

April 7, 1929 *Chengtu, West China*

Dear Girls,

The Archangelskys are still here, or rather still in Chengtu. They are in the city for overnight. Mr. A. is going out on a business trip for a week and they both still have dentistry work to be done. Mr. A. had his tonsils out last week and all this medical and dental work takes time.

When I last wrote we had been invited to dinner at General Tien's. We went and had a very interesting time. It was like going into another world--a life, I suppose, of idleness, *mah jong*, gambling, and wine-drinking. After dinner Tien Tai Tai (the wife) took Mrs. A. and me about the establishment. We saw her bedrooms; the room where she keeps her clothing stowed in boxes piled to the ceiling; the garden with rockery and fish pond. She also presented us with photographs of herself and husband. We came home in their little sedan car. We felt like a million dollars rolling along the streets of Chengtu in an electrically lighted car--until we got to the South Gate. Of course the general had ordered the city gates to be especially opened for us, but in passing the guards and the place where soldiers are quartered near the gate, the chauffeur slowed and a whole gang of soldiers piled onto the running boards, almost sticking their elbows in our faces. I didn't mind as I happened to be sitting in the middle, but I could see poor Mrs. Archangelsky was disappointed and disgusted. We all remarked that the incident showed very well how poorly disciplined these generals' armies are.

Now there are reports of war again. I am afraid the fighting down river is preventing foreign mail from getting through. And there is talk of a scrap here in Szechwan, too.

Recently we entertained a German and an Italian besides our Russian friends. For people living in a rather remote part of the world we are quite cosmopolitan, don't you think?

April 25, 1929

Dear Girls,

It is after seven o'clock and *still* Robert is not home from Senate meeting. I'll start this letter and see if that will bring him.

A big mail was wrecked down river. I wonder if there were any letters or parcels for us on it. Everything recently has come through splendidly, and I hope nothing for us was on that ill-fated steamer. Of course the unsettled political conditions may be interfering with mail, too. We don't get much news but we know the Nationalists are having their troubles. The Szechwan generals are out for a scrap also. They have been *la fu*-ing (impressing) coolies badly so that our gatekeeper has been afraid to go out on the street.

This afternoon some petty officers sauntered onto our place with the old-time air of owning the earth. It just seems as if I couldn't go through those trying days again. They soon went away and did us no harm. It is just a matter of not letting these things annoy you....

Later

Robert finally came home from Senate and we had supper at quarter to eight. The great question these days is the government registration of the University. This involves many problems, one of which is military training. You may be sure Friends will oppose that to the end.

June 22, 1929 *Shan Hsi Kai, Chengtu*

Dear Fannie,

You'll see by the heading I am not at home. I am living in the city opposite the Methodist Episcopal Mission Hospital pending developments. And it is so *hot*. Moreover I have dysentery, not badly, but enough to make me feel punk. This is the third or fourth year in succession I've had dysentery in June. It is the bane of one's existence in hot weather in the Orient. The doctor has shot emetine into my arms until they're lame and sore.

Robert brought Dorothy in to visit me yesterday and it did me good to see her--abounding energy as ever--and Robert says she eats like a little pig. I am thankful she is keeping well. I have told Mrs. Wang to bathe her twice a day, if necessary, to keep down the prickly heat.

June 30, 1929

Dearest Fannie,

Robert has been coming in every evening for a week and sleeping here. Dr. Marian* also sleeps here. She is out on another case this evening, however, so it might be my fate for the event to come off tonight.

We have had some rainy cool weather since I wrote last but now it is hot again. Most folk are getting off to the hills.

Unfortunately Dorothy was exposed to the measles a week ago and when the new baby comes we'll have to keep them apart. How we are ever to manage I don't know. I wish I could "park" her with you!

Commencement was last Monday. I did not attend the exercises, of course, though I surely wanted to see the first girl graduates get their degrees.

July 15, 1929

Our new little daughter finally arrived a quarter of an hour after midnight on July fifth--almost a Fourth of July baby. Of course we all proceeded to fall in love with Margaret Ruth at once.

August 19, 1929 *Behludin, West China*

Dear Girls,

We got away from Chengtu on July 23rd, arriving here the evening of the 24th...after the usual nightmarish trip.

Whenever the chairs were put down in a village the people crowded about as they always do. That is what wears me out. Every time after

---

**Marian Manly, M.D.*

we went on I'd say to myself, "Now next time I'll keep cool and not fret."...But the next time I'd forget my good resolutions and begin to get tense. Of course, the trouble is that one fears disease, vermin at least. Anything from fleas and lice to smallpox is quite possible. Conflicts of this sort wear on one in a country like this. On the one hand I'd like to be friendly with the people, whom we supposedly are here to help; on the other, I am in terror lest they give the children some sickness. When one is tired and hot it isn't pleasant to be the center of a curious crowd. I think I can now have empathy with presidents, kings, and the like!

This week Robert is going off on a trip into the mountains. Will be gone five or six days. Dr. Manly (the father) is with us for a few days and will go, too. Dr. Marian Manly has also been our guest.

December 12, 1929

We are much elated over the prospect of having Dorothy in nursery school, starting with the new year. There will be nine children in the class. It is a new project being run under the auspices of the Canadian School for Missionaries' Children. This school is reopening after having been closed for three years. Before the "exodus" there were over a hundred children enrolled. We are hoping we may be able to keep Dorothy in this school throughout our next term which will bring her to the age of thirteen or fourteen. It has been a very good school. The texts used are Canadian and the school is kept to Ontario standards. We are thankful at the prospect of keeping the family together for some years to come.

Anti-Christian agitation has resumed, this time caused when some students from a neighboring school tried to take a picture of one of our girl students as she was coming out from her class. Several other girls were with her at the time. They and the only male student nearby at the time succeeded in getting the film...whereupon the proctor of the outside school later came around with some of his students to complain to the authorities that their school had been insulted. And so the storm began to brew.

On a number of occasions groups of unfriendly students, anywhere from ten to two hundred, have come onto the campus to *lao* and make a row, yelling and marking up walks and buildings with "Down with Imperialism!", "Strike Down Christianity!", and special attacks on Lincoln Dsang, the Chinese vice-president, as "chief foreign slave." A large company of them surrounded several of the Middle School boys and tried to force them to kneel down and say, "Down with

Christianity!'' They replied that they could kill them but they would not comply.

One other rather outstanding event comes to mind. A few days ago we heard Manila by radio. Two Chinese gentlemen were here enroute to the tribes country* on a geographic mission and they used their radio each evening to get the correct time from Manila.

**Area bordering Tibet.*

A Life Given for Many
1930

January 5, 1930 *Chengtu, West China*

Dear Home Folks,

In my last letter I mentioned a resumption of anti-Christian agitation. The agitation finally spent itself and there was less disturbance at Christmas time than in the past several years although the antis did capture the Chinese pastor of one of the city churches on Christmas Day and march him through the streets. They are reported to be saving their thunder for the time, now close at hand, when several of the denominations will be holding their annual meetings in Chengtu. We shall see....If the National government manages to hold together I do not anticipate any trouble. It is of course in the interim between the fall of one government and the establishment of a new one that vicious elements may be expected to be especially troublesome.

This past week has seen the arrival of several families, one of whom has been absent four years. The campus seems as it did before the "exodus." In the evening there are lights once more all along the Canadian Crescent (the curved road along which the Canadian missionaries live). I tell you it is good! With the exception of Mrs. Lewis, I have been here longer than any other foreign woman. (Dr. and Mrs. Lewis* are both over seventy and having already spent the greater part of their lives in China would really choose to remain here until the end.) I feel somewhat like an old mossback. But at last I can say, "*Next* year--furlough!"

**Dr. and Mrs. Spencer Lewis of the Methodist Mission.*

January 6, 1930

For the last two or three days snow has been flying and this morning we gathered up enough to make ice cream, using a borrowed freezer. The Dyes and a guest are coming in to help us eat it.

January 12, 1930

We can talk or think of little these days but the coming Friends deputation. We expect them to arrive on the sixteenth and are busy with plans and preparations. We expect to entertain the two American Friends, Gilbert Bowles and Carolena Wood, in our home. It is almost too good to be true and I shall not breathe really freely until they are actually here.

Especially with as many foreigners about as there are just now with the annual meetings in session, our campus seems like a little bit of homeland in the midst of China. The children returning to the Canadian School (school for missionaries' children) give a decided home touch, a touch we sadly missed when the "evacuation" took them away. Our house is at one side of the campus facing the country so that we have reminders of the land in which we live. Often we hear the cymbals and pipes accompanying a wedding or funeral procession. (I am never quite sure which it is unless I can see, for all the music sounds very much alike to my untrained ears.) Only two or three nights ago we heard drums booming and cymbals clanging all night long, and at least once a great burst of firecrackers snapping and crackling. Our nearest Chinese neighbors in a farmhouse a few rods away were doing honor to their ancestors.

January 31, 1930 *Chengtu, West China*

Dear Alice, Fannie, and Grace,

The deputation from abroad has come and gone taking Robert with them to Yearly Meeting, which is being held in Tungchwan this year, so I am alone these days. I did feel very much alone at first after all the bustle and flurry of entertaining guests and running to meetings. The deputation's visit was ridiculously short. Five days to see the University and Chengtu!

Yesterday was Chinese New Year and the streets and countryside were full of people strolling about in bright new attire. Everybody must have an entire new outfit, if possible, and some new portion at the very least. The babies all come out in the brightest and gayest of caps. Firecrackers were booming at intervals during the night and day, but the Chinese tell me it is not like the "good old days" when there was scarcely a lull at any time, day or night.

While the deputation was here there was fighting one night in the city. The man who was managing the arsenal was requested to resign; when he refused he was ousted forcibly and later shot. There has been no new outbreak of anti-foreign or anti-Christian persecution except that about two weeks ago Dr. Peterson (M.E.M.) was attacked by a student-patient. Fortunately, the boy did not get the eye he aimed for, and infection from the wound did not reach the eye as was first feared. I suppose there is no doctor in West China who has done more for the people. Probably the boy was a bit demented. He was a student in the Silk School, one of the schools active in the agitation directed against our schools a few weeks ago.

Margaret Ruth is getting on towards seven months. She is much as Dorothy was at this age, dark eyes, pink cheeks, ready with a smile. Many remark upon her good nature and of course my bosom swells with pride. Dorothy is enthusiastic about nursery school. She is away each morning for two hours.

February 28, 1930 *Chengtu, Szechwan*

Dear Girls,

The Sewells got off today for their furlough. That is, they are settled on their little native boat down river at the "Thunder God Temple." They'll pull out tomorrow morning early. The river is now at its lowest, and at first the men will have to pole the boat; later they will row. Coming up river the trackers pull the boat. Do you remember pictures of the men straining and bent almost on all fours? It is interesting and exciting especially in the rapids. The singing of the rowers is something never to be forgotten. They stand to row and sing in unison and in time with the long sweep of the oars. Deep and full, their singing is hauntingly melancholy and beautiful.

Men working together carrying a heavy load also have songs or chants of rather another sort. I have seen and heard men (eight or twelve) carrying a coffin past the house and chanting as they went. The rhythm helps them to keep in step.

Mrs. Wang, whom we have had for three years, has given notice. I shall miss her greatly. I do not expect to find another woman who can look after the children so well. Mrs. Wang says she is going back to her old home and her sons will take care of her, "her feet ache all the time." I should like to have kept her until furlough.

June 1, 1930 *Chengtu, Szechwan*

Dear Ones at Home,

I don't know how much or how accurate "news" is being disseminated by the Associated Press re the attack on Dr. Clifford M. Stubbs. Perhaps we should try to relate what has happened.

Last Friday evening (May 30th) at about nine o'clock Clifford Stubbs was attacked and badly wounded by unknown assailants on the University campus in front of Hart College. His assailants evidently pushed him off his bicycle and then stabbed him seven times. The most serious wounds are two in the side below the arm, one where the knife cut the inner lining of the lung.

Clifford has no recollection of the encounter. He probably was stunned by a blow and lost consciousness until the whole affair was over. A carrying pole and fan were found at the scene. The bicycle which he was riding has not yet been found. Nothing was stolen from his person.

He was discovered by students not more than ten minutes after the attack. Three doctors were there immediately, and he was carried home where his wounds were dressed at once. The following morning (yesterday) he was taken to the Si Shen Tsi Hospital (U.C.C.M. Men's Hospital) and the wounds were sewn up. The report this morning is encouraging.

Later

Robert has returned from being in the city all day. Clifford's condition is very serious. Hemorrhage of the brain has set in due to the blows on the head. We are very worried and sad.

Jack, their boy, is with the Havermales.* We have taken temporarily August Lovegren, a boy of eight who goes to the Canadian School and has been living with Jack. The two Stubbs girls are in England.

Monday, June 2, 1930

Clifford died last evening shortly after seven o'clock.

Communists are suspected, but two or three of the assailants were finally traced because of Clifford's bicycle, which they took, and they claim that simple robbery was the motive. The bicycle was sold for thirty silver dollars. So Clifford was sacrificed for thirty pieces of silver! As you know, Clifford lived in our home for a number of months. We knew him well and miss him terribly. His advice on mission problems was invaluable. As head of the Science Department in the

---

**Members of the Methodist Episcopal Mission.*

University he was doing a magnificent piece of work. He was one of the two or three foreign members of the University Cabinet. I will not attempt to tell all the places he was filling, but everywhere his forward-looking Christian outlook made him a leader. He understood and loved the Chinese.

The local authorities were of course notified at once of the crime. They are sympathetic and are probably doing all they can to locate the criminals. General Den, at least, seems to attach political significance to the deed, that is, he sees in it an attempt to embarrass the present political combination. Others see significance in the date, May 30th.* Sometime about noon on the 30th some students (from other schools than our own) began to gather near the clock tower, which at times has been a meeting place for radicals. A member of the faculty immediately notified the police authorities in the city (or some official there) who sent a body of men out. The students apparently posted lookouts because the group dispersed suddenly, with most heading to the east. There is another clue. A few minutes before the incident, one of our students saw three or four men hiding near a hedge at the point where Clifford was attacked. The student hesitated, then went on and was not molested.

The University students are greatly shocked by the attack, for Dr. Stubbs was loved and respected by all. He was, to my mind, nearly an ideal missionary, and China never had a more loyal friend.

Dastardly deeds are being done all the time, but it hits hard when one of our own close friends is the target. Why should it be Clifford Stubbs of all people, a man so able and so much needed!

August 5, 1930 — *Behludin [White Deer Summit]*

Dear Girls,

You have asked about Mrs. Wang's successor. We have a good woman. Mrs. Wang was exceptional when it came to disciplining children but in other respects I am well pleased with Pen Da Niang. She is a good needlewoman.

We have been up here on this glorious mountain top for several weeks now, and oh! the air is so good and it is so peaceful and quiet. We look down on the plain, or up to the massive peaks, and it is hard to realize with all this beauty and quiet about us that we are living in a

**On May 30, 1925, in Shanghai, twelve Chinese students, one a Szechwanese, were killed by British police. This caused spread of anti-foreign feeling throughout China.*

land shaken and confused. It is good to be away from it all for a time and calm our souls and minds.

Following the tragic loss of Clifford Stubbs, the officials advised the building of a wall about the campus. Otherwise they claimed they could not protect us foreigners. The campus has become more and more a pleasure park (that in itself is not a bad thing) and a meeting place for radicals. Marauders have begun to destroy trees viciously. Of course there is always thieving. Things were coming to such a pass that the University authorities really had too little control over the property, so they decided to try to close the place in. Our own students were very anxious to have this done. Immediately the erection of walls and fences commenced.

Then the opposition began: "The foreigners are making a new concession," "They are building a city wall" (the campus comprises some 150 acres), "They are training soldiers for defense." (Military police were stationed on the property at the strong urging of the officials, although Friends at the University *strongly* protested.) There was much agitation and publicity against us in the newspapers and the opposition grew until a parade was formed on August 1. More sympathizers joined the marchers as they proceeded until at the University they tore down all the newly erected walls and fences. The officials seem either to have decided that the University was going too far in closing everything up tight, or they are afraid to oppose the radical elements. Reports from down river are not reassuring. (Chiang Kai Shek is reported to be losing. If the Communists get the upper hand the party in control locally is doomed, unless they are opportunists and jump in the right direction at the right moment.) So it goes. We shall have to see what the next days bring forth.

On the one hand, I have had misgivings from the first when I knew the wall was contemplated, because of what we stand for in our life in China--friendliness for all; but on the other hand, I have a sense of disappointment now that the wall-building has seemed to fail because it *would* have been a relief to be free from rude stragglers and the rest. They have crowded us off the walks, they have been insulting, they have subjected our children to unpleasantness that is far from desirable, (I have known outside students to stoop down and hiss in Dorothy's face), they take our flowers, tearing down and breaking off great branches of shrubbery. Perhaps all these things are inconsequential but they do wear on one. But please remember it is our Chinese colleagues who suffer the worst. Dsang Lin Gao (Lincoln Dsang), the acting president, continually receives letters threatening his life, and the newspapers carry all sorts of nasty criticism of him--a "foreign slave."

Since writing the above we have learned that a second mob came to the campus early on the morning of August 4 and broke down the big, heavy gate at the river. After firing shots in the air and much yelling, they pushed down some of the wall around the Library and some around the Church Missionary Society (English Church) property. As these walls were blocking no roads, such lawless action can only be construed as wanton destruction.

August 22, 1930

Dear Girls,

We have not had any very recent news from down river. The past news that the "Reds" had taken Changsha and burned consulates, foreign business property and Yale-in-China gave me the same queer, sinking feeling that I had when I heard of the Nanking outrages. For a moment one wonders when our turn is coming. Since, of course, we have heard that Chiang Kai Shek has retaken Changsha.

October 11, 1930 *Chengtu, West China*

Dear Grace,

I'll let Robert give an account of the trip home from Behludin:

We encountered about the maximum of bad roads on the way down from the mountain, as it had been raining for days and rained each of the three days we were on the road. The "road" was a sea of mud and in one place I waded up to my knees in water. In places I gained greatly by making wide detours on the narrow dikes between the rice fields. About noon of the third day I had hired a man whom I picked up by the wayside to carry my bicycle. We came to an especially abominable stretch of road and I again tried a detour. Some passersby told me that by taking a certain path I could regain the big road farther on, so I went on, the man carrying the bicycle not far from me, he on the big road. The small path turned quite away from the road and I found a big irrigation ditch twenty feet wide between me and the bicycle carrier. I didn't want to go back and besides, the road which the man had been toiling over was atrocious. I took off my clothes, wound them into a bundle with my watch buried in the middle of my canvas hat, and waded in. After a couple of steps the bottom went out from under me. I floundered across, holding my clothes as high as possible, and soon found footing again. I couldn't avoid getting my clothes somewhat wet, for I didn't think of swimming on my back. By the time I got dressed and regained the road the carrier was out of sight, but when I reached the end of the road I found him washing the bicycle. It needed washing, for the water and mud had got into all the bearings, so I left it in the shop as I passed through Chengtu city.

We found our house and its contents unmolested, for which we were very thankful, for at the time when the radicals started to push down walls and the authorities dared not deal with them, it seemed very likely that they might go on and loot the whole place. Fortunately they pushed down several tens of rods of wall and let it go at that. Since we came down matters seem pretty quiet. I say the house was unmolested. This is not quite true, for the caretaker whom we had left in charge had contrived to open one of the windows of our coal room in the basement and possibly eight or ten dollars worth of coal was gone. We had to sack him.

R.L.S.

November 2, 1930 *Chengtu, West China*

Dear Folks at Home,

Just think! In two and one-half months we shall be starting on our homeward trek. If there is a more excited family than ours, I don't know where to find it. It *is* thrilling to have the time so near, but what a mad rush there is going to be. We have sailings on the North German Lloyd *Saarbrucken* leaving Shanghai on March third. The Havermales of our campus community sail on the same boat. *Don't send any more letters to Chengtu.*

We are due at Port Said on April sixth and are arranging to have four weeks in Palestine and Egypt and take the next boat, the *Coblenz*, on to Genoa. Won't it be great to be with Katherine* in Palestine?

The Communists, eight days ago, staged a coup at Hanchow, a day's journey away. Colonel Tao escaped because his bodyguard remained true, but rumor says his wife and son are missing. Several subordinate officers were killed, the yamen looted, also the municipal hospital. Colonel Tao was really doing a good piece of work in Hanchow, making a modern city of it with good park, library, hospital, kindergarten, etc.

December 6, 1930 *West China Union University*
Chengtu, West China

Dear Ones at Home,

A few weeks ago we had a Communist outbreak (which I reported in previous letter) and a counter agitation. Apparently the coup at

**Katherine Haviland, a very dear college friend.*

Hanchow was a bit premature, so two other threatened cities, Chengtu and Sintu, were awake to the trouble and headed it off. The authorities here soon began a weeding out of radicals. For a full week we had a regular reign of terror. At least fifty were executed, many of them students. Two neighboring schools, which no doubt were hotbeds of Communism, were searched and cleaned out. The students were lined up, the roll called, and as there were responses to certain names those particular students were told to stand aside. Then they were simply taken to one side and shot. There were young girls among those who were executed.

Our students were in terror for their lives. On the one hand they feared the Communists, on the other the soldiers. Should our dormitories be searched they feared some little thing might be construed as evidence of their complicity. Some few students of pink hue, if not a deep red, decided it was a good time to move out. But the terror of the students was pitiful. It is hard to understand, unless you have lived in this country, the hopelessness and helplessness of this people. They have nothing back of them, nothing stable or sure to which they can flee.

This evening I have been reading a rather long report of one of our Friends missionaries who lives in Suining. He has, among other things, told of the difficulties they have there in holding their meetings for worship. All year the meeting house and school premises have been occupied by soldiers. They have had to hold their meetings while the soldiers at the same time occupied the gallery "eating, sleeping, gambling, and quarreling while our meetings have been going on." Doesn't it sound rather like the early days of Quakerism?

It is thrilling to be thinking and planning for going home at last. En route down river we expect to attend Szechwan Yearly Meeting which is at Chungking this year, opening January thirty-first.

Furlough Ahead
1931

February 7, 1931 *Tsang Pin Kai*
Chungking, Szechwan

Dear Girls,

...We were thirteen days reaching Chungking and some of the days in the second week were bitter cold because of hard up-river winds which not only retarded our progress but penetrated our little native boat as if it were a sieve. These native boats have only woven bamboo covers and although we had had wooden doors especially made for the front and back there were plenty of places for the wind to come through. We pasted paper over most of the holes but it was a losing battle. Also we had a *ho pen* (charcoal fire in a brazier). But all of us got colds. At Luchow we called a foreign doctor to see Margaret Ruth. He said she probably had bronchitis. Now her cough is practically gone and she is as happy and full of spirit as one could wish.

We came through the bandit country with nary a sight of one of the gentlemen unless it was a nest of them we ran into the last evening before arriving at Chungking. It was a beautiful moonlit night and we were anxious to go on until late to make time. However at some dinky little place or other there was a rain of shots, probably not fired directly at us but round about us, and we were called in to shore. The captain was ordered ashore for "trial." It appears that it was against orders to pass this point after six o'clock, though how anybody was to know of such a ruling I have yet to discover. Two or three soldiers with guns and belts of cartridges came onto the boat and pried into our things. They are so awfully bumptious and rude it just made me *furious*, ordering me to open this and open that. I simply was so mad I didn't think to be scared! Meanwhile Robert was on shore to see what could be done for the captain; we were afraid they might beat him up. Soon Robert came back, also more "inspectors."

All the while we (Dorothy and I) were trying to get our supper eaten. Dorothy was sitting on a stretcher bed, one end of which rested on a steamer trunk. The bed, the little table from which we were eating, my chair, the *ho pen*, all had to be moved to get into the steamer trunk and to lift floor boards so they could see down into the hold of the boat. The next thing we knew, after having settled down once more, the imposters wanted four dollars and fifty cents to pay for the cartridges they had used in stopping us! Robert spent the evening in negotiations and got them to compromise somewhat, but plainly it was a hold-up. This is what folk have to put up with all the time. How can trade or anything else flourish?!! We were glad to get out of the place early the next morning.

February 8, 1931

We got in at Chungking last Sunday afternoon. I was impressed by the imposing sky-line. The city has grown and developed in the seven years and the approach by boat is fairly pleasing. But close at hand I found the shacks still clinging to the city wall, flimsy dwelling places of the beggar class, supported by poles stuck in rocks and sand along the bank of the river. And there are still the appalling steps from the river up into the city, filthy and wet from the constant stream of water carriers who must supply this great city with river water. All the way up into the city and on to Tsang Pin Kai, where we are stopping, are steps, steps, steps. The streets are narrow alleys often just wide enough for two small sedan chairs to pass. At night the rats scurry about under foot. What a contrast to our wide, modern streets in Chengtu which are open and airy! I don't see how they can ever make common use of rickshas and automobiles here. But the other day we heard and saw an airplane overhead! Even Chungking is being modernized.

It has been pleasant being here with the English Friends. Robert especially has had many invitations to meals with the Chinese. He used to live here and was well known in former years.

Yearly Meeting closed Thursday evening and Central Executive followed. This smaller meeting, which really has the responsibility for managing Yearly Meeting affairs, closed last evening. Foreign Friends will begin to leave for home tomorrow and we shall soon be left here alone. Since fall this house has been occupied by Mr. and Mrs. Li and family. They kindly gave up most of their rooms for use of foreign

Friends at Yearly Meeting, and Leonard and Laura Walker came on from Tungliang to act as host and hostess. All of us have been more or less camping out, using our camp beds and equipment which must always accompany us in travel in West China. Tomorrow morning the Walkers leave and I shall then be hostess for Leonard Wigham, Dr. Davidson and whoever else may be left.

We do not know yet when we shall get away. We are waiting for a satisfactory steamer. The river is very low and we are anxious to be off.

February 26, 1931 *The* Pao Wu *on the Yangtse River below Chin Kiang*

Dear Girls,

This is our sixth boat and tomorrow we are due to arrive at Shanghai. There, I hope we shall find letters waiting for us. I have had no word from any of you since we left Chengtu more than five weeks ago.

We have had varied experiences since leaving Chungking. Because the water in the upper Yangtse was very low we feared to wait for a really good boat and took our chances on a small steamer called the *Suiting*--no heat, no accommodations for foreigners, no food. We had a Chinese captain. It was a British boat, however. We were glad to accept the captain's bathroom as a cabin! Dorothy slept in the bath tub! I had a camp cot bed beside her with the baby's basket on a shelf at my head. There was then just room for us to get in and stand. Robert slept on the bridge. The cook, our Pen Si, had prepared food for us and we had some tinned stuff which I warmed on a Sterno stove. (Pen Si bade us goodbye at Chungking.)

The *Suiting* would not have been too bad except that we had bitter cold weather. There was no place to exercise except on a tiny deck and the bridge which was colder than our bathroom cabin. We had snow from Fuchow down through the gorges and all the way to Nanking. We spent three days and nights on this little boat, arriving at Ichang Sunday afternoon.* At Ichang the water front is lined with foreign

---

**An account of an incident on one of those days aboard the* Suiting*: At the Chin Tan (rapid) there was an eight-foot drop--somewhat like going over a narrow dam. Our family stood huddled on the bridge. All three helmsmen were at the wheel holding it firmly and the pilot, tall and gaunt in his black Chinese gown and with serious and stern face, stood with arm upraised and forefinger uplifted to indicate quickly which turn to make. We took the plunge and the bow struck the water below, sending spray flying high up onto the bridge. We had made it! We were safe!*

buildings and since the shore and everything else was covered with deep snow I had a feeling that I already had reached New England. The Squires at the China Inland Mission Home took us in. How different things look when you are going up river and when you are going down! Going up, Ichang seemed like an outpost, with quaint and primitive water jugs, stoves, lamps. Coming down, the sight of Mrs. Squires' motherly face warmed my heart and the simple old-fashioned "home" seemed like a bit of Paradise. The children were as happy as kittens there. We were in Ichang one day.

The next boat between Ichang and Hankow was quite proper and comfortable. We travelled first class and ate like royalty. At Hankow there was another wait of two days. Hankow was buried in snow, piled high on either side of the street, but there we were in the palatial Lutheran Mission Home with hot-water heated bedroom, sitting room and private bath. So life becomes more luxurious with each advance. I did not see much of Hankow as I had to stay with the children, but to sit in the window and watch city traffic there in the foreign concession was play for all three of us. It is like a foreign country; it *is* a foreign country, in China!

The next boat brought us to Nanking. Rachel Mostrom* was at the dock to meet us and we all bundled into a carriage and drove to the "Quakerage" five miles from the river, where we had a perfectly wonderful time. Rachel is the first friend of former days that I have seen for over seven years. She is doing fine work at Nanking.

The next morning, a glorious sunny day, we took an auto ride for a sight-seeing trip. First we went to Purple Mountain and saw Sun Yat Sen's mausoleum. It is beautiful, and the view from the steps in front is magnificent. Then we drove to Ginling College and looked about rather thoroughly. I was very much interested because of my great interest in our Woman's College at Chengtu. Ginling has an almost ideal location and very beautiful buildings of Chinese type.

Dorothy is enjoying the journey very much. She has a good appetite and has been well except for colds. Just now she has a bad one. The baby has not done so well. There have been moments when I have felt we should never have started out with so young a child. We consulted a good doctor in Nanking who looked her over thoroughly. He found nothing wrong but her tonsils, and I, of course, knew her weakness there. But at any rate having a consultation with a doctor has reassured

---

**An acquaintance from New England Yearly Meeting who crossed the Pacific with us in 1923.*

me and given me courage to go on. I suppose I worry unnecessarily.

This *Pao Wu* is the best boat we have had yet. We travel* intermediate but the food and all are excellent. Apples, bananas--what a treat for us!

The pounding of the engines makes the boat joggle badly and I have been too sleepy to write a very good letter.

INTERLUDE

The sea voyage on the *Saarbrucken* was a delight, the service excellent and company on shipboard cosmopolitan and interesting. Port calls at Hongkong, Manila, Singapore, Belawan (on Sumatra), Colombo and on through the Red Sea and the Suez Canal enabled us to see life "as it is" with different peoples in varying environments. A month in the Middle East (Egypt, Palestine, Syria) was a great joy and satisfaction due to the guidance and help of good friends in Cairo and especially at Ramallah.

The *Coblenz* took us from Port Said to Genoa. Then by train we went to Milan (saw cathedral) and on through the Italian Alps to lovely Kandersteg, Switzerland, where the children and I spent several days while Robert was exploring Martin Luther country in Germany. After he rejoined us at Mainz the family had a good boat trip down the Rhine. Then it was on to Rotterdam and London where we adults attended Yearly Meeting. We also had a few days in Birmingham, a weekend with Margaret Stubbs in Saffron Walden and a visit with the Rodwells (formerly of Chengtu) at Derby.

After a brief visit in Dublin we sailed on the *Cleveland* from Galway to Boston. It was June and we were home again in New England with fields of fragrant new-mown hay, clover, daisies and buttercups!

Furlough time went quickly, partly spent in study at Hartford and partly in visiting families and other relatives in Maine, Connecticut and New York. In October 1931 my dear sister Grace, whom we had hoped could be with us in Hartford, died of cancer. By later summer 1932 our family of four was starting across the United States anticipating visits with relatives in California and our return to China.

**A memorable feature of steamer travel on the Yangtze is the soundings for depth. "One hears the lead splash the water and then the depth shouted in a high, shrill tone, 'Twa fee' [Twelve feet] or whatever. This is repeated again and again with the engine at low speed until the vessel works her way into deeper water."*

Robert Simkin's notes

The Simkin family at Ventnor, New Jersey in the winter of 1931–32.

四川書简

Birth Throes of a New Nation 1932 – 1940

Man has a thousand schemes,
Heaven has one.

Chinese epigram

The Return Journey 1932

September 28, 1932 S.S. President Taft

Dear Home Folks,

We are due at Yokohama Friday morning (September 30) and have a day in port. We'll probably run up to Tokyo. It's too bad I'll miss Esther Rhodes again; she is at home on short furlough.

October 2, 1932

We have had two perfect days in the Japan Inland Sea. It certainly is lovely to be speeding along over the blue water with green wooded mountains on either side, sometimes close at hand, sometimes farther away. There has been beautiful sunshine and a balmy air so that we could sit out on deck in summer clothes. I wouldn't mind having a prolonged ocean voyage of this sort. Perhaps you'll remember that most of this trip by the northern route is very cold.

On the thirtieth we were in port at Yokohama all day so we went up to Tokyo to visit Gilbert and Minnie Bowles, who received us most hospitably. We looked over the girls' school and then at noon Minnie Bowles arranged for the Japanese maid and a Japanese boy who lives there with them to look after the children while we adults went to the Imperial Hotel (a very fashionable hotel by the way) to a luncheon of the Pan-Pacific Club. Japanese, Chinese, Americans meet there together weekly in the interest of amicable relations between Pacific countries. The "new" Ambassador Grew spoke briefly; I thought very well. He married a daughter, or granddaughter, of Commodore Perry, so Gilbert Bowles whispered in my ear. Afterwards we talked informally with a number of people. One was Mr. Thoburn Brumbaugh who usually writes some good stuff in the *Christian Century*.

Last night we were at Kobe. That is, we docked at about five o'clock and sailed again at midnight. Robert and I went ashore in the evening to look up some people we had heard about while in Paradise, California. We found that the Oxfords had gone home to America but another family in residence received us and showed us about the school where they are teaching English to several hundred young Japanese men.

Japan does not give me quite the thrill it did in 1923. Of course it is interesting to see the men and women especially in the beautiful kimonos, and the Japanese wooden clogs. But Japan is very similar to China in many respects and it seemed familiar to me this time, not strange and odd.

We're due at Shanghai on Tuesday, October 4. Robert writes of future travel plans:

October 13, 1932 *Shanghai, China*

Dear Folks,

I am writing on the Yangtze Rapid Steamer *Ichang* on which we have taken passage direct to Chungking. We shall not have the bother of transferring from steamer to steamer at Hankow and Ichang as we usually do. Our freight from Philadelphia, Hartford, and Portland all arrived on time and is on this boat with us. We have had to wait several days beyond the time required to attend to our business, as the boat has postponed sailing from day to day, but now we think she will sail about midnight. We have been very fortunate during this long wait in being the guests of Mr. and Mrs. C.C. Boynton. Mr. Boynton was a classmate of mine at Union Theological Seminary and is now a Secretary of the China Christian Council.

The *Ichang* is one of the best of the Yangtze Rapids fleet. It seems tiny when compared with the *President Taft* on which we crossed the Pacific but I think we shall be very comfortable. We do not know how we shall travel from Chungking to Chengtu. By the overland route it is three hundred miles, but those who have more recently come from Szechwan advise that we take a small tub of a steamer from Chungking to Suifu, which is nearly half of the circuitous river route,* and small native junk from there two weeks to Chengtu. Serious fighting has broken out between Liu Hsiang, the warlord in Chungking, and his uncle, Liu Wen Hwei, who is the most powerful general in Chengtu. Their opposing armies are drawn up along a line more than a hundred

**The river describes an arc of 1745 li, or about 500 miles.*

miles long, across which we shall have to pass by whatever road we travel after leaving Chungking. The general disorder which accompanies warfare is not conducive to safe travel, but we shall hope for the best. The trouble may be over by the time we get there. It always is best to go on as far as one can for conditions usually look worse at a distance.

Robert L. Simkin

P.S. Already it seems like being ''back home.'' One would know this to be China from the sound and the smell alone--even if blindfolded.

Margaret

October 23, 1932 — *On board* Ichang

Dear Folks at Home,

...We got this ''through'' steamer and we have enjoyed the trip up the Yangtze very much....We had beautiful weather coming through the gorges. And oh, what grandeur and wild beauty! There were the expected dangerous currents, the roar of the rapids, and the great whirlpools fatal to any fragile craft caught in their fiercely swirling water, but it is the majestic beauty of the mountains rising steeply from the water's edge that I shall remember most.

Robert has facts to add about navigation on the upper Yangtze:

Dear Friends,

We were fortunate in securing a through steamer from Shanghai to Chungking. It was one of the larger ones on the upper river and drew about nine feet. The captain told me he had come down when the water was 170 feet above low water mark in the gorges. In February 1931 when we went down it was a few inches below the zero mark. About 1870 it rose in the gorges to more than 250 feet and virtually washed away some of the cities on its banks. October and late April are the best times for navigation. When we came it registered 24 feet at Ichang and 77 feet in one of the gorges. At the Tingling Rapid we barely managed to get up. We were steaming at least fourteen knots per hour and were failing to make any progress at all. The pilot sent for the chief engineer and asked what was the trouble. The engines were doing all that they were capable of, yet for a short time it seemed as if we were actually slipping back. Finally the boat swung over slightly where the current was a little less swift and we began to gain. This rapid is particularly dangerous, as there are two lines of submerged rocks between which it is difficult to pass safely. During the year about six steamers have been wrecked on the Ichang-Chungking run. We saw two in trouble, one of them abandoned until the low water when she will be broken up and the pieces taken to Shanghai to be used in a complete rebuilding.

Robert L. Simkin

November 6, 1932 *Wen Feng Ta School*
Chungking, Szechwan

Dear Home Folks,

We arrived in Chungking on the 24th of October and here we still are. If we could only know how soon this warfare is going to clear up! I feel rather restless. If I knew we were to be here some time I could resign myself and settle down to a more or less satisfactory mode of living. But always, or rather intermittently, there is the hope that the situation may clear and we shall soon be able to go on. Dr. Crawford,* whom we saw the other evening, is trying to be optimistic. At any rate, his news from home in Chengtu was reassuring about warfare in that immediate vicinity. Robert has gone to the city today and perhaps he will bring us some more news....

November 13, 1932 *Temporarily at Wen Feng Ta*
Chungking, West China

Dear Ones at Home,

I am beginning to feel rather at home in Chungking. We have now been here nearly three weeks. And still our departure for Chengtu looks remote.

It is all because of this terrible warfare. To show to what an extent warfare has gone in West China let me say that we frequently hear airplanes (war craft) flying overhead. For days they have been going on to Luchow to drop bombs on that luckless city. These planes belong to Liu Hsiang, the Chungking general, and Luchow thus far is held by the 24th army, Liu Wen Hwei's, the Chengtu general. Liu Wen Hwei has no planes. We heard today, I don't know how authentic the account is, that the planes first dropped notices over Luchow warning civilians to flee, but the 24th army refused to let the people leave the city. What wretched business war is!

Leonard Wigham writes from Suining that the 24th army has been driven from that city, but no less than four other armies have come in to take its place. The town and countryside have to feed all these soldiers and food is getting terribly dear. Thus far he has been able to

---

**Canadian Mission member and neighbor in Chengtu.*

keep the soldiers off his premises although many requests have already come for the use of the Mission house. Suining lies on the overland route to Chengtu, and some foreigners are undertaking to go through that way, but we hesitate to try it. First, we have considerable baggage and the cost of transporting our supplies overland would be prohibitive and we therefore feel it is wiser to go by boat and personally conduct the boxes, stoves, and all the rest through customs and other barriers. Second, there must be some point between Suining and Chengtu which is contested ground. We just can't think of subjecting the children to situations that might well arise in getting through the lines....

November 23, 1932 *Still at Chungking, Szechwan*

Dear Home Folks,

I wish I had definite news and plans for procedure to write of. You have no idea how hard it is to get trustworthy news of conditions in the rest of the province. We hear all kinds of rumors, but don't know what to believe.

Has Luchow fallen? If so, perhaps we can venture forth on a boat next week. We shall have to feel our way along. Even if Luchow has fallen, which seems likely, other cities on the river, such as Suifu, may be in a state of seige. Suifu is a city we must also pass but at any rate we shall be that much nearer Chengtu.

There are reports of fighting around Chengtu, but letters of an earlier date do not mention such an attack. We have received several welcoming letters from Chengtu, however, to make us happy....

Robert's diary and bits from my letters give the story of our journey from Chungking to Chengtu.

November 25, 1932 [Diary],

Miss Jack and Dr. and Mrs. Hoffman* of the Canadian Mission are engaging a large boat, as they have a lot of freight. We are negotiating for a smaller one belonging to Captain Ho. The Canadian party wants to start Monday but we cannot get ready so soon as we have to attend a funeral tomorrow.

November 28, 1932,

Finally secured Ho's boat and took it down to the steamer pontoon to load our freight. We came within a SQUEAK of dropping our cookstove

---

**Hoffmans, new recruits.*

into fifteen feet of water. The junk swung away from the pontoon and the stove slipped down between. I grabbed the crate and held it from slipping completely over the edge until some of the men came and pulled it back up. At another time I had a narrow escape myself. The four-foot sloping border of the pontoon has no rail. As I walked along the edge I slipped on some grease from a leaky tin of lubricating oil and started straight for the water. I only *just* managed to stop as I reached the brink!

We had scarcely started loading when the *likin* (local customs) officers descended upon us. "What is in this box? What in that?" After I had opened four cases on the deck, exposed to the rain, they went away and I hoped we were rid of them. Not so! Back they came to the attack. We had paid $167 (Mex.) duty in Shanghai and the customs officials in Shanghai had given us a paper stating that our goods were free of duty from there on, but this paper was of no avail. I finally prevailed upon the inspectors to permit us to transfer the goods to the junk on condition that the junk should not leave the pontoon without their permission. It was dark when we got things aboard so I left them in charge of our cook and started back to the city. Margaret and the children were still on the hills. I picked my way carefully along the slippery shore. Suddenly my underpinning went out, lantern, briefcase and open umbrella described incredible arcs in space and I made a "forced landing" face upward, ending in total darkness! In falling I arched my body on hands and feet, so I didn't get excessively muddy. Nothing was really broken and a boy helped me relight the lantern. I crossed the ferry and soon found myself in the warmth and cheer of the Canadian Mission Home.

A trip to the pontoon next morning failed to free the junk. A missionary friend suggested that an application to the head of the Bureau of Navigation might help. He phoned and got a promise that a messenger would be sent to investigate. I went with this messenger to the pontoon and a consultation ensued, after which the *likin* officials suggested that I apply to General Liu Hsiang's office for a pass. The messenger kindly undertook to apply for this pass for me, but still the junk was not allowed to budge. About four o'clock the Bureau of Navigation sent a letter which had been issued by the Eastern Szechwan General Tax Office. Thus armed I made my fourth trip to the pontoon. The *likin* office stamped the paper and told me the junk might now go free.

A new difficulty arose before we could get together our oarsmen, who had gone ashore to drink tea. The road tax officials came aboard and said that the junk could not be released until the paper had been stamped by their central office in Chungking city more than a mile beyond the ferry. When I reached that office it was closed, so nothing can be done till tomorrow.

November 29, 1932

Better success today. Took my letter to the road tax office which gave me a paper to go with it. This the pontoon officials recognized and freed the junk about 11 a.m. I spent the day rearranging cases so as to occupy less room in the hold and loading freight belonging to other missionaries who wish it taken to Chengtu in our care. Slept on the boat and discovered that the captain is an opium smoker. He and another boatman smoked opium until after midnight. The Canadian party left this afternoon. Perhaps we can overtake them at Luchow.

November 30, 1932,

Margaret and the children came down from the hills this morning.

R.L.S.

December 2, 1932

We spent November 30th on our junk digging down into numerous trunks and boxes and pulling out winter clothing, blankets and bedding. The next day the captain still had made no move to set forth. Budge he would not! Miss Jack's boat had given extra money because of an excessive amount of freight and our captain thought he would hold us up for more money. (The contract called for $290 (Mex.) from Chungking to Chengtu.) He complained about our huge amount of freight and was very ugly indeed. We are carrying baggage for others besides ourselves.

Finally, Robert and he went up to the Canadian Agency through which the arrangement had been made, and after Gordon Jones had threatened to hire another boat, he at last came to terms. By noon on December 1, we had actually pushed off. By night, we had covered about five *li* of our 1745 *li* journey and still were almost in sight of Chungking! But it was a beginning!

M.T.S.

Robert's diary continues with the story.

December 2, 1932,

We have a crew of twelve men and a boy. Eight of these pull from the shore by a cable of split and braided bamboo. The captain's son, a lad of nineteen, poles at the front, and an old pirate (the captain) stands on a high board at the stern, hand on tiller. These two seem very unskillful and have twice today run us on rocks, producing minor leaks which had to be caulked. The captain spends most of his time smoking opium or making the air blue with vile oaths whenever anything goes wrong. It is a very badly managed boat, and I fear we shall have trouble before we reach Chengtu....

December 3

Last night some men who we suspected were robbers boarded a boat near us with much angry shouting and commotion. I hastily dressed so as to be ready if they came to us, but it proved to be a false alarm.

December 4

Rainy and cold all day, but we travelled sixty *li*. The captain has not yet closed the back of the boat to keep out the cold. In rainy weather travel by boat is better, however, than by sedan chair. Our stove is a great boon on a day like this.

December 6

Yesterday we made 115 *li*. We had a favoring wind so we could use the sail. This afternoon we tied up at 2:30, and so lost three hours of daylight because bandits were reported to be at the next anchorage and it was too late to reach the one beyond.

December 9

Dorothy and I took a long walk yesterday by the river. The country is beautiful. Wheat, peas, a kind of coarse bean and many vegetables grow all winter long, so many of the fields are green. We saw the poppy, the source of opium. We passed a group of thirty-nine men washing sand for gold. Mud, stones and water are poured into a rocking bamboo basket. The water carries the mud down over a sloping bed of deeply grooved wood. Tiny particles of gold find their way down into these grooves and are later washed more carefully.

We stopped at 4 p.m. at a place which I did not like because it was separated from a village by a wide expanse of stony beach, in summer entirely covered by high water. Only three other boats were there, and it was too far from the village to expect any help in case of robbers. To go on, however, seemed still less safe, as the boatmen said the next sixty *li* was robber country with no proper anchorages at all. I was awake at 12 and at 1 o'clock. (A flashlight is a great comfort.) At two the trackers got up, lighted their fire, packed away their bedding and mat shelter, and started out. I lay awake listening to the shouts of the men and the rush of the rapid water. I was now less concerned about robbers than about the possibility of a wreck as it was dark and the men had told me that there were many rapids in this section. At 3:45 we moored at a sandbank and the trackers came aboard and had breakfast, squatting on their haunches as they usually do at their meals. As they were eating, someone on shore challenged us. "It's a foreigner's boat," went back the reply. Were our challengers local militia or robbers? Who could tell? After half an hour we were again challenged, this time more insistently, with a demand that we send up one of our men. Two men came down to the water and asked some questions. Probably they were militia. At any rate they didn't rob us, but it is the constant uncertainty which keeps a fellow guessing. Our trackers didn't dare to stir from the place until after six when it became light, lest we be shot at as we were by local militia last year when we journeyed down river.

For over two hours our trackers sat huddled together at the front of the boat, with totally inadequate cotton clothing, shelterless in the biting cold wind. From their sneezing we knew they were taking cold. One said, "*Len de teo*" (Shivering cold). Half of them have "graveyard coughs." You can hardly imagine the unspeakably hard living conditions of many of the poor people. Only today one of the trackers in boarding the boat to row across river slipped from a rock and plunged into the bitter cold water. This is his second dunking since leaving Chungking.

December 13

We reached Luchow December 10 and had a very happy day visiting the three families of missionaries there. They had a very strenuous time when airplanes were daily bombing the city. Some of the bombs were "made in U.S.A." It is a shame that Americans should enrich themselves by selling such instruments of destruction. We overtook the Canadian party at Luchow and have since travelled together.

This morning we had a great scare. Suddenly we ran on a rock. A big seam opened in the forward compartment and the water spurted in. After the trackers pulled us off a regular flood poured in. We bailed furiously, a second bailing scoop was brought from the other boat, and pails, washbasins, and a saucepan were all quickly requisitioned. Nevertheless the compartment was soon swimming with water. For a time it looked as if we were going to have a repetition of our complete wreck the last time we went up river. The men managed, however, to check the water with a cotton quilt until they could stuff the seam with cotton. Then they bailed out, caulked the seam carefully, nailed a board over the place and caulked the edges of this board. Only the two boxes which were in this forward compartment got wet and they contain things which will not suffer greatly. A partition right across the boat prevented the water's filling the other compartments which contain our trunks and supplies for seven years.

We are thinking seriously of changing to another junk, as this one is so very poorly managed. The difficulty is that we paid, as is the custom, two thirds of the passage money in advance, and if we should transfer we should not get back anything from this opium sot. He seems to have spent all his money and has not even brought enough to buy necessary equipment for the journey. Twice today he has begged me for additional money to buy bamboo rope, although I had already advanced more than the contract specified. I have compromised by advancing part of what he asks, as otherwise we fear he will try to use too poor a rope in some rapid and wreck us.

December 15

We have had two beautiful sunshiny days. Thus far the temporary repairs have held well. Today we went through a *big* rapid. Some of the trackers from the other boat were helping ours, but we hung in the rapids for minutes, unable to gain. Just then a breeze came up, we raised the sail and the additional push got us through. We are nearly half way to Chengtu and hope to reach Suifu tomorrow.

December 16, 1932

Arrived at Suifu this afternoon and got some letters. Chengtu has had a terrible time, street fighting throughout the city.

Conditions on the river ahead are bad. The Duncans on their way out from Batang arrived at Suifu half an hour before we did. They were fired upon near Chien Wei. Thinking that their boat carried an attacking party, the 21st army continued to fire even when Mr. Duncan advanced waving an American flag. Mrs. Duncan and the children sought shelter behind a small hill, and finally Mr. Duncan convinced the soldiers that he was not an enemy. We do not crave a similar experience, so we shall wait a few days until travel seems safer.

December 18

Since word has come that there is a lull in the fighting we plan to go on tomorrow.

R.L.S.

December 18, 1932 [*M.T.S.*]

With the Wood family
Suifu, West China

We are having a perfectly lovely respite from our boat journey. After sixteen days on our junk we arrived here and as conditions up the river at Kiating and Chengtu are too uncertain (or worse!) we are off the boat for the time being. Robert has returned to the junk both nights to sleep and watch our goods, but the children and I have been completely enjoying this hospitable home. You've no idea how good an American home looks after being "on the road."

We are the guests of Chester and Dorothy Wood, two fine New Englanders. They came out in 1920 (American Baptist Mission) and were students of Robert's when he taught in the Language School. We like them tremendously. They are such comfortable folk. The Woods have the great gift as host and hostess of making you feel as if you were conferring a great privilege by staying with them. Besides Dot and Chet there are four little Woods--aged eleven years to five weeks! As they are the only foreign children in Suifu they have given Dorothy and Margaret a warm welcome too, and our children have been having the time of their young lives. The Wood family are urging us to stay over Christmas. Wouldn't we just love to!

M.T.S.

December 23, 1932 [*M.T.S.*] *Chien Wei*

Tonight we are anchored here at Chien Wei. (1155 *li* from Chungking and still 590 *li* to Chengtu. A *li* equals approximately one-third of a mile.) Soldier inspectors who came aboard earlier this evening informed us that the enemy line is but five *li* farther up the river! Now we must hold a council of peace (if not of war) to determine our next move. (Will give result later.)

You'll be interested in our domestic arrangements. Irene Hutchinson wrote that our old cook, Pen Si, was willing to come to Chungking to meet us, that he quite expected that we'd take him on. I had quite decided, however, that it was time for a change. So we employed another man in Chungking and he started out on the boat journey with us. Before a week was up, we knew he would never do. In the first place, he was not well and altogether he made Pen Si appear a paragon of perfection. Fortunately there was another cook aboard, a young man who had agreed to help us to work his passage back up river to Suifu. I liked his energy and ability to manage, and after finding that he would be willing to cook and buy for us all the way to Chengtu, we arranged with Liu Si to leave us at Ho Chiang and to return to Chungking and thereupon Bao Si took charge. Bao Si is as careful about keeping things neat and is as energetic as old Liu Si was dirty and shiftless. He is also very kind and helpful with the children. We like him very much, but unfortunately we have many reasons to believe that he indulges in opium so we cannot keep him permanetly.

Once we got a good "boy" at the helm and things on the boat organized we have pretty much enjoyed our river journey.

We have our new foreign coal-burning cook stove set up with the smoke pipe running out through a hole in the bamboo matting covering the boat. It is great for cooking (cook has even baked bread) and also radiates much welcome heat. Opposite the stove is a big packing box which we use as a dining table.

Often we can get out and walk and this gets us warm. One of the great delights of our Szechwan winters is the fresh greenness of the countryside with young peas, beans, and other crops. And the graceful bamboo is always beautiful. We are enjoying the delicious loose-skinned oranges which grow throughout this region.

It is nearly three months since we have had any word from you. Trust all is well.

M.T.S.

Robert tells what happened to us after leaving Suifu.

December 19, 1932 [*Diary*]

We did not get started today until noon as the captain had dismissed some of his trackers and could not easily get together a crew. Darkness therefore fell before we reached Su Mao Pin. I went on shore with a lantern to light the trackers and help pull. We almost reached the village, when in darkness the boat turned too much broadside to the current, dragging us backward until we had to let go or be pulled into the river. Down raced the boat, and I in hot pursuit. For a time I lost ground and wondered where if ever I should find my family. At last the few men on board managed to row into a back current and stop the boat. The trackers finally made their way down in the dark over great rocks and slippery boulders, and we started to recover the ground lost. A second time the boat all but pulled away in the rapid. We slackened the rope and ran to get a better standing ground and so checked it. The captain's right hand, however, got caught and severely crushed under the tracking rope.

Robert L. Simkin

Margaret writes:

On the morning of December 24, Robert and Miss Jack went up to the city of Chien Wei scaling the city wall on a ladder as the city gates were not open. They found the place under martial law, and after numerous adventures got a pass which would let us through the lines of the 21st army (Liu Hsiang's). This took all forenoon.Finally we were on our way again and soon in "No Man's Land." We had no trouble whatever. I think I heard two shots, one of which was fired at ducks. As we approached the line of the 24th army (Liu Wen Hwei's), another pass had to be secured. This was accomplished without too great difficulty, although Robert got into the water to his waist because a plank (put out by a small boat for him to cross on) broke beneath his weight. Fortunately our boat was near and he could change to dry clothing at once.

So we have come merrily on our way. During the first part of our journey, between Chungking and Chien Wei, I was impressed by the scarcity of soldiers (one usually sees them about everywhere when travelling in West China). I suppose they are all at the front. And as we have passed through the country it has seemed peaceful enough. That is so true of China. Folk five miles away may be passing through agonizing experiences but life near at hand goes on about as normal. What other people on earth could go through what the Chinese have endured and still survive?! Such a patient people!

December 28, 1932 [*Margaret writes*] *Kiating*

We got here yesterday about 2 p.m., went to the Quentins and found the foreign community eating Christmas dinner! Room was made for Robert and me at the table and we shared in the Christmas pudding, mince pie and other goodies. Dorothy and Margaret went off to play with the children, who had eaten earlier. After dinner there was a beautiful Christmas tree and old Santa Claus came to entertain the children. So we had a real taste of a "home" Christmas after all! We had already celebrated the day on the boat. We had gathered some green stuff, while off on shore for a walk, and decorated (?) the boat. The children hung up their stockings on Christmas Eve. Christmas morning they found a gingerbread man sticking out of each one. There was also a bit of candy, an orange, and some remembrances from the other boat and Suifu friends. Christmas night we were invited to Miss Jack's boat for supper. It is sometimes quite fun to see what can be done with a little of nothing. The children were quite happy.

Here at Kiating we realize more of what this terrible civil war means. There are thousands of wounded soldiers in the city and they are still being brought in. The foreign hospital is caring for them as best it can. Those badly wounded they cannot help. They have no x-ray, they can't probe for bullets. But they are dressing minor wounds. On the field iodine is applied but the men come in with old and obviously far from sterile dressings. The school (mission) just below the house is filled with soldiers.

This is what happened. The 21st army attacked the city, the seige lasting nearly a week. Finally the 21st had to withdraw because of lack of ammunition. Everybody seems to fear another attack. It seems we have slipped through at the opportune time.

Matters are quieter at Chengtu now, but they have had a dreadful time there. Our Shi Nie Kai (Industrial Street) School was right on the line and soldiers used the premises, firing from the roofs. When leaving, they looted the place. Mr. Wu and the servant put in a terrible night and lost most of their possessions. Of course there was considerable destruction to property. What is to happen? How are repairs to be made? The people in that section, the patrons of the school, will perhaps help but they themselves have been looted.

Our story continues with Robert's diary.

December 30, 1932

Last night we went to bed fairly easy in our minds as we thought we were at a safe anchorage. About eleven there was a sudden outcry followed by a lot of talking on the shore. Our cook said it was the local militia, so I turned over and went to sleep. About two I was awakened by more talking. Several men with guns and a lantern walked along the bank past our boat. I heard one of them say, "Come ashore, Li Laoban, we want to talk with you." Supposing they were the local militia I went to sleep again. This morning we learned that they were robbers and had relieved Captain Li of $258. Perhaps they knew that he was treasurer for the fleet of salt junks and also that the guards were not armed. They did not molest us. I was a little nervous, however, about leaving the family and going back to hunt up the other two boats.* Two or three miles down river I found them both coming slowly through a rapid. When they assured me that they were all right I hurried back and overtook our boat soon after ten. Both on the down trip and on the return I heard some shooting, but nothing came of it. We stopped this afternoon at two but the other boats have not appeared. Tonight we are again anchored with the salt junks as it is probable that they will not be robbed again so soon.

December 31, 1932

Miss Jack's boat arrived after dark last night, but tied up across river from us. The freight boat has not yet come. We are very anxious about it. Rainy and bitterly cold all day. We arrived very early at Han

---

**Miss Jack's boat and one from Kiating containing freight for the University.*

Yang Ba, eighty *li* from Kiating. Here another boat with a woman captain named Chang is joining us. It is loaded with wood for some of the University people. The war has made it exceedingly difficult to get fuel in Chengtu.

New Year's Day, 1933

With the fuel boat we arrived at Liu Chin Tsang at 1 p.m. and tied up to wait for Miss Jack's boat which is always behind. This time they stuck in shallow water and had to hire a smaller boat (Captain Cheo's) to take off some of their cargo. I went down river to see if I could help. On my way back I met Margaret who had come to tell me that we were in trouble. Soldiers had come aboard our boats and had taken several of our trackers and all of those from the fuel boat except one. For several days there has been a very heavy movement of troops toward Chengtu, hence the impressing of our men. Our cook says that some are even given arms and are forced to go to the front as soldiers. I went into the village to look for these trackers, but apparently they had been hustled off. I tried to find someone in authority, but the place is at sixes and sevens. People told me that soldiers have been passing all day, each group making demands upon the village, so the gentry and all the important men have fled or hidden. We fear that with no one in charge in the village we may be robbed in the night, but it is too late to go on now, and besides, we haven't sufficient trackers to pull our boats.

January 2, 1933

By using our combined crews we had enough men this morning to pull one craft at a time through a troublesome stretch of rapids. It was slow work pulling the big one through, then Cheo's, and then ours. It was impossible to nurse along the fuel boat with its single remaining tracker, so I told the woman captain to return to Han Yang Ba if necessary and wait for more auspicious times. I went on shore to help pull and to keep the men from being taken as many soldiers were passing on the bank of the river. We kept ourselves out of sight as much as possible, hiding behind trees or rushes when we saw soldiers approaching. A soldier took one of our trackers in spite of my protests. He drew his revolver (but did not point it at me), so I had to let go of the tracker, but I followed until we came to the soldier's sergeant who kindly released my man. A second case was more difficult, for here my man was put to carry two rifles in a long line of soldiers on a path only wide enough for single file, and some of the soldiers pushed me out of the path when I attempted to follow. I kept as near as I could to my man for nearly half a mile and finally ran into a group of officers halting for dinner. Among these I recognized the secretary whom we met in the office of Wang in Chien Wei nine days ago. In response to my breathless request for help he came with me and released my man when I pointed him out. I don't care to repeat the experience too many times however. All this afternoon I pulled with our five men whenever we came to swift water, and so we managed to keep going.

January 3, 1933

Early this morning the boatmen called me to save one of the trackers from being taken by the soldiers. We couldn't get near to shore in the shallow water, so I got my feet well soaked, and lost the man after all. The soldiers hustled the man off before I could reach them. We had to go into Chinsen city to get permission to open a pontoon bridge. We have failed to reach Taipingchang (the Village of Peace) and are anchored in the river below the town--not a safe place, so far as one can judge.

All along this section of the river are trenches, dugouts, shelters, sometimes at intervals of less than twenty yards.

January 4, 1933

The big boat (we have begun to call it "the ark") stuck twice today, so we made only 20 *li*. We came to another pontoon bridge. The soldiers guarding it opened it for us and refused the dollar which we usually paid for the service. Had we been able to go on immediately all would have been well, but it was too late to reach Meichow so we tied up just above the bridge. The soldiers saw a chance to "squeeze" us so they came back and demanded six dollars. After a parley we compromised and have paid three.

January 5, 1933

Last night I was glad we were not in so lonely a place as the night before. About eleven I awoke to hear a man calling out something which I did not understand. Then he said, "If you don't answer I shall shoot." Someone came to life and made a reply which apparently satisfied him. The "ark" is still leaking very badly. Half its cargo has been transferred to Cheo's boat, and we tried unsuccessfully at Meichow to get another small one to take the remainder. The ark is always getting stuck in shallow water. Tonight we are tied up just above another pontoon bridge. The place is literally swarming with soldiers and to avoid a repetition of last night's extortion we pulled up stream a couple of hundred yards and tied up. We had just finished supper when ten men came and asked the ark's captain to go on shore.

The captain called me to go with him, but I had no desire to go as I did not know whether they were robbers or not. I therefore asked, "What is your business, that you want us to go ashore?" They replied, "Oh, it is only the captain we want. It has nothing to do with you foreigners." Miss Jack's captain went with them, and, fearing trouble, immediately our three boats pushed off and dropped back to the bridge. We are anchored in midstream.

January 6

We had no further trouble last night. Did these men have some score to settle with the captain, or did they merely wish us to tie up near the bridge? If the latter, why should it have required *ten men* to tell us this? We are anchored this evening in a very lonely spot but there is no possibility of making the next anchorage before dark. Miss Jack and the Hoffmans have lost hope of getting their big ark through, so tomorrow morning I am going back to Taihochang to see if I can secure for them a small boat belonging to Hsiung (Mr. Bear), a friend of their pilot.

January 7

We have had a day of it--worked hard from dawn till dark and only made eight *li* (two and a half miles). We shouldn't have done that if I hadn't been successful in engaging Hsiung's boat. When I returned from Taihochang the fleet had advanced less than fifty rods. Our boat had broken its rope and had gone back down the rapid. We pulled through the rapid, stuck in a shallow, took off part of our cargo and tried again--without success. By three o'clock Hsiung's boat arrived and began to transfer cargo from the ark, so we went back a second time down the rapid to get Hsiung's boat to take part of our cargo too. Thus lightened we managed to scrape over the shallows. The ark, however, though now practically empty, stuck fast. Finally after breaking several ropes they got her over. The captains say that because of the pontoon bridges and the military restrictions on travel so few boats are moving that no definite channel has been made. Our own boat has leaked badly since we scrubbed over that shallow. The men are bailing and are hunting for the leaks.

Eight or ten men came aboard tonight after we tied up. They were a motley aggregation and had all sorts of weapons so at first we didn't know whether they were local militia or robbers. They were militia and told a story of just missing some robbers last night who came while they had gone across river to inspect some boats.

January 8

A beautiful day. Two pontoon bridges; I think we have passed eight in all. Reached Kiang Keo about one, where we had a very difficult *likin* (local customs) examination, but finally we were allowed to pass. We have waited for Miss Jack who has gone to get rickshas for her party.

January 9

Miss Jack spent last night at the Penshan mission and returned this morning. No autos are running, nor could she get rickshas. She brought one two-man chair and a man to carry bedding for herself and the Hoffmans. They abandoned the ark and set off overland to Chengtu after transferring the last of their goods to Hsiung's boat. Our captain had business which delayed our starting until one o'clock, but we have made 25 *li*. Tomorrow we go through "no man's land" into the territory of the 29th army.

January 10

Made 45 *li* today, and should have done better but for two fuel boats which blocked the channel for three hours. One of them broke its rope six times. Its boatmen calmly cooked and ate dinner as if oblivious of the fact that they were holding up a string of waiting boats. In America a line of autos would have honked their horns with impatience if kept waiting *three minutes*! "No man's land" did not materialize today as the 29th army has retreated toward Chengtu.

January 12

Bitter cold; pulled for a while with the trackers to get warm. At Kiang Keo the captain engaged two young fellows, one to steer and one at the bow to pole. Both are very skillful at finding the channel, but neither ever loses an opportunity of telling the other he is wrong. On this journey we have heard enough oaths to last Methusaleh a lifetime. We are still in the territory of the 24th army.

January 13

Last night's cold drizzle turned to snow, and this morning the world was white--quite unusual for Szechwan. The boatmen were simply overcome by the cold and snow and never moved from our anchorage until after two o'clock.

January 15

Well, here we are at the University in the hospitable home of Dr. and Mrs. Wallace Crawford who are caring for us until we can get settled in our own home. We arrived yesterday afternoon, after forty-four days journey. For thirty-nine of those days we were actually travelling or trying to travel. In the 500 miles either our cargo or our papers were inspected by *likin* officials twenty-five times and by the military fourteen times. At five other points we were permitted to pass *likin* without inspection, probably because we are foreigners. Almost everywhere we met with courteous treatment both from civilians and from the three armies in whose territory we travelled. Again and again where soldiers had received orders to permit no boats to travel we were allowed to pass, and pontoon bridges which had delayed Chinese travellers for a week were forthwith opened for us. I have mentioned the impressing of our trackers by soldiers, but this is the system upon which military leaders depend for moving their troops, and these soldiers treat their own countrymen ten times worse than they do us. Wherever we could reach any higher officer we were always sure of courteous treatment.

Later

The freight boat and the fuel boat which we had to leave behind arrived about ten and twenty days respectively after we did.

We are getting settled and are glad to be back.

Robert L. Simkin

War and Rumors of War 1933 & 1934

January 29, 1933 *Chengtu, West China*

Dear Folks at Home,

We arrived two weeks ago yesterday and are still in the process of getting settled.

Everything about the place is in good condition, except for the wear and tear that two years may be expected to bring. One trunk which came with us was wet at the bottom, but fortunately only washables were damp.

We cannot hope to get fully settled until we get our ''furnace'' and electric lights in. Now that we have passed the Chinese New Year we may hope for workmen to come and install these conveniences. Won't it be great if we can keep warm and have good, convenient lighting?

Many of the homes on the campus now have electric lighting (from the plant in the Medical-Dental building), but ours will be the first to have a furnace (a potbelly railway station stove in the basement with a floor register above it), and we need one. Our one room which we attempt to keep warm (by means of a fireplace) registered 50° yesterday forenoon. Nobody can do efficient or effective work under such conditions. I wear a heavy overcoat all the time while trying to unpack and settle. The ground was white with frost yesterday as it has been many mornings. When snow is flying fireplace heat is inadequate.

While on the subject of cold--our last three days on the boat were *terrible*. Snow lay on the ground three inches thick and our poor trackers refused to budge the first half day of it. Would you like tramping through the snow in bare feet save for thin straw sandals? We bundled up even more than usual, sat on the boat and shivered. It was somewhat like living in a barn through the November cold of a New England winter....

Dorothy has started school. Three other little girls are with her in the beginning class which opened about ten days before our arrival.

Margaret goes to Nursery School, also at the Canadian School. The mothers take hours in turn supervising their play. When Margaret talks to the others in her perfectly good English they answer back in Chinese, though they are all foreign children. (She'll soon be using Chinese, too.)

March 5, 1933
Dear Folks,

I must tell you of a Chinese girl who had real gumption (good New England word). She is the sister of a girl who graduated from our Woman's College in the first class (a girl who herself became a secondary wife). This sister, who has been here in school too, I believe, was teaching at a Methodist Episcopal Mission school in Tzechow. Unknown to her, her parents and family arranged for her marriage to Yang Sen, who had been attracted to her. Now Yang Sen already has so many wives I have quite lost count! The family, however, because he is a big military man with plenty of money, thought they were doing a *fine* thing. Plans progressed merrily. The girl was called home and told what was expected of her. Much to the surprise of the family, the girl refused to fall in with the plans. (Remember the family solidarity that exists in China and that it is far from easy for the individual to stand out against the family.) The girl did everything she could to call a halt. Finally she told her family, "Very well, call the wedding chair if you will, and I will go to the wedding, but when I get there I'll stand up before the guests and all, and tell them that the arrangements for the wedding were made without my knowledge and consent." At last her family saw she was in earnest. They, or the girl, wrote the foreign teachers at Tzechow, a conference was arranged with Yang Sen, and the girl herself met him and explained that she had no desire or intention of entering upon any such relationship with him.

March 26, 1933 *Chengtu, West China*

Dear Home Folks,

...I suppose you feel as I do when I look out on this beautiful and peaceful landscape. How can there be so much trouble in the world? It really seems incredible. As usual one can only half guess at what is seething underneath here in China.

Communism is rampant in some parts of the province. Many of the foreigners of the community were invited the other day to a tea in honor of three China Inland Mission ladies who recently had to flee from their station at Pachow, leaving nearly all their worldly possessions behind. They expect to go back, perhaps before very long, but hardly hope to find much left after the occupancy of the Red Army. We who attended the tea took gifts of various kinds, bed and table linen, towels, and foreign groceries as a surprise shower for them.

April 30, 1933 *Chengtu, West China*

Dear Girls,

...Returning from furlough Mr. Plewman* brought a radio with him, and having obtained a special permit to use it, he is getting all sorts of news from the outside world. I have not seen or heard it myself.

Several weeks ago Shanghai air mail, leaving Shanghai on a Tuesday, arrived in Chungking and was brought to Chengtu by fast auto service arriving here by Friday evening. We were thrilled. Even our part of the world is speeding up....

May 30, 1933

Today is the anniversary of the fatal attack on Dr. Clifford M. Stubbs in 1930. On Sunday there is to be a memorial service in "grateful remembrance for the lives and widespread influence" of Dr. Henry T. Hodgkin and Dr. Stubbs. The influence of these men lives on in West China. I wonder if you can half guess how China needs others like these two.

June 8, 1933 *West China Union University*
Chengtu, West China

Dear Friends at New England Yearly Meeting,

My eyes look out on a different world than in May last year. A man in blue cotton jeans and a big straw hat is manipulating a plow drawn by a ponderous water buffalo in a small field not far away. A soldier in the usual grey cotton uniform runs along a winding path leading to the thatched farm buildings over yonder. What is he seeking? (A very poignant question these days). Women and children in the typical Chinese blue are harvesting wheat in another tiny field, beating the grain against the side of a huge square tub. To the southeast are other

**Canadian Mission member.*

busy groups, for this is spring harvest time and crops must be gathered in at once to prepare the fields for the rice transplanting.

On the city streets, too, how different the life from that in America. See the young laboring man wearing home his new "melon" hat neatly wrapped in paper and cleverly balanced on top of his old one. A crying baby lying on his father's knees in an open doorway is having his head vigorously kneaded by his grandmother (or is it some neighbor woman with a reputation for healing?) while he protests with louder and louder yells. An attractive young matron stands before her door with a roll of straw matting (used on the beds) and beats it with a stick, examining the earth at her feet quite unashamedly and very earnestly at each blow. She is looking for vermin. A frowzy beggar woman squats on the curb, her arms pulled out of her upper garments which she has gathered in front of her. She is busy as can be picking off what the American soldier boys found plenty of in wartime. Here is a square table extending across the sidewalk with a loop of straw ("For Sale" sign) sticking in a crack of its top. Vendors with all sorts of things for sale, from noodles to buttons to flea catchers, jostle us as they go along their way announcing their wares.

A military officer rides past importantly in his ricksha and clangs a bell attached to the floor of his vehicle with a tap of his foot to clear the way. Two of his soldier body-guards, well armed with cartridges and revolvers, run close behind, red in the face from their exertion and the heat of the warm spring day. A string of young men and women, quite evidently students and *very* modern (witness the extreme cut of the gowns and the "frizzed" hair) saunter past, feminine voices rising shrilly. It is all so interesting, this procession of life along the streets of Chengtu. Such variety, such contrasts! What poverty, ignorance, disgusting filth, superstition; what pomp, gay display, and eager acceptance of the new! I never tire of watching and wondering about it all.

The University year is now getting well on toward the close. Besides classroom work we have enjoyed meeting with the Friends student group, who have been holding a series of discussion meetings. The topics have ranged from "How to Choose a Wife"--a matter of special interest and significance in a country where young people are just beginning to make such choices for themselves--to "China's Way Out."

You will remember the warfare which we reported last autumn and winter. After all that awful fighting, with the terrible destruction of life, General Liu Wen Hwei, who for a time was driven from the city, was readmitted upon his agreeing to certain demands. Once within the city, however, he repudiated this agreement and refused to comply with its terms. Once again all were back exactly where they had started! As a consequence, the cudgels are again being raised. Human life, it appears, doesn't figure. It is just as if men could be raised like so much garden stuff and brought forth on demand. Do you know how they work it? Needing men? Bah! Dispatch some armed soldiers to scour the countryside and fetch along coolies, farmers, ricksha pullers, chair carriers, whatnot. Rope them together and march them off. Now put them in uniforms, drill them a bit and send them to the front lines. And keep a gun at their backs, too, lest they run. One wonders how long the common people will endure this sort of thing. Is it strange that Communism finds fertile ground? The Red Army has recently occupied a portion of this province to the northeast, but has now been driven back somewhat. With the ''Reds'' came added terror. People fled for their lives before their advance, leaving their possessions behind. Whole villages and cities were practically deserted except for the very poor. Having nothing to gain or lose, they dared to remain.

June 12, 1933

Dear Ones at Home,

Fortunately we have had beautifully cool weather for most of the spring. However, the last few days have been oppressive with great humidity which is our usual difficulty. These days make us think of Behludin. It doesn't look as if we should get there however. The soldiers have torn out important bridges which we have to cross on the way. Rumors of warfare continue. There has been no fighting in Chengtu itself, but recently there has been a great movement of troops out of the city. Incidentally, the campus is free of them, which is a relief. Perhaps we can get away later in the summer.

Not only have we bus service between Chengtu and Chungking (when the weather is fair and the road passable), but we now have air service! The plane made the first trip in one hour, forty minutes. It carries only air mail. If there should ever be an occasion to reach us quickly you might try air service....

Robert's notes give the military-political situation in full:

June 27, 1933 *Chengtu, West China*

Dear Friends,

Yesterday we graduated twenty-seven students, six of whom were women. Thirteen were graduated in Arts, five in Science, seven in

Medicine and two in Denistry. The Senior High School graduated seventy-seven, and the Junior High about twenty-three. We are fortunate in having no serious interruption to school work, for although fighting between rival generals began a month ago, our work went on. A lot of the students, however, are not able to go home for the summer, as some of the roads are blocked by opposing armies. One of our teachers was to be married May 20th. Invitations were issued and arrangements were made. The bride travelled to Hanchow, thirty miles from here and could get no farther, so the event had to be postponed. (In China it is customary for the bride to go to the home of the bridegroom for the ceremony.) Since the mountain couldn't come to Mohammed, Mohammed has now gone to the mountain, by a circuitous route, and the marriage is to take place this week at Miencheo.

Last winter all of the more powerful generals in the province except General Den were arrayed against Liu Wen Hwei. They fought for nearly three months causing tremendous suffering and loss of life. (We have already written of this.) Had General Den joined in, General Liu would have been eliminated, but he refrained out of friendship. After an inconclusive peace, Liu, who had been driven out of Chengtu, was allowed to return. Then he attacked and seized a lot of territory northwest of Chengtu belonging to Den. Den retreated northwest behind the river and cut the bridges. The two armies have been sitting for over a month on opposite sides of this river, sometimes attacking but neither able to cross the river and gain a decisive victory. For a time it looked as if Liu would win, for the other generals did not come in to help Den, but now it appears they will unite against Liu. Many people fear that if Liu is hard pressed his men will turn Communist, and no one knows what might then happen.

There is a Communist army about seven days northeast of here which has captured several cities. Missionaries fled out of these cities, returned when the Communists were driven back, and some of them are reported to be fleeing again before the second advance of the Communists. People say that almost the entire population of Paoning (seven days' journey from here) has fled toward Tungchwan, Miencheo and Yenting. A few days ago the people started to flee from Tungchwan where our Friends missionaries, Dr. Lucy E. Harris and Miss Tebbutt, are working but General Tien, whose headquarters are there, stopped the exodus and would not let people go.

June 28

Yesterday and the day before General Liu Wen Hwei has been dispatching many troops toward the south and southeast. A telegram from Kiating missionaries says that fighting is expected there soon. The impressing of coolies and school servants to transport the army has been especially severe. This afternoon when some soldiers appeared, over twenty farmers who were raking the rice fields near us scattered in all directions, some of them hiding under the trees in the back of our compound. Last night we could hear big guns at the northwest, beyond the city....

July 4

It looks as if Liu is going to evacuate Chengtu, for he has begun to collect a house tax of two percent on the value of all the houses in the city. People are resisting it, but as soldiers are sent with the tax collectors, it is very difficult to avoid paying. Americans ate supper together at the Woman's College in celebration of the Fourth.

July 8

All day yesterday Liu's men were retreating toward the south....Soldiers have been coming in from Kienchow, over forty miles southeast of here. They have been pressed hard by Liu Hsiang's forces and some of them are in pitiable condition, hungry or sick or utterly exhausted from the double quick march. The able-bodied workmen are hiding as the impressing of carriers for the army is terrible. Liu Wen Hwei's men are getting out as fast as they can. This morning one of Liu Hsiang's fighting planes appeared, flew over the city and then returned to the southeast. A few times we have heard big guns somewhere northwest of Chengtu.

July 9

...It is said that most of Liu Wen Hwei's men are out and that the city gates will be closed for a while for a close inspection of the city by Liu Hsiang's forces. The turnover has been pretty orderly thus far, but not without its alarms. Last night we were awakened shortly before midnight by shots in quick succession, apparently at the bridge near the rear corner of our compound. Was it a band of Communists? We hurriedly dressed so as to be ready for any eventuality. The men came along to our gate--and passed on. This morning we learned that it was only the local militia who were taking charge of the area outside the south gate during the interval between the two regimes.

July 11

Yesterday Mr. Lutley came in from Hsintu, forty *li* north of Chengtu. His family has been here on our campus for about three months since the birth of a new baby, unable to get back home. For two months since the fighting began Mr. Lutley has been unable to get through to Chengtu. He reports that fighting is still going on northwest and west of Chengtu. By retreating from Chengtu and all points east and north, Liu Wen Hwei has greatly shortened his line of defense. The forces of six or seven other generals or sub-generals are pouring into Chengtu from the east, and rivalry among these for the choice "plums" in the city is keen. It is thought, however, that Liu Hsiang, who is expected to arrive today or tomorrow, and Den, who will then come, can straighten things out. The weather remains remarkably cool. All well.

July 12

Impressment has been very bad today. Mr. Small, University construction manager, has lost between twenty and thirty men.

Robert L. Simkin

July 3, 1933 *Chengtu, West China*

Dear Girls,

Our air mail service didn't last long. I think it has stopped because of the military situation. Chungking is in one military area and Chengtu in another. I hope it will be resumed sometime.

Margaret will be four on Wednesday. I wish you could see her! We are inviting her Nursery School friends in for ice cream.

Yes, we even have an ice box now. We can't afford to take ice regularly, but we have it occasionally and when it is hot it does help to have cool drinking water and appetizing cold food. We dare not put the ice into the water or food but use it only for cooling.

August 1, 1933 *Behludin, West China*

Dear Alice and Fannie,

We finally left Chengtu just a week ago today and arrived here last Wednesday. The heat was getting bad and we were glad to get away. I long for the change itself as much as escape from the heat and mosquitoes. Here it is cool and quiet

For the "first time in history" Robert did not attempt the trip on foot or by bicycle. He had a *wha gan*, a light chair without covering, borne by four men. He seems to mind exertion more than he used to, tires more easily. But let me tell you that anyone who attempts to walk or cycle across the roads of the plain in the terrific heat needs to be as strong as an ox. As a matter of fact, we drew two reasonably comfortable days, but the trip at its best is exhausting.

The children rode in a double chair, facing one another, and felt it was a great adventure.

We were able to get away from Chengtu at all because Liu Wen Hwei retreated west and southwest of Chengtu leaving the city and this region northwest of Chengtu out of the fighting area. We saw along the road, a two days' journey, some of the devastating results of this civil warfare. All the first forenoon we were continually meeting wounded soldiers being carried on stretchers. Some were minus limbs and one poor fellow I remember especially because of his suffering. There he was being carried along on the simplest and meanest of stretchers pretty well exposed to the boiling sun. At Lung Chiao we had to scramble across an improvised log bridge. At this same town, the main bridge across the big river had been almost entirely demolished, only the piers remaining, and we had to be ferried across the rather swift stream. It will take months to replace that bridge destroyed so quickly by the military.

Sunday, August 27, 1933 *Behludin, West China*

There has come a break in the weather. Our lovely sunshine and clear views have gone, but we have some rain in our rain barrels and that is a good thing for we were entirely out of water. (We depend upon the rain water for everything but drinking and cooking purposes.)

...We plan to go back to Chengtu a week from tomorrow. School opens the thirteenth of September.

We have invited Arnold and Lois Vaught to live with us while doing language study. You'll remember they are the young American Friends living at the school on the Chungking Hills. They have never been given a proper chance for language study, were thrust right into school work. Arnold has done pretty well but Lois has found it almost too much for her. We could see the difference in her (in contrast to what she was when we first met in England) while there with them in the winter. She seemed simply crushed by the many burdens and problems. She felt she had made little progress in the language. I have felt very concerned about her ever since and have been trying to persuade them to leave Chungking for a period of language study. I think Lois is really considering coming to us for a time. Arnold can't leave until Alfred Davidson returns from England to take up the school work. They are a fine couple.

September 22, 1933 *Chengtu, West China*

Dear Folks at Home,

It is some time since I have written. The last time was at Behludin. We had expected to come down on the fourth, but early on the morning of the second our *amah* was taken very ill--a miscarriage. The poor woman nearly died from loss of blood. However we got a doctor on the case right away. Of course our departure was delayed and we did not leave until the eighth. The patient was taken directly to the hospital on our arrival in Chengtu. She has since been discharged and is now at home recuperating. Fortunately, her little boy (thirteen years old according to Chinese reckoning) had gone to the mountain with her, although he started out without our knowledge or consent. He acted as his mother's nurse. No wonder youngsters in China know so much about life.

The extra days at Behludin, once the *amah* was over the worst, gave me a chance for a day's trip to a paper mill on *Tien Tai* (Heavenly Platform), a mountain just opposite us. There was a jolly party of us and we did enjoy the trip so much. It was beautiful down in the valley, beside the tumbling mountain stream, under the big trees. We passed through one beautiful ravine the sides of which were covered with giant bracken. Another joy was the open slopes covered with the wild anemone, some pure white with yellow centers, some a delicate pink, others rose deepening almost to a magenta.

The paper mill itself was interesting. Bamboo stalks are soaked in great reservoirs (out of doors) in a lime solution. Then the stalks are cut up and pounded. The fibrous material obtained is put into great vats, probably again with lime, and steamed until a pulp results. These vats, too, are out of doors with great fires beneath. The most interesting part of the process was seeing the men dip into the great tubs of the pulp and water solution and lift up a thin film of the pulp on a sort of screen of finely woven silk (the twisted silk threads composing the screen are laquered to make them durable) then drop this film off at one side by a turn of the screen. Each dipping makes a large sheet of thin cream-colored paper. After the piles (composed of many layers of these films) have dried out considerably, a man separates the sheets and spreads them on great drying ovens where they quickly become thoroughly dry. Of course everything is done by manual labor.

Classes began on the thirteenth. This year there is a Russian girl from Peiping (Peking) in the Woman's College. She has come to study dentistry. We also have two students from Korea. Cora Lenox, wife of a young Baptist doctor, is completing her medical course here. We are becoming more and more international.

The generals here are said to be dickering with the Nanking government as to how much military and financial aid Nanking will send them as a condition of their prosecuting the war against the Reds.

You'll be interested in what Robert has written concerning the movement of the Communist army--and other things.

October 27, 1933 *Chengtu, West China*

Dear Friends,

For a long time there has been apprehension caused by the advance of the Communist army in the eastern part of Szechwan. For a time this army threatened Tungchwan. Recently they have taken a city not far east of Suining and have been reported to be threatening Hochow, two days north of Chungking. If Hochow should be captured, Tungliang, where there is a Friends station, would be in a very precarious position as a forced march could reach Tungliang in a few hours. The Communists have also thrust toward Wanhsien which is on the river between Ichang and Chungking. Some fear that Szechwan will be cut off by the occupation of the Yangtze, the primary avenue of communication. It is also feared that the great numbers of soldiers who are ill paid and ill provisioned will turn over to the Communists and take what they want from the people. Superstition also enters the problem for the Communists have spread rumors of their invincibility. We are told that commanders are afraid to order their troops to attack the Communists.

Of course anything might happen but I do not think the situation is as serious--for us in Chengtu--as some seem to consider it. I say "for us in Chengtu." It has already proved serious for a number of the China Inland Mission stations in the northeast of the province from which the missionaries have had to flee. When they returned to one of these stations the missionaries reported thirty-six pits in a grove adjoining the mission in which hundreds of bodies had been buried, and a similar pit in their own back garden containing the bodies of thirty or forty children. It is no wonder that on the approach of the Communists all except the poorest people flee in terror. It seems hardly probable that, with such examples of what their coming means, their opponents will permit them to occupy the central part of the province including such big cities as Chungking and Chengtu.

Having said all this, perhaps I have conveyed the idea that we are living in a greater state of anxiety than is actually the case. The matter really occupies a very small proportion of our thought. It emphasizes, however, the necessity of getting on with our work of spreading a Life and a Spirit which shall do away with this sort of thing.

Robert L. Simkin

November 1, 1933

...Frank Dickinson, or "Dick," is having a tough time with rinderpest in his herd of well-bred cattle. The other day he had lost twelve of his herd of about thirty-five and a lot of other animals were critically ill. This is very discouraging after spending some years to breed better stock from several imported animals. Seven years ago he had a similar epidemic. This time he has ordered vaccine from India, but apparently because of slow communications it has not arrived. Many Chinese round about are losing their animals too. A farmer nearby who has several well-bred animals from Dick's imported stock has thus far escaped, as his cows are not with the others. We get milk from this farmer.

Due to an earthquake which occurred in August our irrigation streams recently have been full of the muddiest water you would care to see, and where the current is less swift several inches of sediment were deposited. In the mountains a whole hillside slid off into the river carrying with it an entire village. The water backed up behind this mass of rock and earth and then finally broke through, bringing death and destruction to many people in the valleys below. A lot of the refugees have come down to Chengtu. A collection has been made for their relief.

Crops on the plain have been good this year and consequently rice is less expensive than usual. For Chinese in this part of the country the Lord's Prayer might well read, "Give us this day our daily rice." They are fortunate to be able to raise at least one other crop during the winter. The fields have recently been plowed and the wheat will soon be planted to be harvested early in May. Since our house is on the edge of the University campus farthest from the city, we see a good deal of the farming operations. In September and October we see great flocks of ducks, sometimes two thousand in a flock. The young ducks are hatched by placing the eggs in warmed rice chaff. At some distance from the mountains the irrigation water gets warmer than near the foot of the hills so the rice harvest is a little earlier there. Several men will start out with a big flock of ducks, driving them through the rice fields just after the harvest where they pick up many fallen kernels and other food. The men carry a tiny bamboo shelter for themselves and a roll of bamboo fencing with which to enclose the flock at night. They follow the progressive harvest until they reach Chengtu or some other city where the ducks are big enough to sell.

Dorothy is in second grade in the Canadian School and Margaret is in the nursery school, so we are all in school. The children are growing fast. All are well.

Robert L. Simkin

December 14, 1933 *Chengtu, West China*

Dear Folks at Home,

The advance of the Communists in the eastern part of the province seems to have been somewhat checked. At least we do not hear so much about it and we therefore breathe more freely.

At last the University has been admitted to full registration under the national government and we are now a part of the recognized system of education. (Originally we were under the Regents of New York State.) About the middle of November we celebrated the event with an "At Home." It is estimated that on one afternoon ten thousand (10,000) persons visited the University including library and museums. Located as we are there is an unusual opportunity to gather an important collection of objects bearing upon the archaeology and ethnology of western China and Tibet. All this has become of increasing interest and value.

Dr. Crawford left this morning with the University ambulance to meet William and Hilda Sewell and their two children in Chungking. Because little Erica is an invalid, travel is a great problem for them.

We now have airplane service thrice a week to Chungking and back, connecting at Chungking with the plane to Hankow. The pilot, Mr. Mitchell, and Mrs. Mitchell are at present living here on the campus at the Manlys. He goes down about eleven and returns around four, carrying mail and five passengers. Quite a difference between this and our forty-four days between Chungking and here. It is quite likely Leonard and Hilda Tomkinson and their little girl may come by plane day after tomorrow. They are joining the Friends Mission and will live at Green Dragon Street in the city. They come from work in Anhwei province and are to be our guests until they settle into their new home.

Robert L. Simkin

January 4, 1934 *Chengtu, Szechwan*

Dear Home Folks,

The Tomkinsons arrived by plane on the nineteenth. Their Shirley, an adopted child, is just ten days older than our Margaret. It was an addition to the Christmas excitement having an extra child about....

Robert writes of guests and lamas:

February 16, 1934 *Chengtu, West China*

Dear Friends,

...Since December 19th we have had guests continuously. First Leonard and Hilda Tomkinson and their daughter, Shirley, then Leonard and Laura Walker of Tungliang came with us from Tungchwan and are still here. They were robbed just south of Suining as they were on their way to Yearly Meeting, losing most of their clothing, fountain pens, glasses, etc. They have therefore had to come here to get fitted for new glasses. Our house consequently has been well used during these two months.

We are glad also to have the prospects of other guests during the coming year. Arnold and Lois Vaught have been appointed to Chengtu for language study and will live with us. We are very happy to have them for they took good care of us when we were marooned in Chungking by the fighting in October 1932. We are expecting that they will be with us also at White Deer Summit (Behludin) during the summer....

The political situation seems rather quiet except that there have recently been rumors that the generals are moving troops and preparing for another war. We hope that we may have a little more respite before the next scrap begins.

A few weeks ago a party of twenty-one lamas from the Tibetan borderland visited Chengtu and spent a day at the University. Some of them knew members of our staff who have stopped at their lamaseries while travelling in the mountains. One of them told how he got into difficulty last summer. In his lamasery the rules were very strict but he himself was more liberal and made arrangements for Mrs. Brown and Mrs. Hibbard to visit his lamasery when they were in the mountains last summer. He felt rather pleased with himself that the rules were becoming more liberal, when lo and behold, a week after they had inspected the lamasery the god showed his displeasure and wrath by a great earthquake which demolished a considerable portion of one of the buildings. Of course it was due to the visit of these two foreign women! His fellow monks took him to task for letting them come and for a time he had a bad time of it. Most of the lamas who come in contact with the missionaries are friendly. Some of them helped to arrange the exhibit of Tibetan articles in the University museum.

Robert L. Simkin

March 24, 1934

Dear Ones at Home,

We had an exceptionally fine Chinese guest the other day, Dr. Chen* who has come here for a little medical study. He expects to go to England for further study in a few months. Dr. Chen is one of the finest of Szechwan Friends.

May 20, 1934

Dear Alice and Fannie,

I believe these past six months have been the quietest we've known for several years as far as outward conditions in the province go. There has been no fighting amongst the warlords and the Communist army, which threatened last autumn to overrun Szechwan, has been driven across the border. Outwardly peace reigns but the present absence of hostilities amongst the provincial overlords and the momentary victory over Communism do not mean the solution or settlement of *real* problems and difficulties. Here, as in other parts of the world, organized government has its own axe to grind and is willfully blind when it comes to seeing and understanding the needs of the people. In this case, those in places of power scarcely profess to care what the populace thinks, let alone suffers. But the people do not forget, and underneath the surface calm, discontent and dissatisfaction spread and fester. The Communist army has been driven away but the ground is fertile and seeds of Communism have already been sown. Communism offers an escape from oppressive, ruinous taxation and it offers relief from deadening poverty.

At one crucial period or another we have heard missionary statesmen say, "*Now* is the time for a great missionary advance if this country, if these people, are ever to know and follow the Christian way of life." Today, once again, some missionary leaders are crying, "These next five years are to be decisive years. Either we must give China Christ, or she will go Red." There is a critical urgency in the situation. Indeed what alone can save China, or the whole world, but the Christ spirit?

I do not think of "save" in any old theological sense of "save from Hell," although I know only too well something of the kind of hell there would be for those who did not fall in line with the Communist program. But I am hoping for a China saved from greed, oppression, fear, disease, poverty, misery, superstition.

**Dr. H.P. Chen of the Friends Hospital, Suining.*

July 22, 1934 *Behludin, West China*

Dear Ones at Home,

Margaret Ruth furnished us with a bit of excitement the other day. Our cottages here are roofed with bark. There is a secondary skirt (or flounce, or ruffle!) around our house at the upper level of the first story. This is not very substantial and the children have been forbidden to climb out on it. However the other day I heard a crash and a cry. I rushed outdoors and found Margaret writhing and crying in pain. I was pretty much frightened and sent for the doctor post haste. I could see the hole in the roof where she had come through but she had managed to get over to the porch a few feet away. I couldn't see that anything was broken but was glad to have Dr. Hayward come and look her over. He found no broken bones and no internal injuries. She went white as a sheet, every bit of color left her cheeks and lips but of course that was due to the shock. The fall was some fifteen feet. She seems to be pretty nearly alright now except for a slight limp and it still hurts her to squat or stoop. I am thankful it has turned out so well. I suppose it is to be reckoned as a minor incident of family life.

We expect Robert, who has been in Suining for a summer institute, day after tomorrow. I hope the weather clears so that he has no trouble getting through. Sometimes after heavy rains the bridges (board planks) are out and it is difficult and dangerous fording the streams; then of course it is far more difficult getting up the mountain over slippery, muddy paths. It will all mean delay if nothing worse.

Here in front of the house a beautiful lily has nine lovely blooms already open or nearly ready to burst. It is not unlike our Easter lilies, only these here are reddish on the outside, but pure white within. These lilies grow wild in the mountains. Last year I set out bulbs of a yellow "spider" lily. I hope these will come up later to furnish us with blooms. The blossoms come up first and the foliage afterward if I remember correctly. These are very pretty lilies, too, but have no fragrance. Some are white, some red, some rose.

July 27, 1934

Robert arrived safely today.

August 18, 1934 *Behludin, West China*

Dear Friends at Home,

We have had a very great deal of rain this season while the U.S.A., we hear, has been suffering from drought. For a time we were pretty well cut off from the rest of the world. Heavy and continual rains, such as have not occurred in my experience in Szechwan and "for a hundred years" say some of the natives, flooded the mountain streams and the rivers in the valleys cutting off all communication. From our cottage we could see how the rivers below us were tearing out new channels, flooding islands and flats and rice fields, washing out the road over which we had come on our way to the mountain, and sweeping away bridges. For five days we had no mail. Finally the courier postman reached us by fording many streams and coming by a circuitous way.

Many Chinese have had their homes swept away and many have lost their lives. It happened that during the days of these torrential rains I was reading Pearl Buck's *The First Wife*, a collection of stories of Chinese life excellently written. I found the section entitled "The Flood" very apropos! Of course Pearl Buck is writing of conditions in central China during the great 1931 flood, but her word pictures made exceedingly vivid what I could imagine was happening in the valleys below us.

Last Monday, Leonard Tomkinson and a Chinese student also summering on the mountain went down to a nearby market town to get firsthand information of conditions. They found in one village that scores of people had had fields either completely washed away or covered over hopelessly with rock and sand. Leonard proposes that our summer community raise a small loan to be used as a rehabilitation fund to aid the folk in neighboring villages. This scheme, a plan for helping people to help themselves, is one that appeals to me. In these days when missions are on the grill of criticism at home, we on the field, too, are thinking very carefully of policies and methods.

I do think this a glorious time in which to be living in the world as a Friend and an adventurer along the Way. There are so many muddles, so many areas in which things have gone wrong, or in which old foundations seem to be tottering (and we're not so sure but what they ought to be)--but it is great to have a part in the experiment of proving to this weary, hardboiled world that love *will* work. I have thought many times what one of my Earlham friends said--"Jesus associated with people because he really loved them and truly enjoyed their company--sinners and all--not because he was primarily and deliberately trying to 'save' them." The help He gave to men and women came as a concomitant of His love for them. So I think we ought to be chiefly concerned with expressing our love and sympathy to all men, of whatever condition or need, and to think less of results. Indeed it is only by this uncalculating giving of oneself in friendship that worthwhile results do come.

August 27, 1934

Since beginning this letter I have been off on a trip to Go Hsien San, a picturesque mountain with many interesting caves. We took along our camp beds and mosquito nets and slept in a temple. On the evening of the full moon we went down the long flight of temple steps to the entrance of the old refuge area where we sat on the crumbling wall under two ancient cedar trees and looked out over the lovely plain below us flooded with moonlight. That same night, after we had crawled into bed, the priests began beating the drum and clanging the bell as they chanted their scriptures.

I was persuaded at the eleventh hour to go on the Cave Mountain (*Go Hsien San*) trip. I guess I was needed as a chaperone for a young nurse. I certainly am glad I went. It is such a picturesque place--a mountain of many wooded pinnacles and interesting caves. I just left all my family responsibilities behind and had a good time. We were gone three days.

Robert's letter gives information concerning the crisis we are facing.

September 24, 1934 *Chengtu, West China*

Dear Friends,

The Friends who are at West China Union University have recently been confronted with a very serious situation which arises from the requirement of the Chinese government that educational institutions in China shall teach military drill.

Of course none of those in charge of the University wish to have military drill but the University is now registered under the national government and it is difficult to disobey orders. With one exception the University has managed to stave off the requirement. For a few weeks in the excitement following the invasion of China by Japan a military instructor came from the city for a few lectures and a little drilling. Due to our furlough Margaret Simkin and I were not in China at that time, and as the matter was discontinued after a few weeks, we did not realize until this month that military training had actually been carried out. Irene Hutchinson, who was the only representative of the Friends Service Council here at the time, protested against it.

Recently the government has been pressing the requirement, and we learned that the University Cabinet had practically decided to carry out its order and introduce military training. This decision came as a great surprise to us for we felt that such an important matter should be considered by the whole faculty. If the entire faculty should consider that there was absolutely no way but to submit to the government requirement, we felt it would then be time for us as Friends to take appropriate action. But the Cabinet apparently felt that if military training was quietly introduced without any fuss the objection would soon peter out. They also tried to lessen the issue by stating that the training would not be compulsory for those who might have conscientious objections.

But this does not really meet our objection. This is a Christian institution and for it to provide military training, whether compulsory or not compulsory, constitutes a denial of our fundamental purpose. The six Friends who are directly members of the staff therefore sent the enclosed letter of protest. The other representatives of Friends approve of this action but did not sign the protest because they are not themselves members of the staff.

The result is still hanging in the balance. Our action apparently had the effect of staying proceedings for a time. Then it was reported that political conditions, Communist menace, etc. are so critical that the University considered further delay practically impossible, yet several days have since passed without the step actually being taken.

We feel much sympathy with the administrative officers of the University for if the government continues to insist that its orders be carried into effect and the University stands out against these orders, the government has the power to close the institution. The University may feel that to acquiesce is the lesser of two evils. In case the University does introduce military training, Margaret Simkin and I feel that we shall have to withdraw from official connection with the University and probably discontinue teaching as well. In the case of Margaret Simkin this would mean discontinuing her service in the University Library. Whether or not the other Friends members of the staff will take the same action we do not know.

For us this is not an easy decision for we realize that if military training is introduced and maintained this may mean severing *for life* our official connection with the University. It is not easy to pull up roots which for a quarter of a century have been striking down into the soil. We are still hoping that it may not be necessary but if worst comes to the worst there seems to be no way but to act in accordance with our own consciences.

Actually the situation may not affect our work so seriously as the above might indicate. Three-fourths of my teaching hours are at present in the Union Middle School. Its principal, S.C. Yang, is a Friend and thus far he has kept military drill out of the Middle School, ignoring the orders of the government. So long as he is successful in keeping military training out of his school I can continue to teach in it. I am also principal of the Friends Middle School Dormitory, which work can still go on. Even though we may not teach in the University there will still be plenty to do unofficially among the University students who now number more than three hundred and fifty. In fact it is possible that our influence might be quite as great as formerly if for conscientious reasons we withdraw.

Fortunately among the Friends missionaries there is a very great unanimity of viewpoint, and there are a number among those who are not Friends who share more or less fully our views.

There is rather alarming news of rapid advances of the Communists in the eastern part of the province. Most of the Church Missionary Society workers in Paoning have been evacuated but we have not heard that the Communists have actually occupied that city. The government authorities in Chengtu are exercising unusual care, closing the gates of the city at nightfall and searching for Communists. Appeals have also been sent to the Central Government for aid.

Robert L. Simkin

The Union University, Chengtu
12th September 1934

The President and General Faculty,
West China Union University

Dear Friends:

We learn with grave concern that the University agrees to introduce military training, and we feel that there must be many who share our apprehension.

Although we recognise the difficulties in which the administrative officers are placed as they face the complex situation, we, as members and representatives of the Society of Friends, cannot acquiesce in the course contemplated. Mindful both of the historic testimony of Friends and of our own responsibility as Christians, we protest against the admission by a Christian institution, even under compulsion, of military training as an integral part of its program. We are opposed to military training, not only in China, but also in our own countries, for we regard the spirit of suspicion, hatred and war, of which such training is an expression, as contrary to the spirit of Christ, and as one of the greatest enemies of mankind.

This is a matter on which we must not compromise. If military training is introduced and maintained, some of us, much as we should regret the step, may have to withdraw from the staff. Also, we believe that the Friends Service Council may find itself unable to continue official participation in the University.

Yours Sincerely,
(Signed) Wm. G. Sewell
Hilda G. Sewell
Robert L. Simkin
Margaret T. Simkin
S.D.Du
Jane Balderston Dye

October 14, 1934 *Chengtu, West China*

Dear Ones at Home,

....Did I write that we are expecting James Thorp, and perhaps Eleanor, early next month? He is with the National Geological Soil Survey. I knew them both at Earlham. She is Juanita Beede's sister.

Dr. Hawks-Pott, president (perhaps now honorary president) of St. John's University, Shanghai, was to have flown here this weekend but failed to make it, perhaps because of bad weather....

So far, military drill has been held off here at the University. I don't know how much longer we can expect it to be put off, but we're hoping for the best.

October 28, 1934 *Chengtu, West China*

Dear Home Folks,

It is already nearly nine o'clock, but I will try to put down something of our happenings.

The thing which looms biggest at the moment is the Sherwood Eddy meetings. He arrived by airplane on Friday (coming from Hankow that day) for a week's meetings with students in Chengtu. He is here under the auspices of the Y.M.C.A. and is addressing students in the schools throughout the city. Tonight's was the first meeting I attended. Hart College gym was packed, with students standing. There were probably nine hundred people. He gave a powerful address interpreted by Lincoln Dsang. He speaks simply but the personality of the man makes a deep impression.

This weekend we have had Betty and Peggy Wood here. You will remember that we stopped with the Woods at Suifu on our way up river. This year they have put their two girls in boarding school here at Canadian School. It is hard for parents and children to be separated....

The Davidsons of Suining, where Robert went for a summer institute, are here for a holiday and medical and dental attention. We therefore have quite a large (foreign) Friends group on the campus--eleven adults. We have weekly meetings together each Monday. Tomorrow they will all come here for tea. We have mission (American Friends are included) matters and problems to talk over. In the evening there will be a meeting for worship at the Friends College with the students and other Chinese Friends. Some weeks there is a study group in addition. It means much to us to have this fellowship. I used to feel lonely in other days when there was only one other Friends family here or at the most two, and other missions were having "family" gatherings.

December 10, 1934 *Chengtu, West China*

Dear Home Folks,

We are still working on the problem of military training in the University and our relation to it. Unfortunately, from our point of view, the University authorities are afraid to disregard government regulations. Then in order to satisfy us they have had to practice deceit! So it is a bad business altogether. What it amounts to at present is this--all official announcements to students and the world at large use the term "military drill," but English minutes and correspondence that goes to the home constituency uses the term "physical drill" to apply to the specific training that is being given. Let me say it in another way: what is actually being given so far is the physical training part of military drill (which Friends do not object to as such), but instead of calling it "physical drill" the University advertises it to the students (and reports it to the government) as "*military drill.*" Does it sound harmless? Does it seem as if Friends ought to let up a little and quit this everlasting stickling over small points (for so our persistent following up of the matter must seem to some)? At first it may appear so. However, we have thought about the whole problem almost weekly together and we are pretty well united in our judgments. We cannot approve this misrepresentation of facts in the first place. But more than that, we see danger ahead. China is likely to get more militaristic, not less. If we as Friends countenance the name, because the thing in fact is harmless, we are likely soon to find ourselves in a position of having to accept the reality along with the name.

And yet we have great sympathy for those upon whom the responsibility of the administration of the University rests so heavily. It is not easy for President Lincoln Dsang, whose very life has been threatened at times. To him, I imagine, it seems well nigh impossible to stand out against the government, not only because it would perhaps mean that the government would close the institution (though personally I feel if we presented the case to the Nanking government as a united body, that is, our conviction that militarism is incompatible with a Christian institution, that the University might be exempted) but more than that, such a stand would lay him open to criticism and attack by his enemies.

And what about the students, for now and then we find one who is giving the whole question serious thought? What is an American to say, an American whose country is perfectly secure, to a Chinese whose land is threatened by Japan without and Communism within? He may very well say, "And what do you know of the need of militarism? *Your* country isn't threatened. We've *got* to make a stand against Japan, or she will swallow us up. We've *got* to arm."....

The Communist Scare 1935

January 8, 1935 — *Chengtu, West China*

Dear Fannie,

Robert is giving examinations this afternoon....

In about ten days now the men will be starting for Yearly Meeting. It is at Tungliang this year at the other end of the province so they will be gone nearly three weeks I expect. They plan to travel by car. It is a pity that Yearly Meeting always comes at the coldest time of the year.

The Chinese are much worried about the Communist advance. But the amazing thing about this country is that you may be on the edge of an active volcano and still you keep going on about your little affairs as if all were well with the world. Here is Robert expecting to start off for Tungliang, so you may conclude we are not excessively upset about the situation.

I was interested to know that you were writing a paper on Kagawa. I want to enclose a picture of Kagawa and Cheng Ching Yi with their arms about each other, these two fine representatives of enemy countries. I have been a great admirer of Kagawa for a long time. Cheng was at Union studying the year I was there.

Robert's letter of January 14, 1935:

The Communists are reported to be gaining ground south of Chungking, pressing northward in an attempt to close the Yangtze and effect a junction with the large body of Communists east of us.* Everybody says that if they occupy central Szechwan it could be utterly impossible for missionaries to carry on their activities in the occupied area. Communists here seem to be very different from Communists in

**Movement of Communists later known as the Long March.*

other countries. They seem to know no method save that of death and destruction. In the early wave of advance in eastern Szechwan only the upper and middle class Chinese evacuated before them, but the lower class people who stayed suffered so terribly that in the second advance, which occurred this autumn, even the beggars fled. Some cities were almost completely evacuated.

The coming of the Communists to Chengtu, even if we should be able to escape with our lives, would make our financial problems serious. However we don't need to live more than one day at a time. For several months, until yesterday, we have had sort of a lull because the Communist army is still more than one hundred and fifty miles away and the local authorities have been very watchful to prevent a local outbreak. Yesterday the news was more unfavorable so the Standing Committee decided to postpone the holding of Yearly Meeting.

In the matter of military training the situation has changed materially. For a long time there remained a hope that military drill might be prevented but now it has been practically adopted. The fear of disobeying the government orders, and thus incurring the threatened penalties, proved too strong for some of our leaders.

To be sure, the University is seeking exemption. H.T. Silcock was asked by cable to approach Quo Tai Chi, Chinese Minister in London, to intercede with the Minister of Education in Nanking on our behalf. It is too early to say whether this and other efforts will be successful.

In the meantime the University opened classes which are sometimes referred to as "physical drill" and "citizenship" but are in part military in character. These have been announced as part of the military training required by the government. Therefore on December 18th and 19th William G. Sewell, Jane B. Dye, Margaret T. Simkin and I resigned our official positions in the administration of the University. When these resignations were presented to the General Faculty on January 9th the following was passed:

> "*Resolved*, That we deeply regret the resignations of the members of the Friends from these positions, but that we accept them in the hope that it will soon be possible for Friends to resume their former positions."

For the present we are going on with our teaching. We have been able to continue our relationship of good will and I think practically all of our colleagues now appreciate the fact that the stand we have taken is the only one consistent for Friends. What our ultimate relationship to the University will be in case exemption cannot be secured is a question for the future. Even should we feel it necessary eventually to resign from the Faculty, I should hope it might be possible for us to live on here and continue our service in an unofficial way. Should the University fully accept military training and all that this would imply it would seem all the more necessary that there should be people here to disseminate Friendly ideals. A few of the students have absented themselves from the military classes and have stated that rather than conform they would sooner forego the seal of the government on their diplomas.

R.L.S.

February 3, 1935 *Chengtu, West China*

Dear Girls,

After our last letters and "scare" news items in American papers about the Reds in Szechwan, I know you will be relieved to hear that we are feeling much more comfortable and secure. We never saw danger immediately ahead but it was near enough to make us consider a bit what course we might take in case the necessity of flight arose.

Our situation now, as compared to 1927, is better in at least two respects. We have radio connections with the outside world. We have airplane service which might be used in case of necessity, although I can hardly conceive of our entire foreign community being evacuated by air. However we are not thinking of evacuating at present. The Reds are being well checked. Should we have to leave it is not now, as it was in 1927, a question of running away from our Chinese Christian friends, for all of them who can get away will do so.

Here in Chengtu the authorities are very cautious, are trying to comb out all Communists. Just as an illustration--one of the girls in the Woman's College, a girl sponsored by Friends (each girl who enters must have some Mission behind her although she herself may have no connection with any church) has been put in jail as a suspect. She is a freshman but has proved herself a very decent sort and we cannot believe she even has Red tendencies. Probably some of her family are Red sympathizers so they have grabbed her too. Poor child! It certainly is tough. I hope to go to see her. She is behind bars but I am told one is allowed to converse in the presence of a guard.

The postponed Yearly Meeting is to come this week. Robert expects to leave on Wednesday and will be gone nearly three weeks.

Tomorrow is Chinese New Year. I hope it is as beautiful a day as we have had today--bright, warm, sunny. On the street today, I saw men carrying racks with "kitchen gods" on them for sale, others carrying racks with the pretty red and gilt fancily cut paper which the Chinese put up over their doors in sets of three--I don't know their significance. Other people had stands out in the street selling hats, the melon hats with knotted button on top--red for happiness, white for mourners.

Everywhere was hustle and bustle like it is on the day before Christmas at home.

March 10, 1935 *West China Union University*
Chengtu, West China

Dear Carl and Hazel,

We are having beautiful spring weather. Cherry blossoms are already gone. Now the peach and plum trees are in full bloom. The lovely magnolia are at their height. Roses are growing by leaps and bounds and will soon offer a profusion of color and fragrance. I love spring anywhere but spring in China is a special miracle. We go so suddenly and completely from winter to warmth and teeming life.

These days the city streets are blossoming out too...with flags. General Chiang Kai-shek is actually in Szechwan and is expected in Chengtu within a few days. He has come to see that the province is put in order, to drive out the Communists, and personally to inspect affairs. So the city "fathers" have ordered every little shop to fly a flag and today police were seeing that all debris was swept up and the streets made spick and span. We hope that Mrs. Chiang Kai-shek is coming along also and that we shall have a chance to entertain her here at the University. Somebody has suggested a University Women's "Tea."

Dr. Lucius Porter of Yenching University is here now (in the interests of the Harvard-Yenching Committee I imagine) and is giving a course of lectures to the Faculty members and friends on Chinese philosophy. I have heard two of these lectures and have enjoyed them in spite of my limited knowledge of the subject. I first saw Dr. Porter at Columbia in 1923, when he was in the United States on sabbatical leave and was lecturing at Columbia on Chinese culture. The other evening Robert and I were at a dinner party where he was a guest of honor and had the pleasure of meeting him personally....

Robert and the others report a good Yearly Meeting. The Chinese took a decided stand on several issues. For one thing, with regard to military training at the University, they have notified the University authorities that if the military drill is still being carried on in July this year they are requesting the Friends Service Council (England) to give a year's notice (necessary according to the constitution) and then to withdraw.

Arising out of our problem (the problem of our relationship to an institution which has military drill) has been the reorganization of a Chengtu Fellowship of Reconciliation. We have had several interesting meetings. There are a good many people, we find, who are not Friends and are interested in peace and opposed to militarism. In face of the recent tendency of the nations of the West to increase armaments we have been glad we could report the American student protests against militarism. We are thankful that in China, too, there are here and there youthful spirits which are afire with the vision of a Better Way. Wallace Wang, Secretary of the Christian Student Movement, has come back from Peiping a convinced pacifist (due perhaps largely to the influence of Lucy Burtt, an English Friend teaching in Yenching University). Wallace is also Chinese secretary of our local F.O.R. and altogether is doing a fine piece of work leading the students to think in world terms.

Recently there was an unfortunate incident involving a fine Korean boy, a dental student in the University. While out walking with two or three companions, a Chinese boy challenged the Korean to throw a stone as high as the flagpole. Unwisely he accepted the challenge and flung a stone toward the Chinese flag. The jingoistic students were quick to label the Korean youth a Japanese spy and excited many of their schoolmates to oppose him and prevent his remaining in the institution. But the one thing I am getting at is this--there were, on the other hand, a number of students, both men and women, who refused to follow the crowd and who remained firm in their defense of the Korean even when it meant being more or less ostracized and their being called traitors to their country. It takes more than a little courage in China to oppose the crowd.

From the few things that I have already mentioned you can see that there is a need and often a welcome in the midst of this rising tide of nationalism for the Friendly way of life.

April 5, 1935

Dear Folks at Home,

We are again having a Communist scare. After General Chiang Kai-Shek got to Szechwan with reinforcements for his national soldiers, people breathed easier and the situation quieted down. In fact we have been without any special apprehension for some weeks. In the past few days, however, the Reds have made fresh advances, have crossed the Kialing River and are approaching Mienchow (a Church Missionary Society station where Arnold and Lois Vaught and Dr. Lucy Harris are. The Maxwells are in Chengtu now, arriving today from Mienchow. The say practically all of Mienchow (30,000 to 40,000 people) have left--fled.

We are greatly concerned about the Vaughts and Dr. Harris at Tungchwan. This morning a telegram came from them. It was dated 3 p.m. yesterday and said, "Excitement intense. Outlook serious." So yesterday they had not yet evacuated, yet rumors come in today that Tungchwan has fallen! Probably it is a false rumor but we are anxious. Doubtless it is very difficult for them to get accurate news but people there have been terror-stricken and have been fleeing for several days. Some Tungchwan refugees have already reached Chengtu. On the first, Arnold wrote that no boat, *whagan* or ricksha could be procured and that if they had to evacuate it would be of necessity on foot. And robbers on the road are very, very bad. Our Friends students here at the University who come from Tungchwan are very anxious about their families. They have no word in most cases and naturally wonder what is happening.

Our situation here in Chengtu is not precarious yet. By the time this reaches you the worst will have happened and if you hear nothing further you need not worry. The outlook is none too good, however.

April 16, 1935 *Chengtu, Szechwan*

Dear Folks at Home,

Sunday, the fourteenth, was such a beautiful day. I wandered about the garden thoroughly enjoying the sunshine and beauty of all the fresh growing things. It seemed the kind of a day so perfect and lovely that nothing could mar its peace and charm. What an unsuspecting mortal I was!

...At about 2:40, Bill Sewell came in to tell us that the Reds had taken Mienchow and that plans were being made to evacuate all foreigners from Chengtu. I felt for a moment as if the sky had fallen!

However we went on to the Canadian School for a scheduled concert and gave ourselves to an hour of beautiful worship in song, the music having been written by Mrs. Brace and practically all the hymns (words) by other West China friends. I thought as I sat there in the well-packed room, where practically all the foreign community had gathered, "Well, if this is to be the end, what a *glorious* end."

By this time, the report that Mienchow had falled was contradicted. However people were still very anxious and they met after the concert to discuss the situation and make plans. I came home with the children and left Robert to deal with that.

The Tomkinsons, who live at Chin Lung Kai, remained at our house overnight and that evening we four adults went over to the Sewells to discuss what *Friends* should do. The Tomkinsons have been exceedingly nervous over the Red menace right along--quite justifiably so and they felt that we ought to fall in with the general plans and make ready to evacuate at once. We all believed that Hilda Sewell, who is expecting a baby in June, ought to have early consideration and should be among the first to go. As for our own family, Robert and I could not see that we ought to hurry away, although we agreed that it would not be wise nor right to remain on in case of actual Red advance close to Chengtu. We should certainly choose to be well out of the way before the Communists actually arrived in this vicinity. Robert suggested that if worst came to worst we could move out in ricksha and on bicycle, one child riding with me in the ricksha (if we could get somebody to pull it!) and Robert taking the other child with him on the wheel.

I think we all felt pretty sober and tense that night but I for one slept well, except that I was awakened by dogs barking and then got to thinking of what I would choose to take with us if we could gather up a few things to have on the road. I remembered for one thing that I had no shoes suitable for tramping miles over Chinese roads and thought to myself I will select the most likely pair in the morning and get the cook to take them right out on the street for repair.

I ought to say that all that Sunday a great state of panic existed among the Chinese in the city, or so we were told....During the late afternoon a number of students came in for advice and reassurance. Some talked of plans to move the University to Tzechow! By Wednesday noon a good number of Chinese families of University teachers, and between ten and twenty foreign women and children, including Hilda Sewell and Erica, had evacuated Chengtu....And then yesterday, Thursday, the news was worse than ever. The 28th army had fought a fierce battle and been repulsed and there were all sorts of rumors about the Reds holding Chungpa, etc. Orders came from the official in the city for all women and children to leave (this was not the first but the order was re-emphasized). The Canadians are certainly working in that direction. For one thing their mission is so large that they cannot afford to wait until a situation becomes acute before starting things moving.

By evening today (April 19) about eighty foreigners, including children, had evacuated Chengtu. There are still a good many of us left but other parties are going within the next few days. Dr. Janet Kilborn and children, the Walmsleys and the Willmotts are expecting to leave on Monday or Tuesday, I think. I am not certain whether any of the men are going.

Is the situation as serious as some are inclined to feel? I am sure I do not know but, at least in my calmer moments,I find it hard to believe that the Reds will succeed in taking Chengtu. How can anyone say, as some do, that their objective is this capital?...

We are doing some packing. I have two steamer trunks partly filled with blankets and winter clothing ready to move to the city if it seems wise to send a few things in to Chin Lung Kai. The city officials at first would promise no protection to the University but now I am told they guarantee protection as long as the Reds keep away! The plan in general is for about twenty men to stay on the campus as long as possible to hold the property. Robert feels that his place is here for the present and I am not inclined to leave him.

I have been several days at this letter. It is now Saturday, April 20th. The big plane which was expected today to take another large party to Chungking has not arrived for some reason. However we are recovering from Thursday's scare, ascending another peak of confidence to be followed by still another slump I suppose. Still the news is decidedly better today.

It is hard to be a consistent Quaker when one lies in the possible path of an oncoming Communist army which has won the reputation of being utterly heartless in its program of destruction and annihilation. I can't help but be glad when we hear they have been repulsed or defeated. It seems as if Christianity the world over has failed in not having given them an inkling that we are working for some of the ends they are pressing toward (though they appear to be pursuing them crazily in China). There persists in the back of my mind a bit of guilt. We give them an excuse for associating us with imperialism and self-seeking capitalism simply by maintaining our own standards of living in this land where millions live in desperate poverty.

Here is Robert's letter.

April 14, 1935

Dear Friends,

The situation is very different from that of 1927. Then it was the Chinese--or a portion of them--who were agitating against the foreigners; now nearly all of the middle and upper class Chinese are quaking in their shoes. To be sure, the Communists are not very near

Chengtu as yet, still nearly a hundred miles away, yet the terror which they inspire is very potent. They are also said to be very mobile and if they really break through it is thought that we should be in real danger. The authorities are preparing for a three-month siege of the city and say that if foreigners do not evacuate they should at least move into the city which is surrounded by a wall about twenty feet high. It is a question whether some of the government soldiers, if hard pressed, might not turn over and join the Communists in which case one could never say what might eventuate.

Should foreigners move into the city because the authorities can probably not protect the University which is outside the city wall? Some plan to send some of their goods in so that they may not only have things needed in case they themselves move in but that, if houses outside are looted, they may at least have a chance of saving a part of their possessions. We have not yet fully settled the question, but we are inclined to decide not to move in.

R.L.S.

May 9, 1935 *Chengtu, Szechwan*

Dear Folks at Home,

...We are still here in Chengtu and moving along peacefully. I don't know that the political situation has improved except that the 28th and 29th armies, which were making a stand against the Reds, have been reinforced by the 21st army and Nationalist troops. This has greatly changed the general morale; the local officials have ceased to urge foreigners to leave so here we still are. And thankful enough you may be sure. Most people who evacuated are remaining away as the situation does not warrant their return. But we who are here are going on happily and comfortably. The nervous tension is gone at least for the time being. Whether we shall be able to get away for the summer is a question, but I am still hoping.

...It has been interesting to see the airplanes over our heads these last few weeks. One day there were eight Nationalist planes flying in formation. Yesterday a bi-plane went through great maneuvers directly over the campus, performing apparently for our benefit.

The girl who was taken as a Red suspect was released from jail soon after Jane Dye and I went to see her. Our visit of course had no connection. We believe the girl herself is innocent. Probably she has family connections who are involved.

June 1, 1935 *Chengtu, Szechwan*

Dear Girls,

...The Canadian Mission executive is meeting this evening to try to decide whether or not to bring back their people who evacuated. We are thankful we didn't go. I think it will be a couple of years (based on word of people from Nationalist government who are studying the situation) before the province is clear of Reds. We are quite safe for the present anyhow.

June 19, 1935

Dear Ones at Home,

Generalissimo and Madame Chiang have arrived in Chengtu and plan to stay for some time, I am told. (There is reference to Chengtu becoming China's capital! A jest?) The Chiangs' coming is helping to restore confidence. The Red advance in Szechwan has given the Nationalist government the excuse to dispatch troops to this province and it is no secret that General Chiang hopes to join Szechwan into closer union with the national government. A few months ago in Chungking there was the formal ceremony of taking over the provincial government by representatives from Nanking. If Chiang Kai-shek by his visit can make the union a *reality* it will be all to the good.

Last Wednesday the Generalissimo and Madame Chiang invited the entire mssionary (Protestant) community to their place in the city. The reception was held out of doors. Mrs. Mullett* who knew Madame Chiang in Shanghai--teaching English to her sister's children--introduced each of us in turn to the Madame, and Mr. Brace, Y.M.C.A. secretary, introduced us to the Generalissimo. Then we were seated at long rows of tables arranged in a U shape.

There tea was served us and both Generalissimo and Madame Chiang spoke, the former in Chinese, the latter in English with a well modulated voice. She is a charming person. I was quite captivated by her graces. They both thanked the missionaries for what they are doing. Everybody, I believe, was well impressed and many quite touched by their sincerity. There was a very real strength in both their faces. They are real persons, I think. If we cannot agree with their entire program, I feel we should support them to the limit of our consciences because of what they are and for what they are trying to do. They are the hope of China at the moment. They are humble, too.

**Canadian Mission.*

We were greatly impressed by the naturalness and sincerity with which they referred to the Church and Jesus--"our Church," they said. The Madame spoke of how Jesus had to stand alone, deserted by all and betrayed by one of his own close followers. Think of actually hearing Chinese political leaders referring to Christ as their model and identifying themselves so intimately with the Church! It was certainly a new experience. Madame Chiang was quite clear in stating that they could not hope to build a new China unless they began at the very bottom and changed individual character. She referred to the four hundred and seventy wars (470!) of Szechwan in the last twenty years--all due to selfishness. (I don't know where she got these figures but there certainly have been plenty of wars.)

We are in the midst of our busy time--exams, commencement, etc.

Dr. Luther R. Weigle, dean of the Yale Divinity School, and Dr. Miao from Shanghai arrived today. Tomorrow they open a conference on the theological training of leaders. This is followed in five days by a religious education conference in which I am particularly interested. Then we have a Sunday School Institute. I am helping get ready a Peace Education exhibition for the latter.

This noon we had a stag dinner at our house for Mr. Lo, the head man at Chin Kang Lin near Behludin. We had heard rumors of our bungalows being occupied by soldiers, Reds or otherwise. He says this is not true and that the area is now clear of bandits. If, after a few weeks the Reds are driven still further back, we may be able to get to the mountains for a little time after all.

June 30, 1935 *Chengtu, Szechwan*

Dear Sisters,

Commencement for 1935 is over as far as the University is concerned. It was an especially interesting Commencement. Generalissimo and Madame Chiang were both present and spoke, and lent an added blaze of glory. But more gratifying than that was the ovation given by students and teachers to Mr. Chu, a Miao tribesman, when he received his diploma and degree. Mr. Chu is a man of sterling character and has won the respect of all. I do not remember the students ever bursting out in more spontaneous or genuine applause than they did for Mr. Chu. It fills one with hope to think they so appreciate true worth and character. The ovation was all the more remarkable because the Szechwanese have the reputation of being extremely provincial (due doubtless to their isolation which is now being broken down by airplane and automobile) and unwilling generally to accept anybody from outside. Yet they received this Miao student--there was no doubt of that--and he a member of a rather despised tribe on the border.

Forty-odd were graduated from the University this June. Eight were Friends students, and of these eight, six are doctors! Two of these doctors are a charming couple, son and daughter-in-law of Yang Sao Chuen (S.C. Yang) who is clerk of our Yearly Meeting. Anna Lu Yang started in the Woman's College in its early days and has kept steadily at it, sometimes in face of great discouragement.

...I think this is the first time that the province has been visited by a Chinese of such national and international prominence as the Chiangs. Ostensibly General Chiang came to supervise in person the campaign against the Communists, but his visit has a far greater significance. He is quietly consolidating the power of the federal government. We hope this means the end of irresponsible government by local feudal warlords. It is very interesting to see happening before our very eyes what took place in Europe centuries ago when feudalism gave way before the more centralized power of the emerging nations.

Chengtu has become important as the headquarters of the most important leader in China. Our city has become--perhaps temporarily--a Mecca for many important personages who fly in a few hours from Hankow or East China on important errands of state.

We are distressed by Japan's "bullying" aggression in the North and have great sympathy for Generalissimo and Madame Chiang in the burden they are carrying. It is a trying time for them. We suspect they are partly in Chengtu to escape the necessity of personal commitment to Japanese demands. Two Japanese gunboats have come up the river to Chungking and I've been told that a certain Japanese representative aboard requested an interview. General Chiang replied that he would send his plane to Chungking to bring said representative to Chengtu where he could be interviewed. The Japanese did not accept!

It looks as if Japan means to take over all of North China just as she did Manchuria (now called Manchukuo).

The Communists northeast of us who in April were threatening Chengtu have worked westward into the mountains and have joined the other group from the southwestern part of Szechwan which advanced northward. Some of them are so near White Deer Summit (Behludin) where we hoped to spend the summer that it is considered unsafe to go. Our good friends, the Manlys, therefore kindly offered to share with us their bungalow at Mt. Omei. We have gratefully accepted the offer.

July 27, 1935 *Mt. Omei Resort*

Dear Folks,

We have been here just a week today and are now well settled into this bungalow which we are sharing with the Manlys.

...Generalissimo and Madame Chiang have come to the mountain also. The general is establishing a military school lower down for the training of officers. The Madame is not well. I do not wonder when I think of the terrific burden these two are carrying. They are striving to unify China and we are in full sympathy with them except for their militaristic program. They are the best leaders in sight--very different from the local warlords to whom we have become accustomed. If only Japan would leave China alone we would feel a new day was dawning.

The Generalissimo has gone to the "Golden Summit" in company with his Australian adviser and Dr. Wallace Crawford* and his son, Donald.

Grace Manly came along with us. She is a lovely girl, extremely likeable. Her sister, Dr. Marian, arrives the first of August. In connection with her midwifery school she has "adopted" a Chinese baby who has been a "practice" child for the girl students. They call her Judy (in Chinese these sounds mean "one saved"). Judy is now about a year old. She is to come to Omei too....

August 17, 1935 *Omeihsien, Szechwan*

Dear Friends at Home,

For hundreds of years devout Buddhists have made pilgrimages to Mt. Omei's peak, called the "Golden Summit." Some walk every step of the way; some are carried on men's backs up the steep path; some, to do penance, even make the ascent by prostrating themselves every few feet. At points along the beautiful road, and also at the summit, are temples where the pilgrims burn incense and *kotow* before the idols. Many hope by their toil and exertion to win the special favor of the gods and to earn merit for themselves.

The Chiangs (for Madame Chiang is a very important part of the team) are doing their best to put Szechwan's house in order. We have sensed a greater feeling of hope than we have ever known in this province. Greed, squeeze, and oppression have been denounced in no uncertain terms and the perpetrators are being brought to justice.

**Canadian Mission neighbor in Chengtu.*

Pleased as we are on the whole with the leadership of Generalissimo and Madame Chiang there is one fly in the ointment. The policy of the central government, and of Generalissimo and Madame Chiang as well, appears to be the complete militarization of the schools in the country. Since our mission schools are registered with the government, they must comply with government regulations. This summer all second year Middle School (High School) boys are required to take a three week course in military drill in order to be allowed to proceed with their academic work in the fall. We have already written what government regulations regarding military training in the University mean to us. These and similar regulations present very serious problems for Friends living in China. What would you do under the circumstances and what is the way out for Chinese Friends?

I think it will mean eventually mission schools will be turned over to the government and the contribution of missions to Chinese life will be along other lines. Foreign missions have led the way in education in China; have set the standards. Now the time has nearly come (has already arrived in some cases) when the government can run schools equal or superior to mission schools. Then mission effort will lead the way in some *new* undertaking. That is the gift of foreign missions to China--to lead the way.

Meanwhile the Simkins will try to carry on in ways they can at the University. When was there ever a greater need for the Friendly way of life? Many times I know I am a poor exemplar of that way but often I am so acutely aware of the need that I am ever so thankful to have even my small part in demonstrating the way of love and goodwill.

Robert's notes of a journey from Mt. Omei to Chengtu;

Many changes in transportation are taking place in West China but the new methods are not always entirely dependable. This year several families (eight adults and nine children) arranged to return from Mt. Omei to Chengtu by Canadian mission truck which was to meet them August 27th at the foot of the mountain. Their plans went wrong. It began to rain, bridges washed out, and the truck could not get through. After waiting two days they succeeded in securing enough carriers to take part of them to the river where they got a small boat to Kiating.

We left the mountain August 30th. The boat which was to meet us failed to appear. Near the river was an open yard used for storing coffin slabs. As this seemed the cleanest place in the small village we put up our camp beds under the wide eaves, trusting to a barricade of tables, etc., and to the deepening darkness to shield us from the prying gaze of the villagers. Fortunately it did not rain so we had a good rest. The following morning we secured a small boat to take us to Kiating where we waited for the larger boat to take us to Chengtu. In Kiating we found the Canadians still waiting for their truck which was detained by a washed out bridge.

We spent the day getting our boat in order. The covered portion is about twenty-five feet by nine feet. It is arranged as follows:

X 6 trackers, captain and wife sleep under moveable mats.	Margaret's camp bed	Box wash stand	Dorothy's camp bed	Judy's crib	4 servants & pilot sleep on the floor	coiled rope & boat gear No roof
	Mar. Ruth's camp bed		Mrs. Manly's couch bed	Dr. W.E. Manly & RLS sleep on the floor	oil tin cookstove	
Moveable roof removed in **daytime.**	Mat partition			Curtain	Mat partition	End of roof

Judy's nurse, Mrs. Liu, and her eight-year-old girl sleep on the floor between the cots after the others have retired. You can see that with eighteen adults, three children and a baby, who eat and sleep on board, the boat is very crowded. We burn charcoal in cooking our food at the back, but the boatmen burn green wood in their stove (marked X) at the front, and often we are well nigh smoked out.

In another boat are the Dryden Phelps family* and in a third are several cows taken to the mountains especially to provide milk.

September 1, 1935

The Manly family came last night after we had put the boat somewhat in order. We didn't get started until nearly noon today so we made only forty *li* even by travelling an hour after dark. We saw what we think was the Canadian truck going to Kiating to get our friends. In the middle of the night I awoke to hear the rain pounding upon the mat roof and there, standing over me, was Dr. Manly trying to stop the leaks. Some he stopped by punching up the mats to form a hillock instead of a crater. Two were stopped only by wedging basins between the matting and the supporting framework in such a way as to collect the drips. Nevertheless we all got a good night's rest.

**Dryden and Margaret Phelps and children, friends in the Baptist Mission.*

September 2, 1935

Still raining hard and the trackers didn't want to go on. We learned that the cowman had a dispute yesterday about the price of his boat and hasn't arrived. He is depending upon selling us milk, and besides we haven't an adequate supply of tinned milk, so we decided to wait for him a while. The Phelpses came over and we had dinner together--a jolly good time. Suddenly there was a great commotion and shouting. We rushed to the back and found the pilot and the servants fishing Dr. Marian's *amah* out of the river. She had fallen between the two boats and went entirely out of sight, but she had presence of mind enough to try to swim so came up and seized a pole put out to her. She had dry clothes to change into.

Yesterday a soldier came alongside the Phelps' boat and asked to get on. Dryden told him no, but he waded out into deep water and caught hold of the boat. Dryden wouldn't let him climb on so he had to wade back to shore. For a long time he followed along the shore. We thought he was perhaps crazy.

...About noon our cowboat overtook us but as it was still raining our men didn't stir until late in the afternoon. We made fifteen *li* before dark. Dorothy has been sick all day with fever, listless and without appetite. We don't know what is the trouble.

September 4, 1935

The weather has cleared and the sun shone very hot. Dorothy's fever continued. We tried to phone from Chinsen but the city had no connection. Dr. W.E. Manly therefore walked (or rode a wheelbarrow) forty *li* ahead and telegraphed for the University ambulance to meet us at Meichow the next morning. He took his bed roll and slept at Meichow.

September 5, 1935

After breakfast I walked to Meichow and found Dr. Manly. (He is D.D., not M.D.) We went forward to a point where the motor road is only half a mile from the river. There Dr. Manly waited to intercept the ambulance while I crossed over to the river to wait for the boats which had pulled up around the city. Finally about one o'clock the boats appeared but no ambulance. Fortunately Dorothy's fever was down somewhat so we were less anxious. Dr. Manly and Dryden Phelps went into the city to telephone about the ambulance but there was no connection. Just then along came a truck in which was a Chinese whom we knew. Dryden hailed it and hastily arranged to ride to Chengtu. If he met the ambulance he was to tell the doctor where we were; if it had not started he was to cancel the call. Soon after he left Dorothy's temperature went up and we were again anxious but after some hours it again dropped. I walked the motor road for some miles then returned to the river and found the boat before dark.

September 6, 1935

Returned to the motor road which I followed as far as Pengsanhsien where two China Inland missionaries live. They had seen or heard nothing of the ambulance but they gave me some valuable advice and some medicine. They have had a lot of experience of living in an isolated station days away from a doctor. They think perhaps the trouble is malaria. When the boats arrived at Pengsanhsien Dorothy was much better so it seemed unnecessary for the ambulance to come at all. Dorothy was even able to join in a happy little supper party in honor of her mother's birthday, in which the occupants of both boats joined.

September 7, 1935

We made only forty-five *li* today. It has evidently rained heavily up country for the river is in flood and almost the color of tomato soup. This afternoon the bodies of a man and two children floated past. No attempt is made to get these bodies as it would involve the expense of burial. On Tuesday within ten minutes I counted the bodies of five animals washed up on shore. The high water makes it difficult for the trackers as in many places there is hardly any path at all. However you must not think of a regular towpath like that beside a canal, for the river rises and falls so many feet that in most places a regular towpath is impossible. The men simply beat a path wherever they can catch a foothold. They often wade waist deep across an inlet. In a few places around a cliff a path has been chiseled high up in the perpendicular rock.

This afternoon when I was out walking on shore the two boats were being towed tandem to avoid the inconvenience of passing a second towline outside a row of trees right at the water's edge. Suddenly our boat (leading) swung out too far, was caught broadside by the current and pulled the men backward. There was lively work for a minute. They cut the rope attaching the second boat, a tracker waded out and caught a new towline for it, our trackers first checked our boat by getting a hitch around a tree, then slackened the rope and ran back until the boat could be maneuvered into a bay where it was turned and once more headed upstream. In the melee one of my strong bamboo chair poles fell overboard but I followed it downstream a quarter of a mile. A tracker from another boat saw it coming, swam out and recovered it for me.

September 8, 1935

We awoke this morning to find it raining. Rather late the trackers pushed back the mat covering and prepared to start, but twice just as they were setting out the rain increased and drove them back to the boat. We therefore made only twelve *li* today. We could have done much more, as we stopped long before dark, but we couldn't reach the next town and the boatmen said that because of robbers it was unsafe to tie up just wherever darkness might overtake us. Dorothy continues to improve so we are no longer anxious about her. Dr. Manly, however, has developed a severe cold, probably because he had insufficient clothing for the sudden change in temperature the night he went to call for the ambulance.

September 9, 1935

Dr. Manly's cold and fever are worse but today we advanced half of our remaining distance so we hope to get home tomorrow.

September 22, 1935

The boats arrived at Chengtu at 6 p.m. September 10th. Shortly after noon on that day I left the boat and walked overland to the University so when the rest of the party arrived I was at the river with men and carts to meet them. We hustled our things off and got everything up to the house and the men all paid off by about eight. We found everything in pretty good shape and our neighbors, Mr. and Mrs. Gerald Bell* had a good supper awaiting us. The University opened the following morning so both we and the children, notwithstanding our delays, were in time for the opening of our respective schools. It was Margaret Ruth's first day in primary school.

Unfortunately Dr. Manly's cold still proves obstinate but Dorothy has practically recovered. We still are not certain what she had. We learned that the ambulance did not come because it was temporarily out of repair and one of the doctors was ill when our telegram arrived. Dr. Best started out in another car a day later, but was stopped at the Chengtu city gate by Dryden's message that "the trip was no longer necessary."

I have been delayed in completing this because the Friends Service Council accounts and statement had to be attended to first. The work of the school term is now well under way. It's good to be back.

Robert L. Simkin

Canadian Mission.

September 22, 1935 *Chengtu, Szechwan*

Dear Folks,

...It was good to get back after the tedious boat journey. We are now quite well settled and ready for guests expected this week. Dr. and Mrs. Henry Davidson, English Friends at Suining (he is actually Irish) are due tomorrow or the next day. Arnold and Lois Vaught will come from Tungchwan a few days later.

...You ask, "Do the Chinese actually worship Sun Yat Sen as a god?" I suppose some might say "yes." I doubt if they do. It is just a patriotic gesture--this bowing three times to the great hero's picture. Bowing three times is a common ceremony. When Robert and I return from furlough and visit the Industrial Street Primary School, the children stand up and in unison bob their heads at us three times and we bob back! At our University commencement there was the ceremony of bowing to Sun Yat Sen's picture. General Chiang Kai-shek was on the platform and set the example, standing at attention in stiff military posture. Then there is also a period--definitely timed by watch--for meditation while standing before the picture. I suppose there are those who think people are worshipping the departed hero; perhaps it does mean that to some. I felt that I could quite heartily enter into the occasion of quiet. It seemed quite Quakerly to pause, close eyes and turn thoughts to God. It seems to me the occasion *can* be made one of personal consecration--to country if you like, but something higher if one has it in him.

This is quite a defense! I don't mean that I believe the ceremony is tremendously vital, but there are so many far worse things in China to tackle and work against. Why worry about trifles!...

October 6, 1935 *Chengtu, West China*

Dear Girls,

...World news is not good. Italy at war with Abyssinia, Japan trying to start a rumpus at Swatow. Here in Szechwan we are in the midst of an era of militarization. The uniform is *the* thing.

As far as the problem of military drill at the University is concerned the situation looks rather hopeful. Dr. Beech, the chancellor, reported to us last evening of an interview he had with the Generalissimo. Dr. Beech, I think, did a good piece of work. He presented the case of Friends very clearly. He pointed out the dilemma the University is in--bound by agreement with Friends from the early days of its inception *not* to have military drill and upon becoming a registered institution bound to follow government regulations. Dr. Beech asked the general what we (the University) were to do. He in fact outlined in his letter, which he left with the general, three possible ways out: (1) For the government to provide the military training, not the University; (2) For the government to provide it during the holidays apart from the University; (3) For the University to substitute physical training, discipline, and a course in citizenship.

Dr. Beech reports the Generalissimo as saying that he does not seek to make students military minded, but he wants to put some stamina into Chinese youth--teach them how to stand and move and to hear and take orders. If you were as familiar as we with the slouchy, hollow-chested, strolling, sauntering type of Chinese youth, you would see and feel that there is considerable point to the general's concern to "buck up" the young of China. I dislike all the regimentation while at the same time I am glad to see (among the Middle School boys particularly) a better carriage, a snappiness, a new alertness....

November 12, 1935

Dear Folks at Home,

...We are now having difficulty because of military drill in the Middle School. I ought to say first that the situation as far as the University is concerned seems better at the moment. Through the really valiant efforts of President Dsang and Dr. Beech the government is apparently going to exempt the University itself from offering such training. The University is to provide physical drill and discipline; the government will provide military drill. But now the situation has become acute in the Middle School. The boys *are* drilling and Robert has decided to resign his teaching. We feel great sympathy for S.C. Yang, a Friend, who is the school principal. I think he has a good deal of conviction but he can't see his way clear to stand out. Of course the price to pay is much greater for him than for us. It is an economic question with him. Moreover the school has a debt of $2,000 and more, which he rightly feels he could not get out from under and put on somebody else's shoulders. It is very difficult for him.

The Reds are again advancing in Szechwan but we have had no cause for concern.

Friends cannot hope to stay the rising tide of nationalism in China. Militarization of the whole school system seems inevitable. It may mean that Friends will have to withdraw from educational work for a time at least.

November 21, 1935 *Chengtu, West China*

Dear Home Folks,

What a mess the world is in! Japan continues on her high-handed course in North China. The latest report here is that five provinces in the North have set up an independent state. Japan, of course, is back of all this. She will continue to pull the strings.

The Red situation is again not good in Szechwan. We are told that the foreigners are evacuating Kiating. Yachow is already reported to be in state of seige at the hands of the Reds. Nobody here in Chengtu seems to be anxious about the local situation.

P.S. Later air news indicates that the coup in North China did not come off. General Doihara (Japanese) seems rather to have overstepped his prerogative. He is now resigning.

Mounting Japanese Aggression
1936

February 13, 1936 *Chengtu, West China*

Dear Friends at Home,

Somehow we have been caught up in a succession of activities and commonplace duties and I fear have failed to inform you of developments here. Indeed we ourselves are almost breathless trying to keep up with the rapid swing of events.

History is being made before our eyes. I do not pretend to understand the full significance of what is taking place or to be able to interpret it to you but there are certain things which stand out too prominently to be missed.

Chengtu is now within eight hours of Shanghai. Four days each week a plane flies from our city to the great metropolis on the coast. By radio we have the news of the world as promptly as do New York or London. The government, moreover, is erecting a large broadcasting plant south of the city and adjacent to our University. A new day of transportation and communication is dawning in West China.

Equally amazing, if not so tangible, is the growing unity and increasing purposefulness which we sense in the students, on the street, and among people everywhere. If we have felt in the past that China lacked cohesion, we are aware now of something drawing this great people together into a oneness.

This may be due to the closer relationship which now exists between Szechwan and the national government and all the regimentation issuing from Nanking. I believe, however, that there is more than this compulsion from without; I believe that there is an inner drive--is it fear? or is it desperation?--welding this people into a nation.

In Chinese eyes Manchuria is still a part of China and Japan's more recent aggression in forcing the "autonomous" ("Japanomous" has been suggested as more apt) government movement in the northern provinces is like a terrific stab. The world must not believe for a minute that this movement in the North is in any way acceptable to the Chinese. The National Government is wise enough to see that any violent protest would for the present only spell greater disaster but the youth of the land, rather to the embarassment of the recognized authorities, refuse to be curbed and so we hear of student demonstrations, strikes, etc. I am told that the students of one of the Peiping (Peking) universities are still on strike. Because of our remoteness from the scene of conflict our students' resentment has not (to date) crystalized into an "uprising." Why are the United States and England so loud in their denunciation of Italy's aggression in Ethiopia and so silent with regard to Japan? To China it seems all too apparent that the nations really care only when their economic interests are involved.

We wish there were some way to get a message to Friends and other lovers of goodwill, justice and righteousness in Japan. At present censorship makes free correspondence between the two countries impossible. We are thankful that S.H. Fang* on his way home from England was able to visit Japan as an emissary of goodwill and then bring to Friends here in West China helpful and enthusiastic reports of his visit. We need more of such emissaries. But if there were a thousand such, could the tide be held back?

I have already mentioned the regimentation going on about us. Mere children in the primary schools are being organized into boy and girl scout troops, put into uniform, taught to march to the beat of the drum, and to drill in military formation. This sort of thing extends throughout the entire school system from kindergarten to university. There are multitudinous flag raisings and flag lowerings in the morning and at sundown which are carried out with grave ceremony. The straighter shoulders, the erecter carriage of the Chinese student, and his new purposefulness are in themselves things to rejoice over but one trembles to contemplate what this NEW DISCIPLINE in its full significance may mean for the future of China. Multiply what we see here in Chengtu by all the schools of all the cities of the province and the nation--and consider.

**Prominent Chengtu Friend and W.C.U.U. faculty member.*

...The University now provides a course in "disciplinary physical training" taught by an instructor appointed by the government. Definite military drill is to be provided by the government at vacation time entirely apart from the University.

The first half of the program, for which the University is responsible, has been in progress for several months. What are our conclusions? Are we satisfied?

We do feel very grateful to all who have cooperated in making possible this degree of exemption. In a country where national feeling and military spirit are running high to have obtained even this exemption is no mean accomplishment.

Unfortunately terms mean very little. Most students stirred by an intense national spirit in response to Japan's aggression are *for* military drill rather than *against* it, and in their thinking and speech they recognize little distinction between "disciplinary physical training" and "military drill." For them the training they are receiving may well be a step toward the goal of preparedness for national defense. In fact this special course is still popularly known on the campus as "military drill." In saying all this I hope I do not seem to be casting aspersions on anybody. I have the greatest confidence in the sincerity of those who have tried to find a way out. But goodwill and peace are things of the spirit and no amount of legislation and special terminology for courses will solve the real issue. We are too well aware that in this rather remarkable concession granted the University by the government we have merely touched the outer fringe of this tremendous problem.

How can we, a small group of Friends and pacifists, hope to influence the growing military spirit? In these latter days I have come to realize as I never had before what a "high calling" that of being a pacifist is. What tremendous discipline of spirit and life it demands! Intellectual conviction is not enough. The *whole* life must be a positive expression of love and goodwill.

February 17, 1936 *Chengtu, West China*

Dear Folks at Home,

We have entertained the Browns just back from furlough. I lived with them my first summer at Behludin. Homer Brown has taken up a new line while at home--the study of psychiatry. Psychiatry of course is not new but its use by ministers and religious workers *is* new. Homer feels that the church has failed dismally in not helping mental ill health. Many doctors now see that religion has a very definite contribution to make to those suffering from neuroses. We know that here in China the ministry as a profession is rather looked down upon by doctors and other professionals. I think that Homer hopes to place religion and the ministry on a plane where they command respect....

March 9, 1936

Since writing the above, the coup of young mutineers has taken place in Japan. This does not auger well for China.

Over the radio also has come the news that Germany, in defiance of the Versailles and Locarno treaties, has refortified that section of the Rhine which had been demilitarized.

April 20, 1936

Dear Ones at Home,

We are counting the days now until Robert arrives. We are looking for him on Thursday or Friday, when he will have been away five weeks visiting Friends meetings....Generalissimo Chiang is in town for the opening of a newly-constructed military school.

May, 1936 *Chengtu, West China*

Dear Friends at Home,

May--and the brilliant sunshine and teeming life of an early summer. What a world of beauty and promise! It *is* good to be alive when "the year's at the spring." One wonders then more than ever why men can think of conquest and war and destruction in a world so sweet and altogether lovely. And yet--we know too well that threatening clouds are even now gathering.

Has the world gone mad? Or is militarism being driven to the wall and making one last violent and arrogant attempt to reinstate itself?

The Japanese militarists in their own country have assassinated their liberal statesmen and in China are pushing forward their program of exploitation.

Chinese merchants are being forced out of honorable business because goods, smuggled in by Japanese, are sold at prices to undercut them. You will have read in the *Christian Century* or elsewhere accounts of the traffic in opium and opium derivatives carried on by unscrupulous Japanese and Koreans in North China under protection of extraterritoriality, and how Chinese are being induced to take heroin and morphine in order that they may acquire the habit and so a demand for the drug be created. More recently we learned that a similar traffic in narcotics is being carried on under cover of extraterritoriality in Amoy, Foochow and other parts of China.

We also have definite information of the imprisonment and torture of Chinese Christians in Manchuria.

In such insidious ways Japanese militarism is attempting to undermine China's morale and is carrying on a definite policy of exploitation and terrorism.

In all fairness, however, I want here to point out two things. Chinese need not purchase opium and bring ruination upon themselves. If men are strong and courageous they *can* resist evil. (However, we know that in the United States men and women need to be safeguarded.) Nor do Chinese *have* to purchase Japanese smuggled goods. They *can* pay more and support their own countrymen. Yet if you know anything of the economic pressure in China, you must see how very difficult such a course would be for the majority of people.

And again, on the other side of the picture, the Japanese people *as a whole* have no means of securing adequate and reliable information of what is going on in China. News services in Japan are strictly controlled and the press drastically censored. Early this year, Mr. X (whose real name it is best not to mention in this letter) went to Japan, on behalf of Christian groups in China interested in better relations between the two countries, to study firsthand the Japanese situation. He found great ignorance and misinformation concerning the actual conditions in China but a surprising openness of mind on the part of selected groups and individuals. The Christian groups especially were "broad in their outlook and in their appreciation of the interests of the Chinese people." Such Japanese were eager for the truth even though the truth was uncomfortable.

One of our greatest needs at the moment is the making of constructive contacts and the building of personal friendships between the nationals of Japan and China.

Meanwhile the army in Japan has great influence and popularity among the unthinking masses of Japanese people. In China, we ourselves are witnessing a period of intense militarization and regimentation.

Unfortunately, the so-called exemption from military training granted to our own West China Union University by the Nanking government has not proven to be what we had hoped. Is it because it was not *really* wanted by a sufficient number? Altogether the situation from our Friendly pacifist viewpoint seems as unsatisfactory as it ever has been. The one bright spot of hope is the present dissatisfaction of students and staff who are learning through bitter experience the meaning of regimentation. The situation is indeed a difficult one.

This year sixty are being graduated from the University. Twenty of these are women. The Woman's College group of graduates is noteworthy because of its international character. A Russian girl from Moukden is graduating in dentistry and an American girl, wife of one of the doctors teaching in the College of Medicine, is graduating in medicine. For the first time Chinese girls are graduating in dentistry, two of them. It has been a joy these past twelve months to see them working at the University Dental Clinic in their crisp white coats, efficient, professional, well-poised, taking their places in a matter-of-fact way beside the men internes.

I wonder if you realize the amazing progress of the womanhood of China. Someone has said that the women of China have advanced further in two decades than the women of other countries in two generations. There is tremendous change from the old, giggling type of school girl to today's self-possessed, capable young college woman.

May 28, 1936

...Our new radio station is completed. I say "our" because it is near the University. It belongs to the government and is second in China only to Nanking's. People here at the University, including Robert, have been asked to broadcast. These days they are testing the machinery with impromptu programs. The present set of towers is for China only. They will soon begin building other towers to broadcast to San Francisco.

October 18, 1936

Dear Alice and Fannie,

About two weeks ago Sino-Japanese relationships looked bad. We thought war was almost certain. Fortunately, the air has cleared since then. Humanly speaking, however, war sooner or later seems to be inevitable.

Certainly there are many good Japanese people who are quite unaware of the true situation and would deplore their country's action if they knew all the facts.

Our good Dr. Chen of Suining (who I consider about the finest of our Chinese Friends) paid a visit to Japan in August on his way home from study in England. At first, he felt he could not go. He said he felt no hate toward Japanese people (one couldn't imagine gentle Dr. Chen hating *anybody*) but he did feel such a burden of injustice that he found it difficult to face them. Friends in England and here urged the visit, however, and after much earnest seeking he felt ready to go. He told the Japanese he met just how he had felt and they were much impressed. There was much frankness on both sides and a general clearing up of misunderstanding. As a result of his visit Japanese Friends want to send representatives to Szechwan for our Yearly Meeting. Certainly exchange visits of the nationals of the two countries are very helpful. However at just about the time of Dr. Chen's visit to Japan a very unfortunate incident occurred right here in Chengtu.

It had been reported that the Japanese would reopen their Chengtu consulate. This incensed certain rabid Chinese patriots and when several Japanese came on a visit, presumably to look over the situation, two were killed and two others injured by a mob. Also, one or two shops supposed to be selling Japanese goods were demolished. Some papers reported that the students of our University were connected with this incident, but this is entirely false, a story probably started to divert attention from a purely Sino-Japanese affair and make it appear to involve other foreign interests. At any rate you can see it would not be very safe for any Japanese to be here just now. Szechwan Friends cannot, under these circumstances, advise visits from Japan, but if some courageous spirit should feel strongly led to come, knowing fully the risk and willing to face it, we, of course, would warmly welcome such a person.

This autumn I have started attending one hour daily class at the language school. I am enjoying it greatly.

December 30, 1936

Dear Alice and Fannie,

...We expected about fifty Middle School boys to a Christmas party on Saturday. Only about one-half that many came; the rest were detained in the city because of the celebration and demonstration in support of Chiang Kai-shek's release.

I wonder what the papers in the United States are saying about the Generalissimo's capture. The London broadcast termed the events as "typically Chinese--could not have happened anywhere else--worthy of the best efforts of Gilbert and Sullivan," etc.

It may be, but we are profoundly thankful that Generalissimo Chiang is again at the helm in Nanking. The news of his release came as a very fitting climax to Christmas Day. Now the Chengtu Chinese newspapers are publishing headlines saying how grateful Madame and Generalissimo Chiang are to the Christian people and for the prayers of the Christian churches. What a contrast to our Christmases of only a few years ago, when we hardly dared hold public Christmas celebrations because of the anti-Christian demonstrations and riots.

The Generalissimo was taken captive by Chang Hsioh Liang, while the former was on a visit to Sian. I wonder if Chang Hsioh Liang rightly estimated the widespread loyalty to Chiang, which has been manifest aplenty since his release, if never before. China seems now to be pretty much united behind Chiang. That is gratifying. In unity lies China's greatest hope. And Chiang Kai-shek is certainly, for the present at least, the only man in sight who can achieve anything like unity. The students here have been most enthusiastic in their demonstrations following the Generalissimo's release.*

**White and Jacoby in* Thunder Out of China *point out that the purpose of Chiang's visit to Sian was to revive the flagging campaign against the Communists. He was kidnapped--"not by Communists but by warlords who refused to fight against Communists any more when they might be fighting against the Japanese." While in captivity Chiang "met the Communists personally for the first time since 1927." What exactly transpired is not generally known "but the results were electric; the civil war came to an abrupt end. Chiang recognized the right of the Communists to govern their own area in the north within the loose framework of the Central Government. Their armies were to be incorporated into the national armies." Positional warfare was to be left to Chiang; the Communists were to "wage guerrilla warfare behind the enemy lines."*

Outbreak of War with Japan 1937

February 21, 1937 *Chengtu, West China*

Dear Ones at Home,

...Two Yearly Meeting delegates have been chosen to attend the FWCC* Conference in the United States next fall....The Committee of Missionaries took one definite step which seems the right one even if distressing. They have passed a minute saying that they believe the time has come for the Friends Service Council to make a definite statement to the Board of Governors that unless conditions ("military training, lectures on methods of warfare, etc.") are greatly changed it cannot continue much longer to participate in the University.

Robert and I are thinking it right to resign entirely from the staff. I have already cut loose. Robert may continue teaching in the Department of Religion even if he resigns from the staff and relinquishes his professorship.

We are going to miss Horace Holder and Dorothy Behenna** greatly. Horace was always dashing in and came regularly for afternoon tea and certain meals on Sundays. He has gone for his second year to Suining. Dorothy B. goes off with the Walkers tomorrow to Tungliang. It is going to seem very quiet without them.

May 23, 1937 *West China Union University*
Chengtu, Szechwan, West China

Dear Friends of New England Yearly Meeting,

I have been reading recently a little book called *God's Candlelights*

---

*Friends World Committee for Consultation.

**Friends Service Council workers.

by Mabel Shaw (Edinburgh House Press, London, 1932). Seldom have I picked up a book that has given me such sheer delight and inspiration. We have long talked and dreamed of an indigenous Christianity, but I have yet to see a more convincing picture of its actual worth and honesty. Mabel Shaw is a missionary to the Bantu people of North Rhodesia, an exceedingly human missionary, and one of the delights of her book is this very humanness. She is somewhat of a poet, too, and alive to the beauty around her. I wish all missionaries could have her creative imagination, her daring and her faith that God will find new and different expression in different peoples. We talk about it, but we fail to act always as if we *believed* it.

I have sometimes thought of the gifts which China has for God and the world. Patient endurance is certainly one. Perhaps this virtue has arisen from economic necessity, but at any rate it is here. Then there is the resilience and abounding good humor of the common people. They have a way of smiling through whatever comes, be it a run of bad weather, hard work, or an invading army.

...I believe the enthusiasm of the students for military training is on the wane. They are not at present demanding it, and although the University did not avail itself fully of the exemption granted it by the Nanking government, military discipline and drill are less to the fore now than a few months ago. However, a large number of third and fourth year students have been ordered to Nanking, at government expense, for two months special training. The lack of openness and frankness on the part of University authorities in facing the situation has been far from satisfactory. The University has found itself in a dilemma: on the one hand, it has desired to appear wholeheartedly loyal to China and to satisfy popular feeling; on the other, it has sought to keep the support of Friends. So Friends here, as in other countries, while trying to follow what they believe to be the highest good, may appear to be lacking in loyalty to the state (as *must* be the case if the state stands for an exclusive Nationalism).

China is in flux. Parties and movements come and go, each demanding and winning loyalty and enthusiasm. Not long ago it was Communism; now it is Nationalism. Ten years ago we were passing through a very trying period of anti-Christian and anti-foreign (anti-British) feeling. Today there is scarcely a murmur of such things. Even anti-Japanese sentiment has lessened. A few days ago we got a letter from Irene Hutchinson telling of an athletic meet in which the Friends High School at Wen Fung Ta, Chungking, participated. The Wen Fung Ta boys did very well, getting the highest aggregate score, but greatly to their disappointment they lost the junior football match by one point. Their opponents, a government school, jeered and shouted at them to go home "and pray about it," and called them foreign slaves! This incident is not typical of the present, however, at least not in Chengtu.

A long period of drought has meant the closing of the Yangtze to all but the smallest river steamers. Mail and freight have been delayed and Chengtu shopkeepers are still waiting for much of their spring stock. But we have *air* connections with Shanghai four times a week, and the prospect of a railway to Chungking in the near future. All this means a good deal to us. Do not conclude, however, that China's entire transportation is being suddenly and completely revolutionized. As I write I look out my window and see a woman riding a wheelbarrow. She is being pushed along the narrow path separating the paddy fields by a toiling brown-skinned bare-backed coolie--just as thousands of China's good country folk riding squeaky wheelbarrows have been pushed along over narrow roads for hundreds of years. But a new day *is* coming!

August 7, 1937 *Behludin, West China*

Dear Everybody at Home,

My letter for New England Friends mentioning a lessened anti-Japanese sentiment was, I fear, out of date by the time it was read. It just goes to show how little prepared we were for Japan's increasing encroachments.* But now war seems inevitable and I am afraid China will get the worst of it. Poor old China! The broadcasts from Tokyo (we get them reported to us from Chengtu) are just pure rot. Japan must think the rest of the world is pretty gullible! Imagine! She says she is only trying to keep peace--it is all China's fault for not disarming her soldiers (in China's own territory!) and a whole lot of other nonsense.

Other nations are too busy with other affairs to make much of a protest and Japan knows it. Besides she is telling the rest of the world to keep hands off!!

We don't know at all what this is going to mean to us. We hope the

---

**Of course it had been evident for years that Japan wanted to keep China subordinate; she was banking on China's disunity. We need not have been surprised that an incident at the Marco Polo Bridge [near Peking] on July 7, 1937, would precipitate outright war. Nevertheless it all came as a shock.*

University will carry on, but if war comes the students will be very restless....

August 22, 1937 *Behludin, West China*

Dear Folks at Home,

Our minds are full of the "war" news these days. I put "war" in quotes because war has not been declared but terrible suffering and bloodshed are going on just the same. We get radio reports sent up here by some of our campus folk who have been in Chengtu all summer:

..."War is not declared and the Japanese ambassador is in Nanking and not planning to withdraw." (Ready, I suppose, to reopen negotiations when China crumples).

..."China is putting up a determined and spirited resistance."

..."It appears the Chinese troops have been given forty-eight hours to accomplish the objective (driving Japanese out of staff headquarters in Honkew Park, Shanghai). They appear to be going at the job with grim determination. They see it as either fight or be enslaved and they choose to fight to the 'bitter end.' "

One very bad feature of the situation is Germany's tendency to side with Japan. Germany has quoted the "Japanese viewpoint to the effect that Japan's intentions are peaceful and friendly--no territorial ambitions--simply desires to unite China, Manchukuo and Japan in a triple pact against Communism." Does Japan think anybody senseless enough to believe her intention is *friendly*? It is a queer way of expressing friendship. I doubt if Germany really believes it. If Germany lines up with Japan we'll soon have other countries taking sides and a world war on our hands. There have been rumors of German representatives in Peiping allying themselves with the Japanese cause. It does not look good.

For once, we in the "wild and woolly" West are safe and unthreatened. It's Shanghai that's taking the blows this time. *And* Nanking. Usually the people at the coast have most fearsome tales to tell of *our* part of the country. Now the reverse.

How mail is to get in and out of the country we don't know, but perhaps via Hongkong.

All foreign banks in Shanghai are closed. Fortunately we have little money in Shanghai at present, Robert foreseeing this eventuality.

We are wondering about many things: When will the Canadian School open? (The principal with new staff is just returning from furlough.) Will Stanley Jones be able to visit Szechwan as planned?

Will Rufus Jones come next spring? How are we to get stores and supplies? Will the Tomkinsons come or not?

September 1, 1937

Shanghai now blockaded! Oh, it's dreadful for poor China.

In view of the hostilities it is quite likely the Tomkinsons will postpone their return to China.

September 26, 1937 *Chengtu, Szechwan*

Dear Ones at Home,

...It is useless to write "news" of the Sino-Japanese situation. You know as well as we what is happening. Will the world put up with Japan's atrocities? China has been disappointed and puzzled by America's stand. But with the terrible air raids on Nanking yesterday we are told the United States is getting indignant. She ought to! There should be some way of outlawing a government such as Japan's. If there were only some way of getting the facts before the people of Japan. But the people are not allowed to know the real truth. Do you hear at home the stuff Japan broadcasts? Short-wave radios are illegal in Japan and the strictest surveillance is kept over everybody and everything there so that the people shall know and hear only what the militants permit them to know and hear.

Persistent letters and advices come from the consular authorities asking us to move out. (We are reminded of 1927.) So far I have heard of no missionaries in Szechwan who are moving. There is no danger at present. The British consul does not seem anxious to get his nationals out. Actually, we are all too busy to worry.

We have a well-stocked storeroom. I have tried to lay in enough foodstuffs (imported variety) to last one year or more. Prices on such supplies are going up rapidly as no more goods can be obtained from Shanghai. Mail, however, comes in...though fairly slowly--by way of Hongkong or Canton, I think.

Robert's postscript:

P.S. I am still able to sell checks on Shanghai, so neither our family nor the Friends Mission for which as Treasurer I have to provide are financially in need.

October 16, 1937 *Chengtu, West China*

Dear Alice and Fannie,

...Last evening we had with us two very fine Chinese from

Nanking--Dr. Chen and his wife. They have come with their three daughters and several grandchildren under more or less refugee conditions. Dr. Chen told us, as we sat in complete darkness last evening while an air-raid drill was going on, about their experiences in Nanking. There, practically every family has a dug-out.

...The Chens say Japan doesn't want the war to last more than six months but China is prepared to carry on for one or more years longer. At the rate both Japanese and Chinese are being slaughtered around Shanghai, one shudders to think of the struggle being prolonged.

Don't worry about air raids. Not very likely so far from the Japanese base.

Robert comments on the Sino-Japanese situation and its meaning:

October 19, 1937

We are so far away from the scene of hostilities that conditions are more or less normal here except that things sent from abroad are rapidly rising in price. A few things such as nails are double the former price.

Two schools near the coast are sending some of their teachers and students to join with us or to be accommodated with living quarters on our campus. As Secretary of the Property Committee I am having additional work in helping to provide living quarters for them. I suppose we are the most favorably located of all the higher educational institutions of China, because we are so far from the coast. It is possible that the Japanese may attempt an air raid on Chengtu, but hardly likely that such a raid could be effective at present from so great a distance. We have had two air raid drills in which all the lights were extinguished for a time.

The Canadians consider conditions sufficiently favorable that they have sent for several families which were prevented from coming, either by cancellation of passage before they left home or by stopping in Japan when they found they could not disembark in Shanghai.

Robert L. Simkin

November 2, 1937

*Dear Alfred,**

Dr. Stanley Jones is expected tomorrow. He is flying from Hongkong. He will be here nine days.

The Chinese feel that the nations of the world ought not to stand by and see Japan, the international robber, robbing China, but that they

---

**Alfred E. Simkin, Robert's brother.*

should tell Japan where to get off. I cannot see how the world is to become a well-ordered international society unless the nations take the same attitude toward a criminal nation as we in America take when we see a criminal robbing a defenseless woman.

The building of the railroad from Chungking to Chengtu is being delayed by the war. Latest report said that the government was going to concentrate on a railroad from Yunnan (south of Szechwan) to Chungking. They are digging out hundreds of graves (thousands?) southeast of Chengtu. I think the plan is to extend the city to the southeast. This is not far from us.

Robert

November 21, 1937

Dear Ones at Home,

It seems now to take a full two months or more for letters to get through. I still think they may come via Hongkong or Canton. The important thing is that we *are* getting mail.

Last week we got the news of Shanghai being taken by the Japanese. It made us all sad and depressed. The Chinese have put up a valiant fight but it is hopeless against the highly mechanized, modernized army and navy of Japan. China's chance is in guerilla warfare and everlastingly sticking at it. Japan wants to get it over quickly. China is willing to prolong the fighting, but at what a terrible cost to both countries as it all goes on.

Government offices have already moved from Nanking. Nanking University is now coming to join us. We already have many students and staffs, or part staffs, from a number of schools all over China. Several foreigners from Nanking University are planning to come. We hope to have a couple, or a single man, in our home to live with us.

Robert is extremely busy with plans for building and housing for all these people.

Some people and schools are building dug-outs as they believe air raids will occur. We will go to our basement if necessary. The Japanese have a long way to come before they drop bombs on us. Nevertheless, it may happen yet.

Since writing last, Stanley Jones has visited Chengtu and given a series of addresses to large groups of students. His messages have been good. Stanley Jones advocates that Christians all over the world refuse to buy Japanese goods. He says, however, for such a boycott to be effective (redemptive) it must cost something to the one imposing it.

A very alive and interesting group discussed this question before Stanley Jones arrived. At a Round Table conference with Dr. Jones which I attended, and at other conferences which I did not attend, the discussion continued. Finally, it was suggested that a group get together around the lunch table just the day before Stanley Jones left and have one more session. The group was invited here and fourteen places at the table were filled. As a result Dr. Jones is going to prepare a second open letter to the Christian people of the world and among other things suggest that all powers give up their military garrisons in China. It is to be pointed out that the Chinese people would be willing for Japan to extend her trade interests in China so long as sovereignty is not affected.

We expect Leonard Tomkinson soon. Hilda and Shirley are not coming at present. We also expect to entertain the Willmotts* for a few days when they arrive.

Robert writes:

December 9, 1937 *Chengtu, West China*

Dear Friends,

Our first-class mail and papers are getting through to us, although often delayed. Thus far we have been able to get funds through the regular channels. We do not know how long these conditions will continue, but up to the present we have not been seriously affected.

The Union Theological College has had a special class of three women and eight men for a month's training, closing next Tuesday. This additional teaching has given me a very full schedule, but the class has been keen and appreciative. All our schools are unusually crowded with refugees from east China. Local developments are taking place very rapidly. I shall hope to write more in detail after the situation becomes normal again. It is stated that a gate will be opened in the city wall between the south and the east gates. This will be almost opposite the University. If this is done we shall be able to eliminate about a mile of distance in reaching the main business section of the city. It will have its disadvantages as well, as it will cause the city to grow all around us where there is now farming area and open space.

We are all well, and aside from the feeling of tragedy which is being enacted about us, life is much as usual.

Robert L. Simkin

**Good friends in the Canadian mission.*

December 19, 1937 — *West China Union University, Chengtu, West China*

*Dear Elsie McCoy:**

Our group here has pretty well come to the conclusion that the right course is an economic boycott of Japan, somewhat as outlined by Stanley Jones in his open letter to America and Great Britain, a copy of which I have sent to Clarence Pickett** and a few others. We would not approve of a campaign to win popular support of boycott, as that could only be accomplished by propaganda and would necessarily result in hatred. We do believe, however, that protest must be made and that it is right for individuals to make such a stand if it is done with honest conviction and with a redemptive purpose. At the same time that we make protest we must be ready to admit and confess our own country's shortcomings and her guilt in her treatment of Japan (Exclusion Act, naval maneuvers, etc.).

America *is* in part responsible for the situation in the Orient today. For her to step out from under that responsibility is distressing beyond measure. The world is now too closely knit together for a nation, and a so-called Christian nation at that, to say, "This is not our affair. We'll mind our own business; let the rest of the world mind theirs!"

For one thing, Christian men and women of America ought for the sake of both China and Japan to make their voices heard above the greed and selfishness of their fellow countrymen who profit by such international crimes. Men and women who love peace and righteousness ought to ask *why* munitions and war materials, such as scrap iron and cotton, are being sent to the Orient. Then they should DO SOMETHING ABOUT IT.

December 19, 1937

Dear Alice and Fannie,

...Thanksgiving is over and Christmas approaching. We are having students from down river in for dinner on Christmas Day at noon and three Cheloo and Central China University families in for family Christmas dinner at night.

...We're well but busy. Everything normal here except for refugee students and people all about us; mail *very slow*; foreign supplies and goods nigh impossible.

**Quaker friend in Wilmington, Ohio.*

***Executive Secretary of the American Friends Service Committee.*

Universities and Colleges Flee from the War Zone 1938

January 17, 1938 *Chengtu, China*

Dear Brother,

Many refugees are arriving, but thus far only the more prosperous people are coming to Chengtu, those who have money enough to make the long trip from east China. The less prosperous people are able to pay transportation only short distances, or they walk and carry their effects as best they can. The suffering in east China is beyond all power to compute.

We are building a group of buildings--two-story made of bamboo lath and plaster with tile roof--to accommodate the staff of Nanking University which is coming to join with us temporarily. These buildings are supposed to house about two hundred persons. We also are putting up a two-story brick building designed by the architect for the new University Hospital which will for the present accommodate about two hundred Nanking University students. These students will eat in the Canadian College gymnasium and we shall put up a temporary kitchen for preparing food. A few members of the staff are beginning to arrive. The majority are in Ichang. It is very difficult to secure transportation up river, but they will come as rapidly as they can.

Robert

January 16, 1938 *Chengtu, West China*

Dear Alice and Fannie,

We now have a guest from Shanghai, more recently from Hankow, in the house. He comes representing the National Christian Council. He is Ronald Rees and we have heard of him for many years through the Sewells as his wife is an English Friend....

...Dr. Wu Yi Fang, president of Ginling College, is here at our Woman's College. We had a Woman's College Board meeting which she attended. It was a fine opportunity to become acquainted. Last Tuesday we had a reception in her honor, to which our women graduates and leading Chinese and foreign women were invited--over one hundred invitations. I consider Dr. Wu one of the world's outstanding women. Maybe you have heard or seen her. She was in America on a speaking tour not long ago. How relieved she was to receive a telegram after her arrival here and learn that the staff and servants and buildings at Ginling were safe after the fall of Nanking.

The Japanese army disgraced itself at Nanking. This war is likely to drag out for some time. China has no thought of giving in.

February 10, 1938 *Chengtu, Szechwan*

Dear Calvin, Alice and Fannie,*

...Nanking University President Chen, who came six weeks ago to reconnoitre, arrived yesterday with a bus load of his staff and their families. Many students also have arrived. We are putting up accommodations for them as rapidly as possible. Meanwhile they are being accommodated temporarily in three of the city's churches.

Yesterday, Wanhsien was bombed by twelve Japanese planes and we expect that sooner or later the Japanese may pay us a visit. If so, we shall take refuge in the basement of our house which is protected better than some houses by a terrace of earth on two sides. The school to which the children go also has a very good basement. Chengtu is very much spread out and it is not likely that the bombers will concentrate on the University which is also very spacious. The suffering caused to the people who have to evacuate from east China is very great.

A young Irishman, educated at the University of Iowa and teaching in the University of Nanking, has evacuated and is living with us. His name is Peter Bannon. He now is a member of the Christian Church working under the Presbyterians. Formerly he was a Roman Catholic.

West China Union University reopens next week and Nanking University hopes to open March first. We are very glad that we can offer them a haven of refuge.

We are so far from the Japanese that if they bomb us it is unlikely they can carry the very heavy bomb. We hear terrible stories of

---

**Alice Miller's husband.*

atrocities by the Japanese in Nanking and elsewhere. Unfortunately many of them seem to be true.

Robert

February 17-25, 1938

West China Union University
Chengtu, Szechwan, China

Dear Friends,

These days we are rather cut off from the outside world; the radio and airplane keep us from feeling completely severed. Are you still writing? For the present, apparently the only *certain* way to get mail to and from the coast is by air. Hongkong is the port by which mail now enters and leaves, and since a direct air route has been recently opened between Hongkong and Chungking we now have good air service all the way from Chengtu to the coast. As for the future--but who dares to say what is ahead?

...If in the past we Szechwanese have been provincial, we are likely soon to be shaken from it. The intelligensia from all over China are coming to our very doors. Rubbing elbows with those who throng the streets of the busy shopping district of Chengtu, it is easy to identify many as "down river" folk because of their different cast of countenance and their un-Szechwanese accent. It is a pity it has taken a tragic war to bring about this mingling, but today Szechwan is a veritable melting pot. And it is good for us to have this culture and progressiveness of other parts of China thrust into our midst.

There has been a great and steadily mounting influx of students and teachers to our campus. Cheeloo University (medical mostly), National Central Univeristy (medical and dental), Nanking University, Ginling College (for women), and Soochow University are officially represented by smaller or greater student and staff units. There also are many students from still other institutions who have found their way here by ones or twos (or more) quite on their own. Some are in very straightened circumstances; others in great distress of mind because they have had no word from their families; still others *know* that everything is gone--homes and dear ones are just no more.

One result of this migration to Szechwan should be the strengthening and stabilizing of the young Szechwan Church. Third and fourth generation Christians, because of their greater experience and richer Christian heritage, will certainly have much to give us.

I can't speak too highly of these wonderful people. They are so courageous and altogether splendid. Although many have lost homes and all their worldly goods there is not a suggestion of defeatism about them, or a complaint or a grumble. I am not ashamed of the Christian leadership in China today. There is magnanimity; there is a spiritual quality that wins our deepest admiration. The Church of China will not, I think, deny Christ and preach hate as did churches in the West during the World War. In spite of the grave national crisis there is a very marked restraint on the part of Christian leaders. They deplore the acts of Japan's militarists; they do not condemn Japan as a whole. Rather, there is compassion for those Japanese people who, like themselves, are victims of this war madness. But of course it is going to be difficult for this spirit to be diffused among rank and file Chinese Christians, especially if the war stretches on and on and Japanese forces encroach upon more and more of China's territory and continue to perpetrate hideous crimes. Yet the truly magnificent spirit of the thoughtful people gives us great hope. Somehow I feel the soul of China is being born out of all this suffering. Certainly we have never loved or respected the people of China as we do today.

(After writing the above, we received a letter from Lucy M. Burtt, an English Friend teaching at Yenching University in Peiping. She too speaks of the gentleness of spirit of certain Christians in the North. I will quote one example:

> *One saintly Christian said to me the other day that he had been thinking perhaps it was directly in the purpose of God that this most recent war of aggression should have fallen upon a people naturally pacific and disinclined to foment national hatred, for it may be, he added, we can be used of God to help the nations of the West to a new understanding of international relationships where national pride and honor are not axiomatically the most important consideration.*)

Like Gaul, China may be divided into three parts: (1) occupied territory, (2) threatened area, (3) free and peaceful. To date, Szechwan has belonged to the third class. Twice within the past week, however, Chungking has experienced an air raid. We have had siren warnings here in Chengtu. Our turn is sure to come, but we can't believe that anything will happen to us. Is that what people always say?

What is going on in the occupied areas? After all discounts are made for propaganda and atrocity stories we are forced to accept news that comes directly from reliable, impartial sources. The accounts of ten thousand (conservative estimate) unarmed persons, in Nanking alone, killed in cold blood, and eight thousand cases (lowest estimate) of rape in that city are too terrible to comprehend. The valiant efforts being made by the remaining handful of missionaries to care for the tens of thousands of refugees and to intercept acts of violence, frequently at great personal risk, will make a thrilling story if it is ever written. A statement of Mr...........is revealing: "Four weeks today. The shells and bombs were almost comfortable, if we had only known it. And what is ahead?"

Letters of the first half of November and second half of December have finally arrived. It *is* good to hear from you all once more. We are grateful for your thought of us.

Margaret

March 12, 1938 *Chengtu, Szechwan, China*

Dear Alice and Fannie,

Dorothy and Margaret are having a good time at school this term. Lewis Walmsley, the principal, and the new teachers are giving the children a rich program. Mrs. Walmsley (Constance) has been directing plays and the community has been invited to the performances.

...I have been helping in the organization of a University Women's Association, being appointed by our Woman's College Board as chairman of the promotion committee. We had an interesting and enthusiastic preliminary meeting on Friday and are working now toward a big gathering in about two weeks. There are so many college women in Chengtu now from all over China that it seems an auspicious time to start such an organization.

...World news is not good. Yesterday we got a special issue of "News from the Air"--our small English newssheet--telling of Germany's coup d'etat in Austria. The sheet is headed--"*Is It War or Surrender?*"--a title to cause shivers of apprehension.

For ten days or more there has been no talk of air raids here. All is quiet. I suppose there'll be other scares likely, but meanwhile we go on happily and comfortably.

April 17, 1938 [*Easter Sunday*] *Chengtu, West China*

Dear Alice and Fannie,

Last weekend we were more than busy because starting on Saturday came the Friends conference with Harry T. Silcock of England. (We were entertained by Harry and Margaret Silcock while in London. They used to be missionaries out here before my day.) He came partly to bring expression of love and sympathy to China from Friends in England, partly to seek the cooperation of Szechwan Friends in relief projects, and partly to meet Chinese students on behalf of the

Universities' China Committee, London, to make known to them new requirements for students desiring to study abroad. Ward Perkins, also of London, who has come with Harry Silcock to China, was our house guest while here. He was formerly a civil service officer in Burma.

...We have had no air raids. The attempts on Chungking cost too much for what the Japanese accomplished. Let's hope they'll think it not worth while to come here. Things have been going better for China the last few days. But conditions in Nanking are truly awful. It is reported in a letter smuggled out of Nanking and written by a Chinese member of the Nanking University staff that there was not a single Chinese woman in Nanking, outside those serving under foreign protection, who had not been violated.

May 20, 1938 *West China Union University*
Chengtu, West China

Dear Friends of New England Yearly Meeting,

Last evening I attended the Senior banquet of our Woman's College. Of all the Senior banquets ever held throughout the world I doubt if there has ever been another quite like this one! Senior women of three institutions banqueted together. Girls of Ginling College, Nanking University, and West China Union University sat intermingled at the long L-shaped table, sang gay songs and had their toasts together. (In addition, there were three Senior representatives from three other institutions.) It is interesting to speculate upon the part these young women are going to play in China's future. At other times in her long history China has been swept by invading armies and has had to build anew, but this is the first time, as was pointed out by a speaker last evening, that China will have an educated womanhood to help in the task of reconstruction.

We have already written of the great westward migration that has been going on during the past nine months in China. Probably a million people have come from the east to Szechwan and other provinces of the west. Bands of students have made the trek by foot, tramping a thousand miles or more.

We marvel at the courage and spirit of these people. Dr. H....., Dean of Dentistry of National Central University (Government) has told us of their new dental building costing a quarter of a million dollars. It had just been finished and completely furnished throughout when it was destroyed by Japanese bombs two weeks before the opening. Dr. H..... was given four days' notice to move staff, students, and equipment to Szechwan. He and his family had a beautiful new home which they had to leave and which has since been looted and burned.

...The Chen Wei Pins are another unusually fine family. Dear Dr. and Mrs. Chen have in their hearts no enmity or bitterness. They are able to take their losses with a smile. Dr. Chen, by the way, during the Boxer uprising in 1900, lost parents, sister and brother. They died for their faith and were beheaded outside the Peking wall. After the outbreak was over, Dr. Chen went to the very villagers who had killed his father and mother and preached in their town for several years. Dr. Chen, who is no longer young, is now working with the soldiers in an organization called the Moral Endeavor Society (something like the Y.M.C.A. in wartime).

I am very thankful that American Friends are joining with Friends of England in relief work in China and looking forward to openings in the work of reconciliation between China and Japan.

...We are very much disappointed that Rufus Jones and party have not been able to come to Szechwan. We so greatly appreciated the visit of Harry Silcock and Ward Perkins.

July 31, 1938

A note from Robert:

...We have just learned that Central Theological College from Wuchang is moving to Chengtu to join with our Union Theological College for the period of the war. They will bring three foreign teachers and fifteen students.

And a note dated the same day from Margaret:

And pandas!! You have probably read about the Giant Panda. Well, our campus has almost been surfeited with them. They live naturally in the Szechwan bamboo thickets where they are captured for shipment abroad. "Dick's"* compound (at the rear of ours) is a way station for them and they have become a common sight. The young ones are amusing and adorable; the big ones are not so attractive. More indolent creatures I've never seen.

August 20, 1938 *Behludin*

...If only the Chinese can hold Hankow. The Japanese are not finding it as easy to seize as they hoped. Meanwhile they are bombing Canton, Changsha and other cities. And still the U.S. or U.S. business interests keep on selling scrap iron and cotton to Japan! It is greed, greed, greed that makes war possible.

**Frank Dickinson, Canadian Mission.*

Well, it is now eleven o'clock and I must get to bed. The wind is blowing and it is somewhat of a wild night but we are all snug and warm within.

September 17, 1938 *Chengtu, West China*

Dear Fannie and Alice,

...Ginling College has moved to Chengtu and to the West China Union University campus in toto. Nanking University continues to dig in and so it goes. It is plain to see that these people do not look for the end of the war in any immediate future.

This evening the air drill sirens have been sounding. If Hankow falls it will bring the Japanese that much nearer. The Chinese are putting up a good resistance, however. Even if they lose Hankow the war will not be finished any more than it was with the fall of Nanking.

I hate to think of the outcome of this war whichever side wins. War never settles anything; it only provides more cause for future war.

Now we are waiting with bated breath to know what is going to happen in Europe. I am glad our furlough is not due just now....

November 6, 1938 *Chengtu, West China*

Dear Alice and Fannie,

...Affairs are not going so well for poor old China. Leonard Tomkinson is most pessimistic--he thinks China should make peace, the earlier the better, and save what she can. Japan's recent overtures are interesting. Up to the present she hasn't suggested she would recognize the *Kuomintang* at all. Leonard thinks Britain is now prodding both countries, urging Japan to offer peace and China to accept peace terms. He also thinks Britain is threatening to withhold further loans to China with which she can continue to prosecute the war. At any rate the prospect is not bright.

November 8, 1938

Japanese planes got to Chengtu today. When the first siren sounded I was at my desk at the Library and I did not think it necessary to leave. (I had wasted several hours on Saturday hanging around after the warnings waiting for the "all clear.") Consequently I kept at work. But when I heard a big hum of planes I said to Alice Lindsay* who was in the office with me, "That sounds like a whole squadron coming," not really thinking it was enemy planes. The roar drew nearer and I stepped to the big window and saw eight of them flying low and coming

*Canadian Mission member.

right toward us. They seemed to go directly over the building. By that time I had sensed they were Japanese planes and moved on into the corridor and then on to the front door of the building. By the time I had reached the door, the planes were over the city and we could hear the put-put-put of machine gunfire. I went back to my desk and worked until twelve o'clock. The Library closes for an hour at noon, so at twelve I picked up my things and started for home. Some of the Nanking University Library staff who share a room in our Library stood on the steps. Many people by that time seemed to be moving about on the campus so I asked, "Has the all clear sounded?" "No," was the reply. Nevertheless I came home. A soldier stood in our lane, stopping people from passing. However I slipped in at our back gate. It was nearly ten o'clock before the "all clear" sounded. This afternoon we learned that seventeen planes came and dropped bombs (evidently not very big ones) on the two air fields. Not much damage was done.

I should explain that the Canadian School students are organized into groups and when the siren sounds they know exactly where to go. Our girls, for example, gather with other children who live in our row of houses. Each group is then escorted by an adult--new people who are doing language study in the same building--to a place of safety. The people on our row, for example, come to our basement, which is fairly well protected. If I had not known the girls were well looked after I should not have felt comfortable about staying at the Library. Besides I had thought it unlikely the Japanese planes would actually come. The day was gray. Perhaps the planes were flying low (I believe I could see machine guns mounted on them) in order to be below the clouds so that they could locate the city.

I suppose we shall have a good many air raid scares and some actual raids in the next few months. If they come to the place of doing great destruction, we shall feel the horror of it all, but as for the present experience, it can be put down merely as a bit of excitement. In any case it is not necessary to worry. The Japanese will probably go for places of military significance and leave us alone. It's despicable business anyhow. Such a beautiful, peaceful countryside. To deliberately rain down death and destruction upon it is unspeakably brutal.

Robert also comments on the war situation.

November 15, 1938 *Chengtu, West China*

Dear Friends,

...Still the war goes on. We wondered whether the loss of Canton and Hankow would lessen the determination of the Chinese to resist. It has been a great shock, but the general opinion seems to be that the war is by no means lost, that China could not expect to be more successful than she has been against the highly mechanized army of Japan. Guerrilla warfare is becoming very effective, and the farther the Japanese penetrate into Chinese territory the more difficult will they find the maintenance of lines of communications with their base.

In Chengtu we are still far removed from the areas of greatest fear and suffering, but we did get a taste of what warfare means last Tuesday when seventeen or eighteen Japanese bombers visited Chengtu and bombed the two airfields. Eight of the planes flew nearly over our house, but I did not see them. It was at least half an hour after the first siren sounded and there seemed little indication of the presence of hostile planes, so I was at work in my study, but when the roar of the eight planes grew ever louder I dived for the basement without stopping to look. Margaret has written that she was at the Library when the planes came.

We have a very good place of refuge compared with most householders, as our house is one of the few which have a basement. Some say that any basement is not so good as a dugout because of the danger of being pinned under a falling building. Here at the University, however, we have difficulty in constructing good dugouts because we are on the Chengtu plain, and the water level (water "table") is only three or four feet below the surface of the ground except during three or four winter months.

All supplies of foreign origin are soaring in price, but so far as local products go we are much less affected. Chengtu has up to the present been a sort of oasis in the desert of terrible suffering. At first there were few indications that the country was at war; now conscription of middle class and especially coolie manpower is coming more and more into evidence.

Including the students and teachers of the various universities which have fled to us for refuge, we number certainly over two thousand. A census including workers and servants would probably show about three thousand on our campus.

If we are bombed (as hundreds of thousands have already been bombed), remember that it will probably be because Americans have furnished Japan with airplanes and with materials to manufacture the bombs.

Robert L. Simkin

December 10, 1938

Dear Alice and Fannie,

Last month I wrote at length about one air raid. There was another raid one week later--none since. Neither resulted in any considerable damage. In one case, however, several children were trampled to death at one city gate, such was the panic of the poor Chinese who thought they'd be safer outside the city and so rushed to the gate.

China is now hoping desperately that Britain will help her by giving credit, and America by an embargo on arms to Japan. Will she be disappointed?

I stopped at this point to help the cook weigh out salt and sugar for brine to cure hams, et cetera. We have over thirty pounds of meat--a ham, pork for bacon, beef for dried beef--that we are going to prepare and smoke. Be thankful you can go to the corner grocery and buy as needed! We also have a "load" of oranges (about 120 pounds) which I have directed the coolie to pack away in rice hulls. We buy from the country in quantity when cheap and pack and use as needed. Since the Nanking people have been here and enthused about our wonderful oranges (both the tight-skinned and the tangerines) I have realized as never before what a blessing it is to be living in this part of China where fruit is plentiful (though limited to certain varieties) and luscious.

...The other evening we had Dr. and Mrs. James Yen in as our guests along with some other friends. Dr. Yen is the well known "Jimmy Yen" of Din Hsien and Mass Education fame. They are now our neighbors and are grand folk. He is a graduate of Yale; his wife is half American and a charming lady.

Robert Writes:
December 29, 1938

Dear Brothers and Sisters,

We have had on the whole a pleasant Christmas notwithstanding a rather extensive robbery. Thieves succeeded in getting away with a large Peking rug, three large flower vases, a large fruit bowl, Damascus brass tray and bowls, and a brass fire set. Margaret's leather handbag with library keys, my old overcoat with all my keys and nearly all of our big tablecloths and best linen also are missing.

Fortunately two or three smaller tablecloths are left so we are not really so badly off as we might be, for we can still set a modest table.

We reported immediately to the police, both local and in the city, but they are not very efficient. The chief of police is reported to have said that he was not much interested in helping foreigners to recover stolen property. At any rate the police leave much to be desired.

The tightening of the blockade sends prices of some goods to double or triple their normal level, but essentials can mostly still be obtained. The war affects our life probably less than the Great War affected the lives of most Americans. We have fairly good health and are glad to be in a position to be of service to the many refugee students and teachers on our campus. We have approximately 1,300 university students, including the students of all our guest-refugee institutions. At present I am overseeing the building of two small houses for Ginling College men teachers and families. Miss Elsie Priest, treasurer of Nanking University, is carrying a large share of the work of our University Bursar's office, and we have three accountants one of whom is very efficient. The University has grown so rapidly that the accounting is a very different matter from what it was when I did the work alone. Several building projects are going forward, the biggest being a large hospital plant.

R.L.S.

Air Alarms and Air Raids
1939

January 10, 1939 *Chengtu, Szechwan*

Dear Alice and Fannie,

Robert has written of the robbery at Christmas time. Worse than the economic loss is being without things we have taken pleasure in gradually collecting. Compared with the people who had their homes destroyed and have lost *everything* it's of small consequence of course.

We realized afresh what a wonderful community we live in when on Christmas morning we opened our Christmas parcels and found a regular linen "shower." I think eight or ten people must have given us luncheon or tea sets--some of them lovelier than any we lost. Jane Dye gave me a dinner size damask tablecloth (one she had used but in excellent condition) so we had a cover for our Christmas dinner parties.

Liao Hung-Yin, who with Dorothy Behenna* was our house guest over Christmas, is a graduate of Oxford, a Friend, and a most interesting person.

January 17, 1939 *Chengtu, Szechwan*

Dear Alice and Fannie,

I suppose China's unpreparedness for modern warfare is nowhere more clearly shown than in the provision for care of the wounded. It would be near the truth to say there is no provision. Men have been left to die on the battlefields or crawl away as best they could. There just hasn't been the organization, equipment, skill or power to care for them in any sort of adequate way. It was out of this need that the

---

**Friends Service Council worker.*

organization, "The National Christian Service Council for Wounded Soldiers in Transit" arose.

War in China stands revealed for what it is. There is no glory in or about it!

We have just received an airmail letter from Arnold Vaught telling of the air raid in Chungking on Sunday. Sixty or eighty small bombs were dropped right within that crowded city and while the bombs were not big and heavy enough to cover large areas, they did a thorough job of destruction where they did hit. Nearby window glass (including that of at least two missionary houses) was shattered by the concussion. One report (not Arnold's letter, as he did not give figures) says there were between three hundred and four hundred persons killed. None of the bombs were dropped near anything that could be considered a military objective.

The air raid alarm was sounded here that day--the first warning comes as soon as planes are seen crossing the Szechwan border. I haven't a doubt the planes will continue to come here and will finally succeed in their errand of widespread death and destruction. This is the Japanese policy of terrorization. It is pretty awful to think that the planes, gasoline and bombs that do this evil come--some of them--from the United States!!!

P.S. We are entertaining a Hungarian lady just now. She is Jewish and married a German Christian. She was educated in Germany and is a bacteriologist by profession. Her husband is a doctor of medicine and both of them are in the employ of the Nationalist Government. She speaks of Chiang Kai-shek as "my chief." They head up some sort of institute formerly in Nanking now moved to Luchow (just above Chungking). She is a very generous soul and an interesting guest. She likes children and has absolutely won Margaret's heart. We all enjoy her.

As one would guess Hitler's name is anathema to her. She says you can't believe the things that are happening in Germany even if you see them with your own eyes!...

February 27, 1939 *Chengtu, Szechwan*

Dear Alice and Fannie and All,

We have been busy with Yearly Meeting, including a house full of foreign guests. After all of them had departed we got the regular guest room ready for a permanent guest, Grace Hickson. She is an Englishwoman, small and white-haired but straight as a ramrod. She is secretary to President Liu of Cheeloo University. Last year Peter* helped us to become Nanking University-minded; this year Miss Hickson is helping us become Cheeloo-minded. There will be many opportunities to make our home an "open house" for Cheeloo folk. They came in later and have not put up buildings (at least not yet) as Nanking has. Consequently the staff is more scattered and they need to be drawn into groups and have chances to get acquainted with other folk. Already we've had several of the Cheeloo girl students in for tea.

We've had the mildest winter I have known in China. Already the willow trees are turning green. My sweet peas are in bud.

Mercifully for us, we have as yet experienced no serious air raids. Should Sian fall and Ichang, one or both, the Japanese forces would then be near enough to cause us grave trouble. So far they are too distant to come to us easily. The two raids last October brought too little return to be profitable to them. Some people are getting a bit jittery and the high schools have been ordered by the government to seek other locations in the country. The Canadian School here on the campus, where Dorothy and Margaret are pupils, is making plans to vacate if necessary. But all this is merely in way of precaution so far! I have heard nothing about the University and all the guest universities moving.

The war for us is rather a paradox. Although there are many students on the campus who have lost homes and parents, or are in great anxiety about them, we of Szechwan have had too little actual experience of the war to know what it really means. Rather to us on this campus it has brought new life and vigor and all the fine enthusiasm of Chinese youth of united and "free" China....

May 9, 1939 *Chengtu, West China*

Dear Home Ones,

If you see in the papers that the Japanese have bombed Chengtu--it isn't true. No doubt they meant to do so, but they failed.

I was awake to hear the siren early Monday morning--I looked at my watch. It was 1:15 a.m. There was beautiful moonlight. Because Chungking had been badly bombed recently I thought it best to get up and partly dress. Robert did the same. I decided not to wake the children unless there was a second warning. However I got a sweater out for each and as I went to put them at the foot of their beds Dorothy

---

**Peter Bannon, an American in his mid-twenties, became like a grown son in the Simkin family.*

aroused and then Margaret. So I told them to get up too. They did not dress but put on dressing gowns and sweaters. Meanwhile Robert and our faithful *amah* were moving about opening casement windows (concussion breaks the glass worse if windows are closed). In the midst of all this the second alarm sounded and we went down to our basement where we found several neighbors already gathered, including one Chinese household who had previously arranged to come to our place in case of raids. We brought chairs down and made ourselves as comfortable as possible. Of course we were desperately sleepy but we waited and waited and still no "all clear." Finally we decided to go back to bed--it was nearly four o'clock. At 4:15 the "all clear" came. It seemed as if I had just dropped off to sleep when the warning came again. (I had not undressed but lay down as I was.) Out we all piled again and down to the basement. The second siren sounded at five and the "all clear" at six. However, I am not sure I was awake to hear it! I slept until nine, but Dorothy got up as usual and was off to school before I came to. Margaret also went off to school later.

What had happened was this. The Japanese planes tried to find Chengtu but failed. The airmen all say that Chengtu is very difficult to locate. Unlike a city at home there are no tall buildings. Many of the dark tile roofs are hidden among the trees. Apparently the planes were flying about for some time trying to locate our honorable city but failing to do so they finally returned to their base.

The experience was such as to make the apprehensive begin again to advocate the moving of schools. Scarcely before we know what is happening the Canadian School is being packed off to Omei. Robert and I first thought our girls should not join the others, but since practically all their schoolmates are going, we have relented. Plans for the summer holidays are still in flux. Robert thinks he ought not to leave for a holiday this year and I have not decided what is best.

Many people seem to think the school will not return to Chengtu for the duration of the war. Jenshow is the place chosen by the Canadians for the fall opening. We are not very happy about sending Dorothy and Margaret there. It may mean that we shall leave for furlough a year earlier if we cannot have proper school facilities for the children. However it is too early to say and many factors enter into the situation.

May 14, 1939

Dear Alice and Fannie,

A well-written account has come from Lois Vaught about Chungking's terrible air raids (mentioned in my last letter). Now

Chungking has had still another raid but, mercifully, it was not so serious as the previous ones. People in Chengtu are somewhat apprehensive but so far this city has escaped. The general opinion is that the campus, which is outside the city, is reasonably safe. It is true that we are near the radio station but certainly it is a much happier place to be than within a crowded city where the danger from fire is so great.

Dorothy and Margaret are leaving for school at Omei at the end of the week.

...I have been helping to organize sewing groups to make garments for war orphans. The University Women's Association has undertaken to supply 1,600 garments. We are enlisting the help of all the campus community. We have a "sewing center" where the women can come three times a week. In connection with the sewing we are going to start preparing "first aid" packets to have ready in case of raids....

May 23, 1939

Dear Alice and Fannie,

Fannie mentions the new highway from Burma to Chungking. Yes, it is all true and we know some people who have travelled over it. That was now several months ago and the road was not entirely completed but it was passable. We must take off our hats to China the way she has pushed her construction work ahead and has refused to give up because the usual avenues of transportation have been cut off.

Perhaps we shall be travelling over this new Burma Road ourselves before many months. We are becoming more and more inclined to the idea of taking furlough in early 1940 instead of 1941 as formerly planned. Robert is very tired and I think it would be a very good thing for him to quit for a while before he has to give up because he is too ill to carry on. You will find that he has aged considerably....

June 12, 1939

Dear Folks at Home,

By this time the world knows that Japanese planes bombed Chengtu last evening. The same modern science that carries news with lightning speed to the uttermost parts of the earth has also made possible the demoniacal business of last night. No! Such things couldn't happen except for the selfishness of men. Oh! Why does America continue to countenance this profit in slaughter?

For some reason we received no proper warning of the coming of the planes. The siren which warns this part of the city and countryside was out of commission. The Chinese planes had gone up while we were eating our supper. We saw students and others running out into the country among the rice fields, our Chinese student "daughter" came in and announced that the enemy planes were known to be in the province. (She and a friend had started out to get their evening meal but had been turned back by the police.) But still there was no siren and we assumed there was time aplenty. There was the noise of planes in the air--a great deal of activity--and Robert went out into our garden to watch them. From our upstairs veranda Grace Hickson and I watched the people scurrying along the paths between the rice fields. When we heard the loud roar of a large number of approaching planes we rushed down stairs and onto the lower porch overlooking the garden. Suddenly, quite unexpectedly, came the thundering, booming crash of bombs. Needless to say, we all made a dash for the basement. Of course by the time we were safely under cover the planes had gone well past! Our servants had proven wiser than ourselves for they were already inside with relatives and friends, some of whom had come out from the city. By the light of my flashlight I discovered that the family of Chinese neighbors and friends, who usually take shelter with us, also were already safe in the basement. The electric power had all been turned off before this and darkness soon fell outside as well.

When we dared to venture forth (no "all clear" sounded as the siren had failed) we found the sky over the city aglow with light. We knew terrible fires had been started. Soon, venturing further, we found that a dormitory some five hundred yards away from us and now occupied by the staff of National Central University (a refugee institution from Nanking) had been partially destroyed. A wall of a corner room had completely collapsed, tiles were broken, ceilings were down, windows blown out. Broken glass, splinters of wood, chunks of plaster, broken tile--all these damages made a number of the apartments utterly uninhabitable. Mercifully most of the folk in this building had taken shelter in the ditches outside and nobody was seriously injured. (This morning one of the families took refuge with us when the alarm of a preliminary warning spread through the town.)

At least four bombs fell on the campus. Two dropped very near the University Library but did not explode to do damage. Another fell on the river bank and wrecked residences and injured many people. The University property most affected in this case was the American Methodist although nearby Friends houses have broken glass and plaster down.

Of those we know, the Chen family suffered the most. Dr. Chen is president of Nanking University. Several members of his family were injured, none of them fatally we believe. One of our girl students in the Woman's College was killed and another seriously wounded. There were other fatalities--people on the road along the river just outside the University wall. Some shrapnel was thrown across the river and wounded people sitting in the tea shops there.

When we got to the Liljestrands*, whose house was badly damaged, we found Mrs. Liljestrand lying on a reclining chair under the trees. She had been wounded in the arm by flying glass. While we were still there some very badly wounded people were brought up from the river. These were laid down on the grass and Miss Sawyer, a nurse, and Dr. Liljestrand gave them first aid treatment while the rest of us held flashlights and helped as best we could. Robert brought some of the wounded up from the river on his back. I saw two or three terrible wound cases. They were taken away for further treatment after the first aid care. I wonder if they even survived the night.

Many of the students had had some training in carrying stretchers. We saw many wounded being carried to the dispensary by such students. There were sixty cases treated at our University dispensary and six brought in dead or dying. Of course the hospitals in the city had many cases too.

All this time we had been aware of the fire raging in the city set by incendiary bombs. The sky was aglow to the zenith.

I have been very glad the children were not here for this experience. Of course if they had been at home I should have stayed with them and not gone about the campus viewing the ruins.

A part of this letter has been written by candlelight as our electricity is still off. A main line is down, I believe....It is now Tuesday afternoon and the letter has been interrupted many times. Twice I have been to the Administration Building where some of us are doing sewing for the war orphans and rolling bandages.

June 28, 1939

Dear Alice and Fannie,

Fannie's letter of May 7 arrived yesterday. We were interested in the clippings re the early May raids in Chungking. R....M...., the United Press correspondent who wrote at least one of the articles, was with us for a few days before Christmas. He is young and out to make

---

**American Methodists.*

sensational news, and rather unprincipled I fear. He got himself in trouble with the national government by releasing statistics about the air force in China. In this case, he hasn't exaggerated the awfulness of the destruction and suffering, but he hasn't given the correct slant always. For example, he says, "Foreign residents had formed a committee to direct relief work but *planned to leave as soon as possible for the interior!*" That's rather amusing to us. The women and small children moved across the river to the bungalows on the hills; the men go back and forth. Arnold, for example, still spends a good part of his time in the city. All the older children able to leave home were here in the Canadian School anyway. I don't think the awfulness of the situation for the suffering populace *could* be exaggerated--people trapped and slowly roasted to death. But now people have learned how to act in raids and besides so many have evacuated that at the time of the last raid there were only ten casualties.

Chungking is on a point between two rivers--on a rocky hill. When incendiary bombs caused fires, people were caught with simply no way of escape. It was terrible. Chengtu is much better off in that respect. The people flee through the gates into the country round about on all sides. On the other hand, much better dugouts can be made in Chungking. There they have tunnelled into the rock under the city. Here on the Chengtu plain it is impossible to dig down many inches before striking water, especially at this time of year.

Dr. Chen Hsu Bin, a Friend and a friend of ours, was telling of his experience on the evening of the eleventh. He had medical work and a residence not very far from the South Gate of the city. Usually his family had not left their home when the air alarm sounded, but on this particular occasion they all went outside the city and took refuge among some graves (graves here are heaped up mounds). As soon as the raid was over they came back to their home. When they reached their gate they found house and everything absolutely gone! There was only a pile of debris left. Dr. Chen tells the story in his nice quiet way--no bitterness, no lamenting....

August 2, 1939 *Gao Si Ti, Szechwan*

Dear Folks at Home,

I am settled at this lovely little summer resort for a few weeks with the girls. I hadn't seen them since the middle of May, when they left for Omei.

This is a lovely spot and as much like Maine as any place I have seen in China. The bungalows are on a series of hills which are all a part of one range, with one or more houses on each hill. The hills are well wooded, chiefly pine, so that I am reminded of Maine, except that there should be a little blue lake tucked away in the midst of it all. We are able to get pure spring water which we can drink without boiling, a real treat. There are views of the plain in one direction and of other mountains in the other, but I miss the grandeur and the inspiration of the towering peaks we see from Behludin. This resort is only about 3,000 feet; Behludin is over a mile high.

Robert is not leaving Chengtu and we have a small cottage to ourselves. I think the experience of being away from home has done the girls good. (I am afraid the experience has to be repeated in the fall. The Canadian School is opening in Jenshow.) I keep turning over in my mind plans for the future. Shall we leave Dorothy at home? Would Margaret do better in school there? Dorothy thinks now that it is going to be hard to leave all her friends in the Canadian School. She doesn't realize that the longer she waits the harder it will be!

August 3, 1939 *Gao Si Ti, Szechwan*

We are now in a part of the province affected by the famine of two or more years ago. We have been much interested in four little Chinese children who are summering here. They were rescued by some Canadian missionaries along with some twenty others at the time of the famine. When Miss Rouse took these four over they were simply skin and bones and too weak to cry, move or show any interest in life. They were literally starved almost to death. Indeed it was a question with one or two of them if they could survive. It would do your heart good to see them now. They are as bonny children as one could wish to see, plump and well cared for. They are sweet and clean and happy. They live in the cottage on the next hill to ours and we often hear them singing their kindergarten songs in the evening at dusk. It is hard to believe that they were once the victims of famine--neglected, miserable, dirty, and sick.

In this peaceful spot we hear little about the war. I keep wondering these moonlight nights if Chengtu is being bombed. Robert has written nothing about it so far. It looks as if it were going to be a long struggle....

I wonder if we shall be in the United States a year from now. It depends upon whether there is a war in Europe and upon conditions in China.

Here is Robert's account of conditions in Chengtu.

August 31, 1939 *Chengtu, West China*

Dear Home Folks,

It is a little after two a.m. and we have just had our second air raid alarm and are waiting for the third before diving for the cellar. We have so good a cellar that several families of the neighbors come to us for shelter. We have not had a real raid since June 11, but in the daytime about ten days ago there was an alarm. A lot of planes apparently started for Chengtu but were prevented from coming by air defenses, so they circled toward the south and unloaded their bombs on Kiating. About one third of Kiating was destroyed by the fires started by the incendiary bombs and the loss of life was heavy. Margaret and the girls heard the planes pass Gao Si Ti where they were spending the summer and heard them return half an hour later, but could not see them although the sky was clear.

As soon as planes enter the province (which is very big) we have the preliminary alarm. This morning I dozed off after this one came. At the siren (four long blasts), we get up and dress and open windows (to prevent their being broken by the terrible suction), and often the third alarm (series of short blasts) never comes. It is often two hours before the "danger past" or "all clear" (continuous siren) sounds. Only when the danger is imminent does the electric company cut out all the lights. We still have lights on this occasion, so we know the danger is not imminent yet....

We have been expecting Margaret and the children home for several days, but a bridge out made it impossible for the Canadian truck to meet the party (of Canadians and our family) as originally arranged, so this has doubtless caused the delay. Perhaps they will come by ricksha and arrive today. Inasmuch as we have this air raid alarm perhaps it is just as well that they are not here yet.

I have not been away this summer because there are continually checks coming in to be signed by the University Bursar.

...At least three of the city gates are being pulled down to make wide exits, and big bricks have been used to form steps diagonally up and over the wall in many other places. For many years there had been no way of entering the city except by the four gates. About eighteen years ago the two "new" gates (New E and New W) were opened but this did not improve our situation. A little over a year ago a second south gate was opened and a permanent bridge was built which made access to the city much more convenient. Now to facilitate quick evacuation of the city a second bridge, a temporary wooden structure but well built on piles, has been constructed. They have not yet opened a highway through the wall but I think that will surely come before long, as the bridge is by far the more difficult matter. There goes the ALL CLEAR siren, so I will close the windows and go back to bed. Not yet three a.m.

August 31, 2:30 p.m.

Planes did not come last night (or this morning). We have not heard what city received their visit.

If war does not break out in Europe we shall probably leave for furlough in January or February and travel by the new auto road from Kunming (Yunnanfu) to Burma, thence via south Europe. If war does break out in Europe, probably the best course is to stay where we are.

Margaret and the children not yet in but expected at any time.

Robert L. Simkin

September 4, 1939 *Chengtu, West China*

Dear Alice and Fannie,

...We find Robert looking a bit rested but thinner than ever. The house is still in considerable confusion as the alterations begun during our absence are far from completion. The greatest delight is the new built-in bathtub made of cement with bits of stone pressed in. It has a stopper and the water runs away of itself--a great delight to Margaret especially.

We are all much under the gloom of the European war. Isn't it heartsickening? With English and Canadians all about us we feel it keenly. The war means we'll probably give up furlough for 1940. In fact Robert more or less talks as if it is given up indefinitely. He is afraid if we get home there'll be no chance to get back!

Even here the China-Japan war news has faded out of the picture. I wonder what the new pact between Germany and Russia is going to mean to the situation in the Far East.

October 4, 1939 *Chengtu, Szechwan*

Dear Alice and Fannie,

We have been busy with guests and the girls to get off to school. Yes, Margaret Ruth went to Jenshow too. This past week when we have been having moonlight nights we have had our sleep broken by air raid alarms. Sunday night we had the urgent alarm and had a real raid but no harm done in the city or this immediate vicinity. Monday night we were up again four hours from midnight on, but no visit that time. It is not so bad for us close to a more or less adequate shelter but think of the poor people who have to come out of the city night after night to seek a safer place in the country. The city gets the preliminary warning before we do and the folk start moving at once. Night after night I am awakened by the sound of voices of these folk streaming past our house. They come carrying their *pu kais* (bed comforters), babies in their arms, lugging a few most valuable possessions. Their voices sound remarkably cheerful, however. Sometimes I hear a name being called and I wonder if some child is lost or has strayed behind in the general confusion. For those of us who have huddled together in our basement shelter night after night there is a spirit of comraderie. The Chinese kiddies bury their heads in their parents' laps and a hush falls upon all of us--an eerie stillness over the whole countryside--as we listen to the drone of the planes coming nearer and nearer and wait in suspense for the heavy thud-thud of falling bombs.

...I think we must go home, starting early in 1941, war or no war in Europe. We shall greatly regret having to give up the European trip as we wanted it to be part of Dorothy's and Margaret's education but that is of small consequence as the world goes today. We sailed from Seattle seven years ago on the seventeenth of last month. It is time we had furlough.

October 6, 1939

We had another air raid warning on the night of the fourth, the seventh night in succession that we've had alarms. I got up and partly dressed, got candle and matches ready and then went back to bed. Robert got up and opened all the windows and remained up and worked at his desk.

The Generalissimo and Madame Chiang are in Chengtu just now. This may be one of the reasons for the frequent threatened air visits. When we don't get the bombs some other city usually does. Suifu, Luchow, Hochow, Suining have all had raids.

October 23, 1939

Another beautiful sunny day, but those fearing air raids during the light of the moon were glad to see the sky cloud over again this evening.

...As English secretary of the International Association of University Women I was invited to a tea to which "women leaders" were called together to meet Madame Chiang. I sat at the table a few feet from the First Lady. Unfortunately for me, her speech was in Chinese, and down river Chinese at that, so I got little of what she was saying.

...It seems to me she is looking better than she did in 1935. She was in poor health then to be sure. She (and the Generalissimo, too, I am told) looks very vigorous, alert and remarkably free from the marks of care. The Generalissimo has aged however.

China seems to be winning victories these days. Morale is certainly good and there is every purpose to fight it out to the finish.

November 19, 1939 *Chengtu, Szechwan*

Dear Alice and Fannie,

...This evening I have been reading a thrilling little booklet--*On Foot to Freedom*--an account of Newton Chiang's trip from Nanking to Chengtu. He and his wife and family of seven boys trekked much of the way by foot. The narrow escapes from bombing, the anxieties, the hardships, the courage and bravery of Newton and his family make a stirring story. He is still a young man--a quiet, most likeable chap. He is closely associated with Frank Price* and comes frequently to our house. It makes me feel again what a great privilege it is to be in China just now and have a chance to meet folk like Newton Chiang. Many of them live among us these days.

The action of the United States in recent weeks--the notification to Japan of the abrogation of the Trade Treaty in January and Ambassador Grew's speech in Tokyo--has brought new courage to China (as I suppose it has brought corresponding discouragement to Japan). China seems to be holding her own well. Transportation to the West (China) still remains a terrific problem but work is constantly being done to solve it. Prices continue to soar but we have plenty of good and delicious things to eat and are comfortable in every way.

If only Dorothy and Margaret could be with us we should be quite happy!

Robert's letters tell of *his* busy life.

November 20, 1939 *West China Union University*
Chengtu, West China

Dear Home Folks,

This year I am not teaching at all as my seven or eight treasureships keep me fairly busy.

Margaret and I have built a small brick two-family house on the Friends Campus which is now rented half to the Provincial Commissioner of Education and half to Mr. and Mrs. Andrew T. Roy,

---

**Dr. and Mrs. Frank Price of the Nanking Theological Seminary [Rural Evangelism Department] became a much loved part of our family.*

refugee teachers from Nanking. If and when the rentals received reimburse us for the expense of erection and maintenance of the house, the house will become the property of the Friends College (Friends Service Council) without cost to them. Expressed in U.S. currency at the then current exchange, the house did not cost us very much, and it has been very interesting to plan and erect it as we thought best.

The housing shortage is so acute that in July when the first project was practically finished, we enlarged our own house by enclosing part of the upstairs and downstairs verandas. Dr. and Mrs. Frank Price occupy these added accommodations and part of the other portion of the house. They have a secretary-helper, Andrew Ho, for whom we enlarged our servants quarters by the addition of a room and the fitting up of another room, so Mr. and Mrs. Ho and their baby girl live on the place in these rooms. Andrew is a student in Nanking University. Since March first we also have had Miss G.M. Hickson (from London) who is also a refugee--from Tsinan in Shantung. We therefore have four institutions represented on our own small compound....

November 30, 1939

Chengtu has been bombed five times, the worst being on June 11th about which Margaret has written you. The last time, on November 4th, fifty-four planes visited the airfield north of the city but did not do much damage. It is rumored that eleven of them failed to return to their base. Twenty-seven of them flew in plain sight from our campus, but having had some experience of counting (three times) the twenty-six planes of the June raid until bombs began to explode, this time I took no chances and dived for the basement without stopping to look-see. We could hear the popping of the machine guns as they fought in the air. Whenever we have an alarm, sometimes in the middle of the night, we have anywhere from twenty to forty persons coming to take refuge in our basement. We feel that Chinese resistance to Japan is stronger than it was a year ago. Of course one can never predict the future with certainty, but we cannot see how Japan can conquer China.

The University campus is a hive of activity. People from (1) National Central University (Government Nanking), (2) University of Nanking, (3) Ginling College (Nanking), (4) Cheeloo University (Tsinan) all maintain some of their organized work on our campus with their own registration and scholastic credits, besides many smaller parts of other institutions whose teachers or students count as W.C.U.U. teachers or students. West China Union University has 556 college students and the Union Middle School 396, besides the students of these guest institutions. In October the West China Union University, not counting building operations or the salaries of most of the foreign missionary staff, paid out over $119,000 (Chinese) on the regular budget. We are a big institution such as we hardly dreamed of in the early days. It is a great privilege to live and work in such an inspiring environment.

Robert L. Simkin

Furlough Once More 1940

February 19, 1940 *Chengtu, West China*

Dear Alice and Fannie,

I have heard of a better way to get letters in quickly. Mark them "Air Mail in China." This means that letters fly in from the coast and avoid the Yunnan railway which the Japanese are trying to disrupt. Already considerable damage has been done so that it will take some weeks to put it in condition again. It is a French railway but the bombing is being done on the Yunnan side, not the French Indo-China side.

Perhaps, though, this war will not last much longer. I suspect we are fed the most favorable news and disheartening things are kept from us here in the West but it certainly looks at present as if the Japanese are getting the worst of it. We are told of dissatisfaction and strife at home in Japan and spreading unrest; here, the Chinese forces, especially the guerrillas, are worrying the Japanese badly.

On Saturday night news came in of the recapture of Nanning by the Chinese. There were great celebrations in the city. We heard firecrackers being set off all night long.

Last night we were awakened by something quite different. At about 1:30 Liu Da Niang called us saying there was a big fire. Robert got up and hastily dressed in old clothes (fortunately). We could see a big blaze from our back windows. I went back to bed and slept until some time between five and six when Robert called to me to come and help him. He was dripping wet, soaked to the skin, and cold of course. He bathed and put on warm dry things. While I had been sleeping *he* had been helping to fight the fire in the Dental Building. He had cut both wrists and one hand quite a bit, nothing serious, but he decided it was best to get a doctor to dress the wounds. He finally got home in time for breakfast. Tonight he has gone to bed early feeling rather hoarse and with a very sore right hand.

The fire is the biggest we've ever had on the campus and is a serious loss to the Dental people and the Pathology Department. All the stock for both West China Union University and National Central Dental Clinics is gone. Think of the expense and the difficulty of replacing it. Results of thirty years of research work on the part of one doctor, at least, lost, too!

...We have been thinking a bit about furlough plans. If the European war continues making it impossible for us to go home by Europe we shall probably leave here about April 1941, getting out of China as best we can, cross the Pacific, visit California relatives, buy a car, and travel leisurely across the United States, helping the girls to learn all the U.S. geography they can.

Robert writes about crops and soaring prices.

April 3, 1940 *Chengtu*

Dear Folks at Portland
and
Dear Brother Alfred,

It has been very cold the past week with frequent rains which have broken the dry weather and have saved a good part of the spring crop. Here on the Chengtu plain, where we have irrigation, we are better off than those in the hills where water cannot be turned on at will. About two weeks ago there was a food riot in Chengtu. The rice crop last summer was good, and we had fine weather for the harvest, so there is really no scarcity of food in this part of China. Some of the less important banks bought up large quantities of rice and stored it in granaries in an attempt to corner the market. Prices soared. The government made plans to prevent these banks from profiteering, so the banks raised the price quickly, hoping to make their profits before the government could curb their activities. At this point the people took a hand, breaking in the windows and doors of the granaries and helping themselves. The government knew that the profiteering banks had no reason on their side, so the people were permitted to work their will with little interference.

Prices in general are soaring, many things costing twice or three times what they did three years ago. Yesterday I paid for nails four dollars per catty (Chinese currency). Three years ago I could have bought these nails for about thirty cents a catty. However one gold dollar which three years ago exchanged for N.C. $3.33 now exchanges for about nineteen dollars, so we are better off than the Chinese who have no U.S.A. gold income....

Robert L. Simkin

April 19, 1940 *Chengtu, West China*

Dear Friends,

Sometimes life seems to be very full of committees and appointments. But there are opportunities of another sort too, and just living one's best each day is what counts after all. (As an example of the "other sort" of opportunities--it has fallen upon me to present the Quaker point of view at one of a series of our community mid-week meetings entitled "My Theology.")

On Saturday next, the new University Student Center is to be formally opened. This building is in part a gift from student-members of the Student Christian Movement in other parts of the world. Thus young men and women in West China are linked with their fellow students around the globe.

The news of the spread of bloodshed and horror in Europe shocks and sobers us. Here in China the undeclared war drags on toward the fourth year. There is much talk in Japan of the establishment of a "new order in Asia" and people there are rallied by the call of a "holy" mission. (To what lengths militarists will go to delude those whose support they demand!) But we fail to find anything *holy* in cruel and destructive air raids, or in the insidious demoralization of men and women through the spread of the drug habit and prostitution.

April 21, 1940

Yesterday afternoon I saw an excellent indoor demonstration given by the physical education department at Ginling College. This included a posture contest, different types of rhythmic work, fencing, Chinese boxing, apparatus work, fundamental gymnastics (done to rhythm), et cetera. Perhaps these girls of Ginling College are hardly typical, as yet, of Chinese young women, but certainly they are an indication of the direction modern Chinese youth are taking. I thought to myself as I watched them, "There is abundant hope for China in such as these." The husky young things were abounding in life and spirit and energy. It was a joy to see their dexterity and stamina; their poise and grace.

April 27, 1940

Dear Alice and Fannie,

Yesterday, the three famous Soong sisters--Madame Chiang

Kai-shek, Madame Sun Yat-Sen, and Madame Kung--were at the University and visited our West China Union University Museum (which is said by those who know to have some very fine things in it, including porcelains and jades). They also visited the University of Nanking citrus fruit projects exhibit and saw the herd of blooded cattle owned by Madame Chiang. They then attended a tea in the Administration Building, where we had the opportunity to shake hands with the famous ladies. Madame Sun has a very sad but sweet face. She wears her hair dressed very severely. The two younger sisters were rather more fashionably dressed, but all wore simple Chinese gowns of black....

P.S. We've had two air raid alarms this week. On Monday evening, we had the table all set and everything ready for a dinner party of ten. The early alarms came before the guests left home and the four "specials" couldn't get here at all. Such a nuisance with complete dinner ready from tomato cocktail to dessert. The second alarm came in the middle of the night--Wednesday, or was it Thursday morning. I was awakened at 12:20 and got back to bed at 2:20. Neither time did the Japanese planes get to Chengtu. Suifu and outskirts of Chungking were bombed but no great damage.

June 12, 1940

Dear Ones at Home,

Two more days and we expect the children home. The full moon is coming on and I am afraid we may be in for some bombings. Chungking has been getting some bad ones which have continued with equal fury throughout this week. We get the alarms here but we carry on much as usual. On the second warning we begin to "sit up and take notice." On the third, or emergency alarm, we flee to cover. However banks and shops close in the city on the *first* warning so business is very much disrupted.

Robert and I went shopping last evening in search of an electric iron, which we did not find. It is interesting to see how the shopkeepers keep in readiness and poised for flight. Most shops have large two-wheeled push carts and in these they store their bundles of goods. When the alarm comes, bang-bang up go the shutters (series of upright boards) across the shop front, and the proprietor trundles his cart with its goods out into the country to a supposed place of safety. The people, I am told, are so well trained now that if the "all clear" sounds while the procession is on the march, the carts are simply turned without any stop, and the trek back to the city begins in reverse.

All this is child's play compared to what is going on in Europe. When my heart leaps to my throat at the dread sound of the roaring planes, I think of the now large proportion of the earth's inhabitants who must have a similar or worse reaction to such a sound.

The Dyes are going home to the U.S.A. for furlough at the end of this month. I wish we were going too! Perhaps the world won't be in a worse state next spring--I certainly hope not.

July 14, 1940 *Behludin*

Dear Alice and Fannie,

The children came home on June fourteenth and we came up here to the mountain on the twenty-eighth.

Chungking, as I wrote you, was having daily air raids (weather permitting) by the middle of June, resulting in terrific destruction of property, but not such a great toll of life because of the rock shelters they are able to build there. Arnold and Lois' house (Friends property in the city) was completely gone after one raid. Only a big crater and splinters left....What I began to say was that some people feared the Japanese would go for Chengtu next and we wondered how we would get along after keeping the children in Jenshow all year and then bringing them home at the most dangerous time. However, although we had plenty of first alarms, we didn't get a single emergency. And now we are out of all that for a time at least.

...The news from Europe has been dreadful. With so many friends and acquaintances and ties with England here, it comes close to us. It has been hard to keep it all from our minds. I am afraid England and all of Europe are in for a bad time.

Japan thought she would take advantage of the critical situation in Europe to push her aggression in Asia. It looked for a time as if Hongkong would go and she demanded that England close the Burma Road and she certainly has designs on French Indo-China! It has looked as if our communications with the outside world would be cut off and our chances of ever getting anything in seemed slimmer and slimmer. However, England has made a firm stand and perhaps entered into some agreement with the United States (?) and the situation at the moment is much less tense....

July 28, 1940 *"Rockynotch," Behludin, Szechwan*

Dear Everybody,

We have had little of interest happen here except that thirty-four Japanese planes went right over us, or close to us, on Wednesday last.

They came from the northwest--Sian--and passed us in a thick mist so that I could not see them, though other people on the mountain saw and counted the silver monsters. We felt sure they were headed for Chengtu but we had to wait for two days before mail could get through. Sure enough, there was a raid on Chengtu city--varying reports say eleven to seventeen fires were started. Bombs were incendiary and very small demolition ones. The Baptist property was damaged. No other mission property suffered.

Twice this spring and summer Chengtu has been saved by a heavy storm coming up and driving the enemy planes away. Just a few days ago this happened. This time Tungchwan, where we held our Yearly Meeting, suffered instead. Our gain was their loss. Rose Tebbutt's* house was reduced to a heap of debris--only the laundry and kitchen continuing to stand. Rose herself was away in the country at the time...

August 25, 1940 *Behludin, Szechwan*

Dear Alice and Fannie,

...We have just heard that Lewis Walmsley, principal of the Canadian School, has granted permission for the opening of a small branch school at Chengtu this coming school year. There will be ten or a dozen children who will attend. We are now planning to keep Margaret at home and let her go to this school. Dorothy enters high school this year and will need to go to Jenshow. She wants to be with her own crowd--I suppose this is a healthy, normal reaction.

The cost of living is mounting rapidly, due partly to the depreciation of Chinese currency and partly to general war conditions. We find the Canadian School a big expense as their charges are in gold and at the present rate of exchange it takes approximately $20 in Chinese money to make one dollar in gold. In pre-war times, exchange was one to three. To give some idea of mounting prices--in late June I bought one pound of baking powder at $11.20 and was very thankful to be able to get it in Chengtu at all, while in early August a pound cost $13.20

...Chungking has been having terrible bombings, with scarcely a building in the city undamaged. Chengtu, so far, has come off easily. Will America's embargo on scrap iron, oil, and war materials take effect in time to save us?

Do you see anything of refugee English children or know of people who have received any?

**A British Quaker worker.*

September 12, 1940 *Chengtu, West China*

Dear Alice and Fannie,

...We had an interesting visit yesterday with Mr. Sollenberger, a young college chap, who has been doing relief work in China the past two years. He is a member of the United Brethren Church. He and another young fellow by the name of Whitaker have been linked with the Friends Center in Shanghai. That is, their support has come from their own constituency, but they have had direction and a spiritual linking with the Center--just as people of other denominations have worked with Friends in Spain and elsewhere. These two young fellows have been working recently in Shensi moving back and forth through Japanese occupied territory, working with the Red Eighth Route Army and in the national government controlled area. They have helped get food to refugees in enemy territory, crossing and recrossing the Japanese lines many times, always at night. The guerrillas know the small paths and would lead them around the sentries but even so they were sometimes shot at.

One night they were travelling on a military freight car with some soldiers. An officer was taken ill with chills and since he had no covers these lads loaned him their heavy steamer rugs. Before the journey was over, fourteen in the car came down with typhus fever, among them these two boys. They were in a Chinese inn two weeks before either a nurse or a doctor came, and were cared for only by a little soldier boy who brought them food and water (which they were too sick to take). Later young Whitaker took ill with amoebic dysentery and just recently with typhoid. Mr. Sollenberger said as he told the story, "With the history of typhus we shouldn't have tried to go into Shensi this last time, but we couldn't foresee what it would mean." He brought Whitaker here to Chengtu terribly ill and he was put in the hospital, but he gradually failed and died on the ninth of September. He was buried Tuesday in the little foreign cemetery south of the campus. Margaret went out with me and a neighbor to arrange flowers on the grave. Robert helped with the burial arrangements. Both boys are sons of missionary parents, the Whitakers living in Shantung now.

October 9, 1940

Dear Alice and Fannie,

...Tonight's paper says, "Washington State Department advises all Americans in Far East return to America immediately!" It certainly sounds as if trouble were brewing. I shouldn't like to get caught here after the long term we have already put in; on the other hand, I can't quite face picking up and getting out in a hurry.

We had two successive days of air raids last week. The first was pretty bad with several hundred casualties. The hospital in the city was filled with the wounded, as was a nearby church. I am glad that Margaret has stood up very well under such business so far. She takes it matter-of-factly as we try to do. Of course she has not seen the horror of it yet as no bombs have fallen near. I hope she may be spared that....

October 20, 1940 *Chengtu, West China*

Dear Ones at Home,

We are coming home! You have perhaps seen in the papers that the State Department has advised Americans to leave the Far East. I am afraid that this means the United States is going to get into the conflict. Probably West China will not be seriously affected, but since our furlough is already more than due, we have decided that we should try to get out while we can. Perhaps by the time we can get ready to leave it will be too late, but we hope not.

As we can, we are dropping our responsibilities here and turning work over to others. Next month (November) we shall begin in earnest to sort and put things away, pack a few necessities and turn over the house to Miss Hickson. By early December, or earlier, we hope to be off, going by truck probably to Chungking, and then flying to Hongkong, *if* we can get passage. Then, *if* we can get an early sailing we *might* be in California in time to spend Christmas with Phil and Edith. Here's hoping!

We do not plan to delay long in California. We shall need to get on east where we can get the girls settled in school. We have sent a clipper letter to the Ventnor, New Jersey, Houses of Fellowship* asking for an apartment for the remainder of the school year, from January to June. If we are able to secure an apartment there we shall have the girls go to school in Atlantic City, either public schools or the Friends private school, and so get what they can out of the school year.

We shall be able to take out very little. One is allowed only a little hand baggage on the plane. But most families who have gone out lately have travelled by plane and consequently have taken little. We shall be no worse off than others.

**Completely furnished apartments rent free for use of missionary families at home on furlough.*

You will understand that this decision to leave this early has been arrived at very recently and the plan I have outlined we may not be able to carry out. Whether we can get plane passage or an early sailing are both a question.

December 1, 1940 *Kowloon [Hongkong], China*

Dear Phil and Edith,

We have arrived this far on our journey home and expect to sail on December 5. This will bring us to San Francisco on the 25th, so we shall be too late to spend Christmas with you. We expect to go first to Robert's brother Henry at Paradise. We hope to be with you for New Year's.

We travelled by truck from Chengtu to Chungking and had a good trip on the whole. The weather was fine and since I was able to ride in the cab with the driver I was not too uncomfortable. Dorothy has been running a fever for some days and it was a bit rough on her. We have since become pretty well convinced the cause is an attack of malaria. She has been taking quinine and is improving.

We flew from Chungking to Hongkong on Thanksgiving Day, starting at 3:15 p.m. After the rise, when we could see the terraced fields and the Yangtze below us, we remained in the clouds almost the entire five-hour flight. Since we were flying the latter part of the trip above "occupied" territory we had no lights whatever in the plane. There was nothing to do but lie back and sleep, which we all did. Later on, the stars came out and still later we saw lights twinkling below. The picture of Hongkong and the bay was enchanting. Strings, festoons, and clusters of brilliant lights, many of them colored, sparkled and glistened. It was the brightness and gaity of many Christmas trees rolled into one. Our great silver bird circled and circled about, coming down lower and lower while we exclaimed in rapture at all the loveliness lying below us.

Hongkong is a delight to us after our eight years in West China--the shops, the smooth, clean wide streets, the bright lights, the bay and the ships. Margaret fairly dances with joy.

We had expected to sail on the twenty-ninth on the *Empress of Russia* but that has been taken over by the admiralty and all sailings on it cancelled. There is nothing for us but third class on the *President Cleveland*, but we think we can manage it after our pioneer training in Szechwan.

It will be so good to see you all. I wish it could be at Christmas, but at least we hope we'll be with you to say "Happy New Year!"

BRIEF INTERLUDE

Furlough time was all too brief. After short visits with relatives in California we travelled across the United States by Greyhound bus to Ventnor, New Jersey, where we were welcomed to the Houses of Fellowship. Ventnor adjoins Atlantic City and its popular boardwalk continues along the Ventnor beach. The sea and sand were a great delight. We were near enough to Philadelphia for Robert to renew old contacts.

With the close of the children's schools we were off to Maine in our own car. It was a joy to see the family again and to share with them, as they joined us by twos or more, the fun of a vacation on the wooded shore of a lovely little lake.

But the situation in the Far East was ominous! Robert felt he must return to China as soon as possible. Should I go too, or remain in the U.S.A. with the children? I felt as if I were being torn in two. If I went back to China how would the girls be cared for? To what schools should they go? It was heartbreaking to leave the children (Dorothy, fifteen and one-half, at Oakwood School; Margaret, twelve and one-half, living with Alice and Calvin Miller and attending a nearby public school), but the final decision was that I should go with Robert. Then came the problem of getting passport provision and steamer reservations.

We saw Dorothy somewhat settled at Oakwood and went on in our car to Richmond, Indiana, where we finally received a passport. As we travelled westward we accepted and filled speaking engagements (about China, of course!). At Wichita, Kansas, headlines were discouraging: "Order U.S. ships off Pacific." (Really it should have read--"Navy ordered U.S. merchant ships in Asiatic waters to put into friendly ports.") It looked as if our sailing would likely be cancelled. However we continued toward California planning to proceed as the way opened (or closed!).

...Problems continued. A telegram on November 3 informed us of British visa difficulties in Hongkong and in securing Penang landing permits. (We had planned to take our car with us and from Penang transfer to a coastwise vessel to Rangoon and then it was to be "over the Burma Road)." Robert refused to be discouraged; he would go to see the British consul in San Francisco and find some way out. We were never quite certain I would be permitted to sail (I half-hoped I'd be forced to remain in the U.S.A with the children) but at the very end both of us were assured passage.

The Simkins travelled on the Yangtze River in boats similiar to these. The boat underway is carrying a sedan chair on its bamboo roof.

四川書简

Wartime Adventures 1941 – 1944

There are ways,
but the Way is uncharted.

Tao Te Ching

A Strange Voyage
1941 & 1942

November 9, 1941 *On Board* S.S. President Grant
San Francisco, Cal.

Dear Ones,

...We are sailing shortly. It is a beautiful day and the harbor should be lovely as we go out the Golden Gate at five p.m.

Our baggage and Pontiac are aboard. Robert and I are in different cabins but they have a full ship and we can't complain.

We have been staying with the James family in Berkeley--Philadelphia Friends. Everybody has been kind and helpful, entertaining us at dinner, advising about securing supplies, bringing us to the dock today.

We have been very busy with last-minute errands--shopping, visas, arrangements for shipping the car. However, I have been thankful to be busy and occupied. This going is not easy.

The way has opened for us as difficulty after difficulty has arisen and then been overcome and I take this to mean that God wants us to go forward.

Perhaps we shall not be permitted to land at Burma--that is the next hurdle. We had to cable ahead for a permit and we shall not know the answer until we get to Manila. Authorities in Burma are not likely to grant us permission to travel in that country if war dangers loom large. We shall be guided by their decision....

December 13, 1941 *Balikpapan, Dutch East Borneo*
On Board ******

Dear Carl and Hazel,

I haven't the faintest idea when or where or how I am to post this after I have it written, but having sat here in this little harbor for five days and knowing still no more of the future than a mere zero it seems best to write some letters and have them ready for posting if that time ever does arrive. To be sure, it is difficult to write of plans when there are none, but perhaps it is just as well we don't know what is ahead....

I would feel greatly relieved if I knew the folks in Portland had received, or would receive shortly, my air mail letter posted in Manila which I asked them to share with you. At Manila we transferred from the *President Grant* to the ***** * and moved on our way Friday, December 5th. Consequently we were away from Manila before the storm broke.** I fear the uncertainty re our whereabouts will prove pretty hard on Dorothy and Margaret. We are, as a matter of fact, quite safe to date. If they only knew it! If possible, I hope the girls will have a sense of security somehow.

Of course I faced the possibility of all this happening before I left, but it is always natural to hope for the best and believe that the evil will not after all fall. Certainly, although we had seen what did happen *might happen*, we had not expected it quite so soon....

Sunday, December 14, 1941

Some of the crew and a number of the special passengers have gone out in small boats to get sand. They will put sand bags around some of the most vulnerable parts of the ship. The other day they painted the boat a battle-ship gray. They also mounted a "Quaker gun"! Perhaps after these preparations are completed we may start forth again....

December 19, 1941 *At Sea*

Dear Margaret,

We have been on board a ship now for nearly six weeks. Some of the time, to be sure, we have not been travelling but just now we are steaming along at a good rate through quiet inland seas toward Java. Tomorrow we should be at Soerabaja. Try to find it on your map.

I have been thinking a great deal about you at this Christmas time although it does not seem a bit like Christmas here because it is so hot.

It has helped a bit to have some children come aboard at Balikpapan. They are Dutch boys and girls and although I can't understand a word they say they dress, look and act just like boys and girls I have known before. The little girls came with dolls in their arms, dolls like yours.

There is one darling, fat, black-eyed Malay baby aboard too. I am

---

**Deletion by censor.*

***Japanese attack on Pearl Harbor.*

sure you would love him. His mother sits on the floor with him--I suspect they sleep on the floor too.

It seems as if the stars and planets in these southern skies shine brighter than elsewhere. Venus is so brilliant; it is a great ball of light and throws a pathway of silver across the water. I have tried to find the Southern Cross but have not discovered it yet.

I hope you are happy and well and are bringing happiness to others as you can do to Dad and me. We love you such heaps.

December 19, 1941 *****

Dear Folks at Home,

...Manila was bustling with life. The streets were crowded. Manila has a decided foreign flavor that Honolulu does not. Honolulu is a modern American city in a tropical setting. Manila has fine buildings of modern design also, but it has, too, buildings of Spanish type architecture. Then everywhere on the streets are the two-wheeled Filipino carriages drawn by small horses. They are picturesque but for comfort and speed I chose the taxis which are plentiful and cheap. We saw women wearing the native Filipino costume but that is by no means universal.

When we left Manila we were supposedly starting off for ***** but events of December 7th have changed that. At least the boat is taking a ***** route. We have been quite safe and continue well....

Our terrible anxiety concerns the Sewells.* We left Hilda and the children in Manila; Bill was awaiting them in Hongkong. We have no way of knowing what has happened to them all.

Until day before yesterday there were only two other women passengers on this boat besides myself. Now we have some fifty Dutch women and children evacuees with us.**

December 26, 1941 *Soerabaja, Java*

Dear Ones at Home,

...Christmas would have been rather desolate but for one special child with us. A fine young couple has a boy of twenty-one months.

**Because of war conditions, Hilda Sewell and children had been advised not to return to China with William Sewell. Instead, they had lived in Whittier, California, awaiting more auspicious times. Then they took passage on the same President Line ship in Los Angeles which we later boarded in San Francisco.*

***They disembarked at Soerabaja.*

They are Swiss, but the young man was born and reared in the Philippines. The pretty young mother told me that she came from Switzerland in 1937 to marry. She hasn't been home since. She speaks English very well but with an attractive accent. Her husband speaks as well as we do (and French, German, Spanish and Russian as well). Well, the little boy is a dear and everybody on board loves him. *He* was the excuse for the little Christmas tree which the bunch of "boys"* on board procured and decorated. They also bought several toys to put around the tree. Yesterday before breakfast we had the fun of watching the little fellow find and undo his presents....At 9:30 Robert led a short devotional service (this at the request of one of the "boys") and that was certainly worthwhile.

But the best part was opening Margaret Ruth's packages and Edith's which we had kept all this while. We thought of you all and tried to picture what you were doing. With us it was Christmas morning; with you it was Christmas Eve. One of the gentlemen passengers (a Standard Oil man) had kindly given me some orchids as a Christmas remembrance and I wore some all day. I think he felt sorry for me as I had stood forlornly leaning on the deck rail. In the evening there were some rather blatant Christmas carols over the loud speaker, records put on by the radio man. In fact, these have been played several evenings.

The first night they put on these carol records I felt rather weepy but a day on shore (the twenty-fourth) helped a good deal. It made me feel more normal seeing the rows of pretty little houses each in its own tiny yard. Life on shipboard is so artificial--a steady diet of it for weeks on end is too much!...

...The trip to the town is very hot. We have to cross the harbor in the ship's open launch. After the dock there is a bit of a walk in the hot sun to the street car line. The town is several miles in from the shore....

We do not know how much longer we shall stay here. There are some indications that the ship may be moving on soon....

December 29, 1941

On Saturday I again took the launch on one of its trips ashore and had a cool ride on the car to the town. How pleasant the trees and plots of green grass looked. Coming "home" at about five o'clock everybody seemed to be out, *amahs* with their fair-haired Dutch charges, big boys

---

**Men being sent by U.S. government to advise and assist in Burma Road transportation.*

and girls playing, women strolling about, and all the folk coming home from work. I thought what a pleasant, comfortable sight and how interesting foreign countries and people are (for there were plenty of dark-skinned Malays about in their native costumes, and two-wheeled carts drawn by small horses, similar to those in Manila, and great bullock carts with high, high wheels). How remote war seemed from that bustling, happy town. It was unthinkable that airplanes could come and make desolation of such a comfortable spot. And yet war is *not* remote. Already the people are building and have built air raid shelters. Every night they, and we on this ship, have a complete black-out. These days there isn't security anywhere, except what security we can build in our hearts!...

Robert writes:

December 29, 1941

Dear Folks,

About twenty-five people have come aboard and we may soon be moving again. We are glad. We do not yet know to what port we shall go, as the officers of the ship are not permitted to tell us. They themselves probably do not know more than one port ahead. We think, however, that we may find ourselves in Columbo or some port in India. If conditions at the port where we first expected to disembark are too serious we may stay in India for some months or for the duration.

On December 20 we sent the following cable: AMERICAN FRIEND RICHMOND INDIANA SAFE INFORM FAMILIES SIMKINS. We hope you received it.

Robert

A number of the passengers who have just come aboard are missionaries, some of them due eventually for India, and some from Sumatra going to America. We welcome their company. We have had no missionary companions since we left Manila.

Robert

January 4, 1942 *At Sea*

Dear Family,

...The last day of the old year was rainy, one of the few continuously rainy days I remember at sea at any time. However, that evening just before the sun sank it cleared and we had one of the most gorgeous sunsets that I have ever seen. We were completely encircled by tinted skies and the west was one blaze of glory. The ocean, reflecting the rose colors, was turned a rich violet. We have had several very beautiful sunsets in this section of the globe, but that night was a masterpiece. It made me think of a sunset we saw once in the lower Yangtze where the river is wide and is dotted with islands. Just now as I write I discover that the ocean, which has been almost as smooth as glass all day, is reflecting the sunset tints in an unusually lovely way. It is an iridescent ocean with streaks of rose and pale green and mauve and turquoise shifting and moving across it.

Later

I went out on deck and leaned on the rail for a long time watching the sky, the clouds and the glassy sea take on different colors. My dears, it was exquisitely lovely! A flying fish came out of that smooth surface, a circle of showering drops falling behind it, and skimmed over the water for an amazingly long distance before disappearing again.

...We are enjoying the India folk aboard very much. I think some of these new India friends will be of help to us when we disembark.

P.S. Eight weeks ago today we left the U.S.A. Seven weeks have passed since we have had any home letters. It seems seven months.

January 13, 1942 *Nearing Calcutta*

Dear Family,

...We arrived at Colombo on January eighth, expecting to disembark there. That morning we had everything packed, even to toothbrushes, ready to leave the boat. We had become quite enthused with the idea of driving our car up through India, visiting Madura, Madras and so on. To be sure we had no visa for India and there might be difficulty in getting licenses to drive, etc., but we were ready to try it. So as soon as we had passed inspection and the captain had given passengers permission to go ashore we boarded the tender and went in to the dock. We were instructed to be sure to go to the American Consul's at four o'clock to learn when the boat was to sail (she might be going within a few hours) and if we were getting the car off and all the baggage there were many preliminary arrangements to be made. First, we visited the shipping company to see the possibility of taking a steamer at Madras or beyond for Rangoon. Then Robert went to the Automobile Association to get information. But at the consul's we learned that our ship, this ship, was to go to Calcutta and not Bombay as we had expected. Of course the only sensible thing to do was to stay right on board!

By eleven a.m. on the ninth we were on the way again. We took the long way round Ceylon. That evening it was pleasant watching the lights along the shore. At least the smaller places do not have black-outs. Since then we have seen nothing on land. On Saturday we saw whales in the distance spouting. I fancy we have at times taken a rather zig-zag course....

...As soon as we reach Calcutta* we plan to see if it is possible to get a steamer to Rangoon, in which case we will transfer our things and go on as soon as possible. Rangoon has air raids, we know, but we have known air raids before. On the whole it seems best to get on to our home as soon as possible. India may be in for it later. Our University appears as safe a place as any! Our ship companions headed for the Adoniram Judson country have offered to help us all they can. We are really fortunate to have travelled with them and to know them pretty well now.

We think of you all and wonder how you are. No letters for eight weeks! I wonder if ours are getting through.

Robert's and my joint account of our next adventure follows.

February 3, 1942 *Municipal Hospital*
Bassein, Burma

Dear Friends,

You perhaps know that in making our decision to return to China we have consciously faced the possibility that we might lose our possessions and even our lives. We were therefore not wholly unprepared for what has actually happened.

We have written of our circuitous route, now seventy-seven days from San Francisco to Burma. On arrival at Madras in India we found a small steamer leaving the next day for Rangoon. We weighed carefully the question whether we should remain in India or should proceed on our way, and decided upon the latter. Besides ourselves there were only two cabin passengers, both Indians, Mrs. Roberts and Dr. Raja, a retired physician. Our cabin, possibly sixteen feet above the water, was on the port side and opened directly to the deck.

Just at dawn on January 22, when only 130 miles from Rangoon, we were awakened by a terrific crash, the explosion of a shell from a submarine. Then followed crash after crash, sixteen or seventeen, as fast as the gunner could load and fire the shells. (Actually, though we did not then know it, our own danger was less because most of the firing was from the starboard side.) In the semi-darkness we groped for

---

**We did not see Calcutta as expected. After anchoring for the night in the Hooghly River, a branch of the Ganges, the ship turned back to sea and followed a southerly course to Madras.*

and put on our clothes, and our lifebelts, and with Mrs. Roberts, who in her fright had rushed to our cabin, we crouched for protection under the window until we heard the order, ''Abandon ship!''

The nearest lifeboat had been lowered, but there was no ladder, and to jump the fourteen or fifteen feet didn't seem attractive. Soon another boat was lowered, but as Margaret climbed down, the rope ladder turned over and she fell into the water.

Robert

When the order came to abandon ship and we went out on the tiny deck I saw the submarine coming around the bow. Vaguely I realized that this was the craft which had been shelling us. It didn't occur to me just then to be afraid that it would do *more* damage. I was too occupied with the dread of going down that swinging rope ladder! Often I had wondered how I'd manage to negotiate such a thing--no time to wonder now. Robert urged me on. Over the rail I *had* to go. Clinging with my hands and feeling for a foothold, I got down nearly to water level when the awkward ladder turned over. Feeling I could cope with it no longer and hoping that I'd land in the lifeboat below I dropped off and fell into the water. The plunge, though a surprise, was not too unpleasant for the water was comfortably warm and I immediately bobbed up again to the surface. I managed to get hold of the rope attached to the sides of the lifeboat and there I clung. Looking up I saw Robert following Mrs. Roberts down the ladder. I heard his exclamation of surprise when he reached the boat and found I was not there. He tried to pull me in, but could not manage it alone.

Margaret

She was in danger of being crushed between the lifeboat and the steamer. As I struggled to help her, the submarine which had now come around to our side fired a shell into the steamer from a distance of about 100 yards. We were splattered with burning fragments. The furled sail and equipment in the end of the lifeboat were set afire.

Robert

I am not clear as to just what happened while I remained in the water. Was I struck on the head and dazed? Once I looked up and to my horror saw the whole end of the lifeboat ablaze. I discovered that my left ring finger was nearly cut through and as Robert bent over me I saw blood trickling down his face. He had been wounded in the back also, but not seriously, he assured me. Finally the captain and the chief engineer (Englishmen) came down the ladder and I soon felt several pairs of strong arms tugging me aboard. By this time the fire had been put out, but a new danger threatened. Corks removed from the bottom of the boat to drain rainwater had not been replaced, and the openings admitted so much seawater that we were swamped. Under other circumstances I should have been terrified in a sinking boat, but now I could sit huddled on the narrow seat and calmly watch the men dip water with the engineer's tin hat and R's sun helmet, and the chief engineer, almost to his hips in red, blood-stained water, grope for the plugs and finally cork the holes just as the waves washed over the sides.

Margaret

We rescued five men clinging to a submerged lifeboat nearby. My briefcase, containing watch, fountain pen, passport, account book, credentials and wallet with thirty-seven dollars, checks, etc. had been put into this life boat. I begged the captain to let me go and try to recover it but he would not permit it. We were near the burning steamer and he feared she might blow up at any moment. Actually she burned until late on the second afternoon, after which we believe she sank.

Of the forty who overcrowded our lifeboat sixteen were wounded, four so badly that they died. The bodies were thrown overboard to lighten the craft and to make room for the living. The captain and the chief engineer set the sail, took turns in navigating, and organized our life. We were put on a ration of half of a large dry biscuit (cracker) and a few swallows of water every twelve hours. This was not so hard for those of us who, being wounded and unable to row, were not expending energy. Seven Indian steerage passengers did not know how to row and a Burmese peasant woman could not be counted upon to help, so the brunt of the hard rowing fell upon the Chinese members of the crew who worked splendidly. Our leaky craft had to be bailed almost constantly day and night. For the entire ninety hours we were never in sight of land.

Robert

There were no drugs in the small first-aid kit to ease the pain of the suffering; the one doctor aboard, Dr. Raja, had a badly injured right arm. Mercifully, two men who were horribly burned died the first forenoon. One poor Chinese lad who lasted until the afternoon of the third day might have been saved, I feel sure, if it had been possible to get him to a hospital. In his delirium he imagined himself back in his old childhood home and we heard him cry out again and again for his *chie chie* (older sister) and for his mother.

Margaret

Usually the wind freshened about nightfall, and the first night in particular I wondered if the boat would outride the waves. On the second and third nights when the wind was favorable and both sail and oars were in use one had the exhilarating sensation of speeding over the crests of the waves. (Actually in nearly four days we travelled probably not more than thirty miles toward our goal.)

Late the second afternoon a steamer appeared. We hoisted the white towel on an oar and waved frantically.* She must have seen us, for she was not far away. We thought she was slackening speed, but she did not stop. Probably she feared the same fate as ours if she delayed. After this our ration was reduced by a third.

Robert

On the second night the chief engineer insisted that he could see the beam of a lighthouse. On the third night its reflection on the sky was visible to us all. Yet it was evident that we were making no appreciable headway. The tide and heavy head wind were too much for us. The Chinese boys, who had to bear the brunt of the rowing, began to look haggard and worn. How long would their strength last? By dint of their present effort we were barely holding our own.

On the fourth morning we salvaged a floating case of Nestle's malted milk, probably from the wreckage of our ship. Eagerly we poured the powder into our hands and licked it up. Another case lifted aboard proved a disappointment. We hoped for oranges, but found well packed in straw a bottle of sulphuric acid! We did not suffer so much, however, from hunger and thirst as from being overcrowded and cramped. There was no room to lie down or stretch out. We dozed or slept as we sat on the hard seats. The burning sun at midday made us long for the nights--beautiful moonlight nights they were--and the cold of the early mornings made us thank God for the return of the sunshine. Fortunately my wounded hand did not pain very severely, but by the end of the fourth day it was an ugly sight.

Margaret

About four p.m. on the fourth day we were overjoyed to see a scout plane approaching. It circled three times, flashed a message which we could not fully understand and then made a beeline for its base. We anchored and rode the heavy swell, hoping for rescue in the morning. About one a.m. there suddenly appeared in the bright moonlight a

**Margaret had seized a bathtowel as she left our cabin. It served as a covering from the hot sun and the chill at night.*

small fast boat which the plane had summoned, coming almost straight toward us. We feared it was an enemy submarine, and the vessel was also suspicious of us. It turned its searchlight on us and then came alongside. The sea was so heavy that it was difficult to get aboard, but soon the transfer was made and we were racing through the waves to safety. At ten the next forenoon we were all landed at Bassein where an ambulance was waiting to take the worst cases to the civil hospital.* One lifeboat had reached land earlier, one had been picked up by a steamer, and the remaining one was rescued a few hours after we were.

Here our wounds are being skillfully treated. Dr. Raja's right forearm (radius) which was broken has been put in a cast. Mrs. Roberts, who occupies the same ward as Margaret, had a piece of shrapnel removed from her head. The first officer, who was in another lifeboat, is slowly recovering after the removal of a huge curled hunk of metal "as big as a hubcap." Margaret's hand is very painful and the bone will require weeks to set properly, but the doctors say the finger will be saved. Her right eyebrow was wounded, but is healing. Two small fragments and some wooden splinters were dug out of my back between the shoulders, and the wound is healing nicely. Possibly there may be a piece of metal in my back near the right hip, but it does not give me much trouble and the doctors say if there is anything there it will work itself out gradually. We have now been here eight days. We think it is better not to delay too long, and inasmuch as it will be possible at several points to get Margaret's hand dressed, the doctors have concurred in a decision to start for Rangoon tomorrow.

Robert

February 4, 1942 *Bassein [Burma] Civil Hospital*

Dear Ones at Home,

Robert (Father) has already written of our experiences, but you will want to know directly from me how we are faring.

I look out on a beautiful world--it is like a June day at home. I sit on the veranda just outside our room. "Our" in this case refers to Mrs.

**The consul telegraphed to Szechwan that we had arrived in Burma "wounded and destitute." As we came off the boat we certainly looked it. On our backs a few scanty garments, grimy and bloodstained, everything else lost. Of course, the banks could not in these times cash personal checks for a stranger, and in my pocket was less than five cents. "Destitute" was an accurate description, sure enough!*

Roberts, a young Indian woman, and myself. The Burmese nurses are very sweet and kind. With one hand practically useless I am somewhat helpless. I said to one of the nurses, who perhaps has done the most for me, "You have been very good to me." She smiled and said American missionaries (Baptist) had brought them good things and given them an education and her inference was that she was glad to do a kindness to me in return. Many of the nurses here were trained in Christian mission hospitals.

Father (Robert) still has one piece of shrapnel in his lower back which is painful on occasion.

Today we go to Rangoon to see the American consul, get new passports and make necessary financial arrangements.

Everything is gone and it is *awful*! This losing everything and going into West China destitute gets me down! Father (Robert) takes that part better, and yet we know what a joy and pride the Pontiac was to him. Two new typewriters gone, too. Every day I think of something else which I shall never see again.

And yet I knew that morning when we were scrambling into a few clothes that nothing else much mattered if we could escape with our lives. And in the lifeboat when it was plain to be seen that we were getting nowhere with the boys' rowing and the likelihood of being picked up grew less and less hopeful, I thought to myself if we could only get to Chengtu and our home, there would be nothing left to be desired. We did manage to escape and we are profoundly thankful.

No letters since San Francisco and I am afraid you are worried about us and I wonder if you are all well. Don't take what has happened to us too hard. We have come through remarkably well, and once my hand gets well I shall be equal to almost anything again.

People here in Bassein have been most kind. We have tea-ed and dined with the Deputy Commissioner and tea-ed with the port officer. People have picked up some old garments for us, but we are difficult fits! I know now what it means to be a destitute refugee!

Later *Irrawaddy Flotilla Company Ltd.*

We are now on a nice steamboat on our way to Rangoon. Apparently we are the only first class passengers and we have the whole front end of the boat to ourselves. We are following the winding Irrawaddy and it is fascinating watching the countryside. Later we slip into a creek, I am told, and go eastward to Rangoon. It is nearly a twenty-four hour run.

Life is really very good. Not a day yet but what I have been able to thank God for many things. Now it is good to be travelling again--*inland*--and seeing new sights....

Robert continues with our story.

February 12, 1942 *Maymyo, Burma*

Dear Margaret and Dorothy,

So long as we remained in southern Burma there was danger that the road to our destination might be cut, so we left Bassein as soon as we were able to travel. Our four days in Rangoon were rather hectic, as the place was the prime objective of attack, and old residents were already making preliminary plans to evacuate. During eighteen alarms, more than a third of which preceded actual raids, we took refuge in six different shelters in the city. On our shopping trips it was almost uncanny the way one or another of three Baptist missionaries was sure to appear, often with a car, to take us to a refuge whenever the alarm sounded. Usually the day alarms did not prove to be actual raids but with several of the night alarms we could hear bombs exploding. None were very near, however, and while we were there no damage of any consequence was done by air attacks. The American aviators and the R.A.F. managed to keep enemy planes away pretty well.

Mother cannot use her left hand which is bandaged to a board and supported by a sling. People along the way are very kind in helping to dress our wounds. My wounds are not troublesome. There is still a piece of shrapnel in my back, but the doctor says it would have caused trouble long ago if it had not been sterile, and that no harm will be done if it does not come out until I reach Chengtu. There I plan to have it removed, a very simple operation. Apparently the piece followed around under the skin for five or six inches without finding any vulnerable spot. The doctor in Rangoon said I have something to scratch my back without having to do it with my fingers!...

Robert writes again.

February 14, 1942 *Maymyo, Burma*

Dear Folks,

After a few days we expect to receive word that a convoy of Friends Ambulance Unit* trucks will be leaving Lashio for Chengtu. We shall go by train to Lashio and then the rest of the way with this group. We are not sorry to delay a little here, as it gives opportunity to get a little

---

**The Friends Ambulance Unit [F.A.U.] is a British-sponsored organization providing alternate service for conscientious objectors to war. In China the F.A.U. Convoy [British, American, Chinese] distributed civilian medical supplies across and behind the lines.*

rest, and the weather which will be cold in China will be becoming a little warmer as the sun gains power.

We enjoyed our journey through Burma, first by steamer for nearly twenty-four hours, and then by truck. Everywhere we see bullock carts, some rickshas in and around Rangoon, many bicycles, many bicycles with side car and in the towns small horse carriages which are called *garis*.

In Burma a snack is brought to one's room sometimes before it becomes light. This snack is called *chota hasri* which means "little breakfast." It consists of tea, toast and a little fruit. At eleven comes "breakfast" which consists of fruit, oatmeal, meat and vegetable. Tea at about 3:30 is like tea in England, America or China, and at 7:30 comes another meal of meat, vegetables, dessert and "sweets" by which is meant some kind of candy. It seems strange to me to have "breakfast" at eleven o'clock.

Because Burma is a semi-torrid place it has been very difficult to find warm clothing suitable for our Szechwan winters, and such clothing as we have been able to purchase has cost from one and a half to five times as much as in America. Probably the wartime conditions have been a factor....

Robert Simkin

February 14, 1942 — *American Baptist Mission Rest House*
Maymyo, Burma

Dear Folks,

...Our four days in Rangoon were somewhat of a nightmare at times. We were very glad of the hospitality of the American Baptist Mission folk at Judson College. We were entertained in a lovely home by fine people and all that was a delight. How soft and restful the beds were, and how good to be in a home with books and magazines and flowers and music! It was a typical college campus mission home, similar to those we know so well at Chengtu. Two men, who were "batching it" together, their families having gone to India, gave freely of their time and their cars escorting us to town and helping us shop. All this doesn't sound nightmarish, does it?

It was the frequent air raid alarms and the disheartening task of rushing about and trying to find a few essentials to make up a part of our losses, which was difficult. Imagine, on the second night--four alarms! We hardly got off to sleep when the siren would go again and down we had to traipse to our shelter. The last night we just camped out for the rest of the raid period and paid no attention to "alerts" and "all-clears." Then there was the almost fruitless search for warm underclothing (there was practically none for Robert and absolutely none for me) and a dash for this and that between day alarms. However, when I left Bassein I could scarcely walk a few steps without being tired out and in Rangoon I *had* to keep going and I was far stronger after the four days than at the beginning....

We had no time for sight-seeing, but every day we passed the golden *Shwe Dagon* pagoda (Burma's most famous pagoda) one or more times, and one evening our host drove us around the lake where we got a lovely view of it from the distance. That huge golden mass showing among the green trees across the water was a beautiful sight.

We also have seen cashew nuts growing on their trees. And papaya--doesn't it taste good when it comes fresh from the tree just outside in the garden!

We came this far in the cab of an F.A.U. truck wtih Eric Inchboard, a likeable English lad of twenty-two years. He was careful in his driving and looked after us well. We were two and one-half days coming here from Rangoon....

Robert Simkin

Robert continues with our Burma experiences

February 25, 1942 *Lashio, Burma*

Dear Dorothy and Margaret,

The American Consul-General in Rangoon, Mr. Lester L. Schnare, who was a fellow passenger most of the way across the Pacific, helped me to secure funds against a bank draft and also has brought us in his car from Maymyo to Lashio when he was travelling this way. Doctors and nurses along the road have freely given their services in dressing our wounds. The Friends Ambulance Unit has advanced funds and kindly has arranged transportation to Chengtu. The list of those who have helped is a long one. Not a few of these have themselves now become refugees. The steamship company paid our hospital expenses at Bassein and provided transportation by comfortable river steamer to Rangoon.

We are only 170 miles from the border of China, and are waiting until a convoy of the Friends Ambulance Unit gets ready to go. We are staying in the home of the Karen pastor of the American Baptist Church. Both in Maymyo and in Lashio water is piped with a faucet at various points along each street, and one of the faucets is in the yard about fifteen feet from our window, so we have a supply of water very close by. I have wished that the Chinese in Chengtu had such a good supply of running water, but perhaps that will come in time....

...We have had a good chance to see Burma, as we already have travelled more than 700 miles through it, of which 600 have been by auto. Lower Burma is flat, but later we passed through about 200 miles of hills which must be very beautiful when the leaves are washed clean. From here on to Kunming we shall have plenty of mountain scenery.... We are very fortunate to have got so far along the road while the way was still open. Burma has become a melting pot and one sees people of all colors....Now we also find many Chinese, whom we can understand. Day before yesterday in about five minutes we met on the street no less than three of my former students who were most cordial. At Maymyo I also found on the train as it stopped at the station a young man who was a former student at the Middle School at Chengtu....Last night after we had been dined by these former students who are now business men and successful in life, as they bade us good night one of them said, "We thank you very much for what you have done for us long ago; we have received a great deal from you."...

Father

March 7, 1942 *Lashio, Burma*

Dear Folks,

While waiting in Maymyo eleven days for a convoy to take us farther we had several alarms but no actual raids. However, Maymyo was bombed a few hours after we left. We have been in Lashio nearly two weeks, during which we have had two or three alarms but no raids. Henry Rodwell, son of John and Dorothy Rodwell who were members of the Friends China Mission, will drive a Friends Ambulance Unit station wagon to Chengtu and will take us clear through to our home. Henry, who was eight and a half when he left Chengtu, is able to understand a good deal and to speak a little Chinese....

March 9, 1942

Last evening we went to the warehouse of the Friends Ambulance Unit and the seventeen men who are here now made and served cocoa and we sat around an open fire in the enclosure and had a short worship meeting. Two members of the Royal Air Force also attended the meeting. Many of the members are people not much interested in the regular mission work of the Society of Friends, as they do not understand it very well and think it consists of ramming doctrines down the throats of people. Some of the men have seen our work in Chungking and find it essentially the same type of service they are interested in....

Robert

April 7, 1942 *Kweiyang, Kweichow*

Dear Alice and Fannie,

At Chungking they have what is called the China Mail Bag. Americans and Canadians can send fifty-word messages, including address of recipient, by air to America and Canada free of charge. Somebody in California picks up the messages and forwards them by mail. We hope to send a message when we reach Chungking. Unless we have to use up some of the precious words in asking for money to be forwarded we'll say something like this: "Both arrived well Chungking. Safe, interesting journey Burma Road by Friends Ambulance Unit station wagon. Depart Chengtu shortly. Danger in Szechwan now slight. Communications closing behind us hinder mails. Much love Dorothy and Margaret. Inform Alfred." Long before this letter reaches you we hope you'll have some such message.

I am getting more and more use of my left hand but it is still stiff and not a bit lovely to look at!

May 10, 1942 *Chengtu, China*

Dear Ones at Home,

We have now been in Chengtu three and a half weeks and have received your two air-mail letters to our great joy--one of February 26 sent to Calcutta and one of April 6....Thus far "Via Capetown" brings the mail through safely and quickly.

Apparently no copy of letter telling of our adventure at sea has gone through so I enclose another copy. Robert's wounds are well healed. He still has two small pieces of shrapnel in his hands which may have to have help in coming out. The Friends Ambulance Unit christened their mobile operating theatre in Kweiyang by taking out one piece from his back (under local anesthetic). My hand is all healed but is still stiff. I can type with some difficulty....

May 24, 1942 *Chengtu, West China*

Dear Alice and Fannie,

Some are quite pessimistic about the general outlook here. We do not share that pessimism but these are days when we must at least face the possibility of being quite cut off. I don't want to worry you or the girls with what may never happen, but on the other hand I feel I must try to say what needs to be said if communication is to be cut short. Whatever takes place try not to be over anxious about us. We shall try always to do the wise thing. We do not have to face problems alone--humanly speaking we are here in a community of people of wisdom and resourcefulness.

We are going to have a family from Kweiyang living with us during the summer who are members of the Wider Quaker Fellowship....

June 22, 1942 *Chengtu, West China*

Dear Folks at Home,

...Sometimes I feel very distressed and restless because of the world situation (who doesn't?) and being separated from our girls, but I have decided I can't become neurotic over these circumstances and it is up to me to get the best out of life out here--by putting the best I have into it--and keep on growing, or our two youngsters will get quite beyond me! It is certain that *they* won't stand still.

It would mean so much if we could get letters through more easily and quickly, but we are thankful for every little crumb which does come. No word at all has come in since I last wrote. Do you receive the China Mail Bag messages? Each family is permitted to send one message per month.

I have written before that Bill and Hilda Sewell are interned in Hongkong.* (Are you getting my letters?) We have absolutely no word from them and we dare not write. One other member of our staff is also detained there. It is one of the many tragedies of wartime.

We have not had a single air raid in Chengtu since our arrival. There have been no alarms since last September. We hope this freedom may continue. We are really quite comfortably well off; we lack no essentials. Having the Haywards with us during the summer as we expect to do will help out with expenses. We have a good garden and that helps a lot. At present we are getting quantities of wax beans and lettuce. Soon there will be corn and tomatoes.

Several of our neighbors have good radios where we all feel free to go and listen in. How different from the old days when the whole world might be turned upside down and we wouldn't know it for months! It is good we now have this way of getting outside news for I never knew us to be so cut off in the way of mail. Besides we have a daily news sheet printed in English. The news is well censored, but what news is not?

The Library and Book Club are still full of good books which I have not yet read, so altogether with our democracy discussion groups and meetings we are not likely to stagnate. As I have so often said, it is a stimulating and supportive community to live in.

**For story of Sewell family's internment see William G. Sewell's* Strange Harmony [*Edinburgh House Press, London 1946*].

July 14, 1942 *Chengtu, West China*

Dear Dorothy and Margaret and Family,

...The Haywards of Kweiyang have arrived for the summer. We like them very much. They have a little girl Gillian. She always eats in her room by herself before we do. Her little dresses aren't much bigger than those you made for your big dolls, Margaret.

P.C. Hsu, China's best known pacifist, is in town now. He has just arrived from "occupied" China. On Sunday evening the Haywards and we were invited with others to Andy Roy's to hear what he had to say. He is to be living in Chengtu and do some teaching this coming school year. Andy Roy was just in to see if we could give him a room. I wish we could but he doesn't want more than breakfasts, and in these days of forced economy we have to have a couple who can share meals and expenses with us....I forgot to say that in addition to Grace Hickson Mr. Robertson* is also eating with us, making six adults regularly....

August 16, 1942 *Chengtu, West China [Free China]*

Dear Ones at Home,

It seems almost an eternity since we said good-bye! I hope the next few years go much more quickly! I wish I'd spent all the time I did shopping for things to bring to China in visiting and having a good time with you all. It is surprising what you can get along without if you have to. What friends have provided together with old things left here take care of our summer needs quite well. I imagine we may find the winter more difficult but we shall have to patch and darn and wear what we have. Others who are at the end of a long term are also wearing much worn and mended clothing. We shall be in good company. A spool of white cotton thread costs fifteen dollars (local currency)....

Robert has been to two Chinese weddings recently. Chinese weddings leave much to be desired. Even at so-called Christian weddings so many of the guests are non-Christians that it is difficult to have any spirit of reverence. We like to think of a wedding ceremony as solemn and sacred, but that seems far from the Chinese mind. The bride comes in at a snail's pace, at least that is the fashion just now, and all during the ceremony the hum of conversation goes on. And of course it's a time for feasting, which is the great Chinese indoor sport. We must try to get across to some of our stronger young Friends the idea that marriage is a sacrament.

**Canadian W.C.U.U. faculty member.*

Each week I spend two to four hours at the canteen for R.A.F. men. The dining room of the Canadian School (the children are still going to school in Jenshow) is used for this purpose. The men come there for tea and for supper. There is a place to read and play games. There are also dancing, singing and other activities. Sometimes we are very busy at the canteen when a lot of boys come in at once and it keeps us hustling to serve their suppers....The men often buy only milk and cookies, or tomato juice, and TEA, of course— a standby with these English boys. They are a quiet, clean crowd of lads. I sometimes wonder if American boys, under similar circumstances, would do their home country and training equal credit.

I am even more interested in the F.A.U. boys. Four came in only last evening, grimy and hot and tired from bringing a convoy of charcoal-burning trucks up the road from Kweiyang. We took two in here, had hot baths for them and gave them their suppers. Some of these boys, both F.A.U. and R.A.F., are very young, in their late teens or early twenties. I fancy that Chengtu and this beautiful campus is a haven to all of them.

Please write, all of you. You have no idea how I long for letters. It was so good to have Edith's of April first.

My hand is still stiff but usable.

September 6, 1942 *Chengtu, West China*

Dear Margaret,

Last week Father and I had supper with the Kilborns. All three girls helped wait table as they have no table-boy now. Some of the R.A.F. boys were there that evening to listen to the radio. Messages were coming over the air from London especially for them.

One evening a group of the F.A.U. boys came along to our place for some music. We had invited Alice Settlemyer to bring her cello and play, also Mr. Rogers, an RAF-er, to sing. All together there were nineteen of us and did we have fun! Vocal solos, cello and piano solos, duets, and group singing. Two of the men are Welsh and their voices were beautiful together....

Robert writes of our concern for the children at home.

September 19, 1942 *Chengtu, West China [Free China]*

Dear Alfred,

Yours of August fourteenth which has just reached us gives much valuable information. It is the first word we had received from you since we left the U.S.A. We didn't know whether any letters had got through from Burma or anything posted since, although the remittance which came so promptly told us you had received the "China Voice" radiogram.

We are very grateful to you all for your willingness to care for Margaret Ruth at Poplar Ridge this year. At the same time we are greatly perturbed to learn that a change is so soon necessary. We are mystified about what can be the reasons for so sudden a decision. Absolutely the only inkling we have had of any impending change was a casual remark in Dorothy's letter of May tenth: "Next year Aunt Fannie is thinking of sending Margie to Oakwood if she can make the eighth grade." Since we had no reason to suppose that things were not going well, your letter was a bolt out of the blue.

Didn't things work out satisfactorily in Portland? Did the responsibility (and we know it *was* a great responsibility) prove too heavy? Have Alice or Fannie been ill, so that a change had to be made? Or was the difficulty financial? Before I left Auburn I ought to have given you power of attorney over the bank account. Although I did more than half expect America to be plunged into hostilities, I simply did not visualize how completely the conflict would paralyze communications by sea and land and air, making it impossible even to *know* what conditions are on the other side of the world, to say nothing of dealing with them satisfactorily. Our loss of all accounts, blank checks, and records has intensified the difficulties.

But is the difficulty financial? Or is it something else? We are WHOLLY IN THE DARK, and this is the matter which touches us as parents most keenly--THE THING which makes our separation from the girls the most difficult, the fact that we cannot enter into their lives or even understand their needs and the needs of the Portland folks and of yourselves in relation to them. All through the long summer vacation we did not even know where Dorothy was, or how she was spending her holidays. The best of letters leave unsaid oceans of things which we are most anxious to know, and you cannot imagine how eagerly we look for any scrap of news which will give us an inkling of how matters are going. Even if news is bad news, we feel that it is better to tell us frankly what the problems and difficulties are.

Margaret T. even wonders whether it is necessary for your sake and for the sake of the girls that she return to America, although under present uncertain and dangerous conditions of travel it is a question if she could successfully accomplish the long and expensive journey. If she should go there would be the same sort of worry about my welfare, with the possibility of a similar lack of news due to interrupted postal communcations. Please pardon my writing thus, but I feel that it is better to express frankly what we think. This does not in any way affect our deep appreciation of what you are all doing on both sides of the family for the girls and for ourselves.

Much love to you all.

Robert L. Simkin

September 19, 1942 *West China Union University Chengtu, Free China*

Dear Alice and Fannie,

Before this reaches you, you should already have received Robert's letter of this date sent by air all the way to Alfred. You will know how much upset we are by the bombshell Alfred dropped in his August letter announcing that it looked as if Margaret Ruth would be moving to Poplar Ridge. You see the announcement came without any explanation whatever and it has left us feeling completely puzzled and baffled. I have scarcely been able to think of anything else for these three days.

We also are hoping to send the following radiogram message by the "China Voice": LATEST PORTLAND LETTER DATED APRIL. IN AUGUST LETTER ALFRED SAYS MARGARET POSSIBLY MOVING. MUCH CONCERNED. PLEASE SEND EXPLANATION AIRMAIL ALL THE WAY, CHARGING OUR ACCOUNT. ARE ALL WELL AND HAPPY? DEEPEST LOVE TO ALL. This should bring an answer within six to seven weeks.

Of course I keep saying to myself I must suspend judgment until facts are at hand, but meanwhile my mind is filled with apprehension about Margaret and you all.

September 21, 1942 *Chengtu, West China [Free China]*

Dear Folks at Home,

So glad I didn't get the other letters off earlier, for today a number of home letters came and the world is looking brighter! These were all written in May.

We are SO THANKFUL for every scrap of news. We read the letters over and over and try to piece this bit of news with that and glean all we possibly can. I feel much enheartened concerning Margaret Ruth.

Fannie, you are such a dear! Planning a home for the girls at their summer vacation time. We don't yet know why you couldn't keep Margaret with you for company, but I trust we shall have all the facts soon which will enable us to see the situation as it really is, and to understand the whys and wherefores. I hope both the girls play their parts when they are with you. It has seemed so important to me that they have the security which comes from having a place to call "home."

We are so grateful for the time Dorothy has had with you, Hazel.* I know it has meant a lot to her. It does to us.

Love and thanks to you all for what you're doing for the girls. I suppose *they* don't appreciate it fully, but I hope they are growing in appreciation and understanding.

November 8, 1942

Dear Fannie,

Within ten days now we have had three home letters and we feel once more in contact with you at home and does it seem good! Letters mailed in Portland on October second arrived here on October thirtieth (just four weeks). *All* mail from the United States whether bearing air postage or not now comes by air from Calcutta into China....When Burma first fell, postal communications were difficult and costly for us because of the surtax but I think it is remarkable how quickly the postal system became regularized and mail began moving normally again. Apparently letters we wrote of the trip over the Burma Road (Lashio to Kunming) and from Kunming to Chungking have not reached you.

Bit by bit we are piecing the situation in Portland together, or rather our picture of it. Under the circumstances I can see now that sending Margaret off to Poplar Ridge**was the only practical thing you could do and I am coming to feel the experience will be good for her. I notice that in one letter she expresses the hope that she may spend Christmas "with Aunt Fannie" and again that she writes you "quite often, about every three days." Evidently she appreciates you and she ought to!

I am glad to have news of the nephews these war days. We see so many young fellows out here. The war certainly has sent the youth of the world far afield. I hope communities elsewhere take as much interest in the boys and have as much concern for their welfare as the campus community here.

**Since Oakwood School [Poughkeepsie] is not too far from Waterbury, Connecticut, it was possible for Dorothy to visit Carl and Hazel Timberlake there on numerous occasions.*

***In Poplar Ridge, New York, Margaret lived with Chester Simkin's family, next door to Alfred Simkin. The move of Margaret was necessary after Calvin and Alice Miller bought a smaller house and could not care for Margaret any longer.*

In spite of the difficulties of travel we occasionally see people from the outside world. Recently we met a Dr. Carpenter from New York, who is out here in the interests of the cooperative movement. As a member also of the American Fellowship of Reconciliation Executive Committee, he told of the present concerns of the F.O.R., and the thinking that is being done in the United States along the lines of future world peace. A few weeks ago we felt a bit closer to the world because of the visit of Wendell Willkie. Robert and I attended a very fine reception given in his honor by the governor. Willkie spoke briefly.

December 6, 1942

Dear Ones at Home,

Winter has come, not snow and frost and ice as you are getting, but raw, damp weather that chills to the marrow. We are thankful for our "furnace." Without burning too much coal we can keep fairly comfortable. We are certainly better off than many. We are still getting chrysanthemums from the garden to make the house look cheerful but even they will soon be gone.

This past week four Parliamentarians, two from the House of Lords and two from the Commons, a British good-will mission, have been visiting Chengtu and creating quite a stir, especially among the English and Canadian people. There have been teas, dinners and speeches galore. Ever since our return we have been aware (in certain quarters) of an undercurrent of Chinese anti-British feeling and this is an attempt to make for mutual understanding between the two countries I suppose. China felt that Britain very much let her down in Burma. There are other factors too, no doubt. The abolishment of extraterritoriality is an attempt at appeasement and an effort to bolster China's pride. Extraterritoriality by rights should have gone long ago.

I have heard only one of the Parliamentarians speak, Mr. Lawson, a commoner and Labor leader. At home he is a Methodist lay preacher in his own little community and he impresses one as being a very earnest man. He told of his own personal experiences, how as a lad he had worked in the mines fourteen hours a day, of his interests in books in spite of his hard life, of his conversion, etc. He has risen from the laboring clases and is not ashamed of it. He went to Oxford and his wife, to whom he admitted he owed much, worked as a domestic servant while he studied.

The campus continues to be a place of great activity. Yesterday there was a big football (rugby) game on the large Canadian field in front of the Canadian School compound, played between the R.A.F. and the joint universities. Crowds of people were out to watch it. At the same time the Ginling College girls were having their Field Day. I went to watch them for a time and saw them doing archery, rounders (similar to baseball), and volley ball. One evening not long ago we saw a good play at the Canadian School by some of the R.A.F. assisted by a number of the younger members of the community. It was Milne's "The Dover Road" and it was very good. The two who took the leading ladies' parts are American girls. Loma Houseley is a lovely person and very lovely to look at. She is a new M.E.M. worker. The other girl we first met in Burma! She was teaching in a school at Mandalay and entertained us over night. When upper Burma was evacuated in the spring she came on to China with the R.A.F.

...The Christmas season comes on apace. We are expecting Marjorie Causer* to be with us for a few days. I think I shall help Yang Si make some Christmas cakes soon. Norman and Muriel Glass, young Friends who were in Kansu with the China Industrial Cooperatives this summer, brought me some Sinkiang raisins. Since we don't have our own precious girls with us we shall put our energies into trying to make someone else happy. But we shall be missing you, Dorothy and Margaret, *very* much.

With special Christmas love to all.

December 16, 1942

Dear Ones at Home,

...It is good to be on terra firma *this* Christmas time. On the whole the world does look brighter, doesn't it? At least one can feel there is a prospect of this war (this global war, as President Roosevelt calls it) coming to an end in the not *too* distant future. I fear it may still be a long struggle though....

There will be at least twelve of us having Christmas dinner together--our own household of five** plus Marjorie Causer, Norman and Muriel Glass, and four R.A.F.s. We thought we might have Brian Harland with us too. He is a new worker for English Friends whom we have agreed to house and care for. However, the poor boy contracted malaria while in India and is now ill in a hospital in Chungking. His temperature went up to over 106! I fear he will not be able to come along until after Christmas. By that time the Tomkinsons may be able to take him in. It is a great problem housing people these days.

**An English girl whom we met in Chungking and who was later "loaned" to Ginling College to teach zoology.*

***Douglas and Imogene Sargent, Grace Hickson and ourselves.*

...We have had quite an influx of transient guests recently. Some of the members of the English Baptist Mission (Grace Hickson's Mission) have been passing through Chengtu on their way to Sian. In the old days we never saw Shensi missionaries passing through here, but it is the only way they can get in now....Another guest is Mr. Madge, just back from furlough in England. His wife couldn't come with him. English women seem to have trouble in getting passports now, as do American women. (I have wondered if my experience, which the Rangoon consul cabled home to the United States, didn't put an end entirely to passports for American women to China.)

From Chengtu to Chungking 1943

January 9, 1943 *Chengtu, Free China*

Dear Ones at Home,

Mr. Robertson who was eating with us last summer and was taken very ill with typhus and pneumonia is now back from Penghsien where he has been convalescing the past few weeks. He is going to take his meals with us again.

Dr. Janet Kilborn is very ill at Jenshow with a cerebral hemorrhage due to high blood pressure. Dr. Leslie has gone down to Jenshow to be with her. On the whole I think there has been a good deal more serious illness in our community than formerly. One reason is that the community is now larger. Some suggest that people have lowered resistance due to war strain.

...Still no real news of the Sewells although we have seen interesting accounts written by those who have been repatriated from Hongkong. Dorothy Behenna was caught in Manila. No word from her either. Imogene's father, a M.E.M. bishop, is now in concentration camp in Shanghai. People in the city are allowed to send in needed clothing and food to the detainees. At present we here feel very far away from the war area.

January 10, 1943 *Chengtu, Free China*

Dear Friends,

It is more than a year since we sailed from the U.S.A. How remote it all seems now! Still I can never quite forget it....I can't forget our seventy-seven days on the sea following a circuitous route and often in complete ignorance of where we were going except as we could judge our direction from the position of the sun and stars, or our unexpectedly turning up at Balikpapen (later when we read in the paper that Balikpapen with its oil wells had fallen into Japanese hands we felt a proprietary interest in the fate of that Dutch outpost on the edge of the jungle) and at Soerabaja, where on entering the harbor we nearly ran into a mine field. What a strange voyage it was! Approaching Calcutta the ship turned south again to Madras where we transferred to a freighter bound for Rangoon. I remember well, as we put out from the dock with ourselves and our car and all our baggage safely aboard, friends on the deck of the big ship towering above us waved goodbye and we waved back confidently and happily....

Unfortunately I kept no notes of our journey over the famous Burma Road. Conditions of travel--long days in the car, eating after the stop at night in poorly lighted inns, often sleeping in the station wagon (without undressing)--made even the most meager note-taking difficult. I can only say that I have no words to describe the wonder of this road. It is a daring engineering feat and takes one through terrain of breath-taking grandeur. It twists its way to the upper heights of range after range; it winds down again to deep gorges. It is its magnitude that astounds me. To pass over one high range, or two or three in succession, is wonderful enough, but to go on day after day and still find lofty heights to climb and descend, until you wonder where the end can be, that is the marvel that makes the experience unforgettable. It was early spring when we crossed the mountains of Yunnan and Kweichow and the loveliness of the fresh foliage, the brilliance of the showy red rhododendron and the fresh beauty of the vari-colored azalea were a great delight. Some open slopes were so covered with bloom that they were like beautiful gardens.

But travel over the Burma Road was also frightfully treacherous. There are no guard rails, shoulders are soft, the road sometimes dangerously narrow. The Friends Ambulance Unit has reported that fifteen hundred trucks had gone over the precipices (none belonging to the F.A.U.); we ourselves saw wreckage of numerous vehicles on slopes below. There have been many fatalities, in one case a personal acquaintance. How fortunate we were to travel in a F.A.U. convoy!...

Robert writes of inflation and wartime conditions.

February 15, 1943 *Chengtu, Free China*

Dear Brothers and Sisters and Friends,

Last term our own institution had 1001 students. I do not know the enrollment of the other four institutions which are associated with us, but when classes close just before the noon hour the roads and paths are crowded. Nearly a year and a half ago National Central University withdrew from our campus and set up its own work, but we still have four refugee institutions because Yenching University has now opened classes and is cooperating with us in many ways. I believe Chengtu is the largest educational centre in Free China, and probably the largest now in any part of China. It is an unusual privilege to be members of such a group.

Many changes have taken place in our life, not the least of which is the different economic standard which has come due to war and as a result of this great influx of people and the difficulty of importing supplies which used to be considered essential. Even articles of food produced locally have risen to unheard of prices.

The demand for housing accommodation, and the necessity as far as possible to increase the number of persons who will share the overhead expenses of each family, have meant that nearly every available space in attics and basements is now pretty fully occupied in nearly every house on the campus and in the city.

Many Chinese have built houses in the suburbs, the city gates have been removed and openings have been made at many points in the city walls so that people can get out into the country in a hurry if necessary. Here in the capital the old sedan chair is rarely seen, its place having been taken by rickshas chiefly. Out in the country the sedan chair may still be found, as well as the more jouncing wheelbarrow, which has no springs. Until recently the rich and the military people who seem to have plenty of money have travelled longer distances chiefly by air or by motor buses, but recently it has been difficult to purchase seats on the planes and motor traffic has increasingly turned to charcoal as a fuel, with the result that a journey of three hundred miles often takes six days where it used to take two, and performance is uncertain at that. These days one may be thankful to be able to stay home.

Robert L. Simkin

Another letter of Robert's:

March 22, 1943 *Chengtu, Free China*

Dear Friends,

At the West China Missionary Conference in 1908 there were in our province only two Chinese leaders who were sufficiently educated as Christians and of real leader calibre to attend and understand the purport of the discussions. S.C. Yang (Yang Sao Chuen) was one of these. Ever since that time he has been a leader in educational and church work. For twenty-five years he acted as principal of the Union Middle School. For many years he was president of the Y.M.C.A. in Chengtu, and clerk of Szechwan Yearly Meeting of Friends. He died a week ago and was buried yesterday. He was a fine and wise leader, excellent in team work and appreciative of the viewpoints of others. His passing brings vividly to mind the great progress which I have witnessed in these thirty-five years. In 1908 S.C. Yang stood out as almost alone; now there are scores or hundreds of well educated Christian leaders who are carrying on the work initiated by the few.

Yearly Meeting begins March 27 at Tungchwan, about one hundred miles northeast of Chengtu. Travel is exceedingly difficult and expensive because of the shortage of gasoline, but the Friends Ambulance Unit is helping to solve our problem by taking a group of us, including Margaret and myself, in one of its trucks which has been converted to burn charcoal....

One of the problems to be considered at Yearly Meeting is a proposal to establish in Chungking, the wartime capital of China, an International Friends Centre. Practically all the buildings belonging to Friends inside that city have been destroyed by bombing, so the Friends Meeting is without a home. The Meeting also has suffered because many of its members have evacuated and are scattered in the surrounding area, some in villages miles distant. There is an opportunity of using a building and plant which another mission cannot at present staff, and Friends are trying to find suitable personnel to take over this plant and use it as a rallying point for our work....

Robert L. Simkin

March 31, 1943 — *Tungchwan, Szechwan*

Dear Ones,

Robert and I both feel clear that I must go home to the girls unless some assurance can be given that loving supervision and guidance is being provided for them. Alfred's letter, and to a lesser degree word from others and the girls themselves, seem to indicate that not all is well. You have all done your best by them and neither side of the family is in a position to "mother and father" the girls this coming school year. Whether I can help them is a question, but if they need me, it is my business to try. If their difficulties have arisen from a sense of insecurity coming from the break in their family life my returning to them might help considerably. On the other hand, there is a certain degree of risk in travelling at this time and if I should lose my life on the way home that wouldn't be any great comfort to the girls. However, provided that transportation is possible with a reasonable assurance of safety I am quite prepared to undertake the journey. There is talk of such transport.

Meanwhile as a result of laying the whole matter before the western Friends gathered here and thinking of the problem in relation to the Chungking Center which they seem to want Robert and me to have a share in, the decision is this: *if* we can be assured that Dorothy and Margaret are being cared for in a wise and loving way and *that they themselves are happy in the arrangement*, we have agreed that I shall stay on for another year or eighteen months and act as matron-hostess at the Friends Centre (formerly the Canadian Mission Business Agency and Home) in Chungking in which the F.A.U. also will cooperate to a certain extent. We shall want guidance from all of you....

Later

We were surprised and delighted to find that Paul Cope, the first *American* Friend member of the F.A.U. to arrive here, is no other than the son of our Atlantic City friends, the Paul Copes. Robert is taking no small satisfaction in the fact that another Haverfordian has at last found his way to our West China Union University home.

March 31, 1943 *Tungchwan, Szechwan*

Dear Dorothy and Margaret,

We arrived here on Friday evening, coming through in one day--due to our conveyance, a F.A.U. truck. Three of the F.A.U. boys have come along and we were a jolly crowd. We had seats along the sides and with cushions at our backs we rode in comfort and style--for China.

On Sunday the F.A.U. boys spoke at the afternoon meeting. The church was packed. Henry Rodwell, who brought us up over the Burma Road, was one of the three and he told a little of what the F.A.U. is, and what it is trying to do. Tom Haley gave some stories of adventure in England, Burma and China. Larry Baker told of his leper colony in Kweichow. This is the story as Larry told it:

The colony was started by women missionaries in a section of Kweichow where there are many lepers. They used to appear on the streets and these women attempted to treat them. After a time some of the number whom they cared for failed to appear. Either they were so mistreated by the people of the town or else they had such fear of contaminating others that they thought it best to stay away. The women felt they must get a place some distance away where the lepers could be isolated and cared for. Thus the work began and a fine colony was developed, buildings put up, farming operations started etc. Then the war came and these women had to leave because they were Germans. The colony was left to its own devices. Some months went by when Larry Baker came along and, seeing the plight of the lepers, undertook to pick up the work again. He has been there ever since, the sole worker among the lepers, giving them the course of treatments, helping them with their organization, living and working with them. Larry is a delightful and lovable person....

April 11, 1943 *Chengtu, Free China*

Dear Fannie and Carl and Hazel,

You tell just the things we want to know. We welcome any information which helps us to understand the home situation better and gives us even an inkling of how the girls are reacting to life. If you all can keep us posted concerning new developments we may be able to help the girls forestall some difficulties.

I am not so sanguine as I was about the chances of my getting home soon. Evidently shipping companies are not desirous of having as passengers women travelling alone. Single men yes, married couples yes, a lone woman only possibly. Perhaps after the Allies have completely driven the Axis forces from Africa, shipping around the Cape and the South Atlantic may be safer. I may have to be reconciled to leaving the girls to make out the best way they can without me. I hope what Carl says--"they have got the stuff"--is true, and that they can weather it.

June 6, 1943 *Chengtu, Free China*

Dear Ones at Home,

It is now definitely decided that we are to go to Chungking. We hope to move about the middle of September. It will be a great change for us and I should not be happy to look forward to such service, especially in the city of Chungking, for an indefinite period, but we feel it is a worthwhile opportunity for us and it will be an interesting enough job to compensate for the drawbacks since we don't expect to put more than eighteen months into it--the time the Canadians will allow us to use the place.

...Four F.A.U. boys came over for outdoor supper with us on the lawn this evening. Think of having four American lads, Friends or friends of Friends, out here! One of the boys is an American-born Chinese, who comes from Worcester, Massachusetts. Chris Evans' father was at Haverford with Robert....

August 29, 1943 *Chengtu, Free China*

Dear Ones at Home,

It is a beautiful summer day and the lawn and garden look fresh and lovely after recent rains. I mean to enjoy the trees and flowers and green grass to the full during the next few days since we shall have nothing but a stone tennis court and ugly walls in Chungking. After living in Chengtu for nearly twenty years and on this huge campus which is like a park, it will be a great change to become a city dweller and a Chungking dweller at that. However, I am comforted by the thought of the river. The Chungking Centre is up above the bank of the Yangtze* and from its verandas one can watch the fascinating movement of boats and ferries, and look across to the hills, still somewhat wooded, on the south bank.

It now looks as if we might get off about the eighth or tenth of next month. We are trying to get ready for a F.A.U. convoy coming from the northwest, which is due in Chengtu about the fourth. The trucks will have to be overhauled here which will take several days. Paul Cope of Atlantic City is in charge of the convoy and it will be pleasant to travel in his care.

...I wonder if I made a mistake in deciding to stay on--travel seems a bit easier now. Perhaps not if I can persuade Dad to come with me at the end of 1944. The Willmotts**have invited us to spend our last Chengtu days with them. They are good to us.

October 12, 1943 *Friends International Centre, Chungking*

Dear Margaret,

...I really like it here. I believe I could watch the boats and the river all day, and at night it is simply lovely with the opposite hills dotted with sparkling lights. There are the familiar Chinese sounds we were used to in Chengtu, children in school saying their lessons, vendors

---

**During the winter months the water of the Yangtze at Chungking recedes leaving a wide space of sand on which people build mat huts. There they live until the water rises in April or May when they move up higher. The annual rise of the river at Chungking is seventy to ninety feet. The river "has been known to rise forty feet in one day and in 1905 it actually reached one hundred and seven feet above the low water mark."*

From Robert Simkin's notes

***Canadian Mission neighbors.*

crying their wares, the sounds of dogs, pigs, hens, ducks and so on, but then there are the river sounds too--boat whistles, the call of trackers pulling native boats, the beating of the drum on the boats to signal the trackers who are pulling from shore. These sounds take me right back to the days and weeks we have spent on the river between here and Chengtu....

You will be glad to hear that Dad has now pretty well decided that he ought to go home with me at the beginning of 1945. For one thing, it costs so much to live here in China these days that we can't afford to stay on.

Liu Da Niang cried when she was getting ready to leave us in Chengtu. I felt like crying myself. She has been such a faithful helper. I am getting to like the woman here but she doesn't take the place of Liu Da Niang.

November 17, 1943 *Friends International Centre*
Chungking, China

Dear Ones at Home,

...We have just been reading a letter written by Dr. William Cadbury of Canton being repatriated on the *Gripsholm*. He mentions Elizabeth Earle on the same ship; she was caught in Manila. She crossed the Pacific with us in 1941. You see if we had not made that transfer at Manila we doubtless should have been interned all this time. Of the two, our experience at sea was on the whole much better, although I can't help but feel a wee bit envious of those who should be arriving in New York early in December in time to spend Christmas with loved ones. They deserve that joy....How happy we should be if we knew the Sewells were being repatriated! The last we heard, two of the children were said to have grown an inch or two but they were exactly the same weight as when they were in Whittier. Two years must seem an eternity in an internment camp.

Last week we had our share of excitement here. We had a very narrow escape from fire. On the river front below us the flimsily built Chinese houses got afire and soon there was a terrific conflagration. Sheets of flame fifty or more feet high shot up beside our godown and close to our east verandas. The fire swept on around to the north and soon we had the flames on two sides of us with moments when it looked as if the fire would spread to the third side. The heat was terrific and if the house had not been made of brick and stone we should most certainly have gone up in smoke. Burning brands fell on the wooden porches and the house really caught in at least six places. The third floor windows were set on fire as was the corner beam supporting the roof. For nearly two hours the men were watching and fighting to keep the fire back. Sometimes when the wind would shift and send the flames in our direction I thought we could not possibly save the place. Our room, in the corner with the fire raging on two sides, was in a most vulnerable spot. I had visions of losing everything and of having to start from scratch again. The city fire department did good work once they got started but they were slow getting the hose ready and the water coming. In the end we had to keep them out or they might have done more damage with water than the fire actually did. There are galvanized iron shutters at the windows and we managed to get most of them closed but the heat was so intense that nearly all of the windows on the north side have many cracked panes of glass. Robert watched the godown attic and had to hold the metal fire shutter closed with his hands and stamp out the sparks that fell through the tile roof. We are certainly thankful that we got through with no more damage. Some of our guests packed up their things and moved out--a sensible thing to do....

December 31, 1943 *Friends International Centre*
Chungking, China

Dear Ones at Home,

Arnold Vaught is here, spending the night, and he and Robert and I are going to a New Year's party given by H.H. Kung at the Victory House. H.H. Kung, you know, is a brother-in-law of Madame Chiang, and quite an important personage in his own right.

We now have been in Chungking three months and feel as much at home here as we ever shall. There is a certain thrill in living in a great war capital but the city has a feverish atmosphere....

Times are hardly normal in Chungking for the costs of all commodities continue to mount. Common laborers are very well off these days for wages are high. Students and teachers are helped by the government to some extent or else they could not manage to live. The sorry thing about it all is that most people are bitten by the money-making bug and apparently there is no limit to profiteering.

...Compared with other Quaker Centres in other parts of the world perhaps the beginning of the Centre here in Chungking is not significant but I do think we are slowly building up something worthwhile. We greatly miss the leadership of Harry Silcock who we had expected would take responsibility for Centre activities....

One helpful Friend is Alfred Liu who studied in the University of Chicago for several years. He is not a bit prepossessing looking, but he is a *very* helpful frequenter of the Centre. He is an electrical engineer and more than once he has given a hand in finding out why a certain electric circuit in the house didn't work and then has helped to put it right. Another helper is a sweet old Chinese gentleman who speaks excellent English and is eagerly working on the problem of developing our Centre book salesroom and reading room. He is uniting with Friends. He is from "down river" like Alfred Liu and has worked with crippled and disabled Chinese soldiers....

Goodbye, China!
1944

January 18, 1944 — *Friends International Centre*
Chungking, Free China

My Precious Ones,

...A good share of my time is taken up with running the Home, a task complicated by wartime rationing and astronomical prices. Different races and nationalities have shared in our family life--Chinese, English, Scotch, Australian, Hungarian, Czech, American, Canadian, and Indian.

Dad is off this morning buying flour. Flour and sugar particularly are rationed and you pay for these commodities in one place and then sometimes have to go miles to another place where they supposedly are available. In fact we have to go (or send) several times perhaps before we can get the flour we need. Dad likes to go himself, if he can manage it, because otherwise the servants call carriers and we have to pay them huge sums whether we get the flour or not. When Dad goes he waits to see if the flour is actually procurable before he has the carriers called....

Arnold Vaught's successor on the American Advisory Committee of the Church Committee for China Relief (what a title!), Mr. Henry, has arrived. The Vaughts will probably be getting off to the U.S.A. next month or early March. I wish we would see ahead to a definite date of *our* leaving. I am terribly interested in the job we have here, but I am longing to be with you girls again....

February 3, 1944 *Friends International Centre*
Chungking

Dear Fannie,

...In one of the letters you wrote of Frank* being in Washington state ready to be shipped out on a Flying Fortress. I keep wondering if some of the nephews may not turn up here in China. Men are certainly coming out here in great numbers. And I tremble to think what is before them, not only in the fighting line but morally. I don't think the impact of wild American youth on China is very good either....

I suppose that Dorothy will be in college somewhere--does she yet know where? We think that Margaret had perhaps better continue at Lincoln as her schooling has been so interrupted already from changing location....

We have some interesting folk here just now--an English couple, Dr. William and Claire Band, who appeared unexpectedly at our door dressed in Communist garb, drab gray cotton, padded and unshapely garments.** They got out of Peiping, or rather Yenching, which is outside the city, just five minutes before the Japanese entered the campus. They fled as they were, leaving the breakfast dishes on the table. That was December 7 (or 8), 1941. They have been treking through north China, through mountains and guerrilla country, through "occupied" territory, and have just arrived here after being on the march for over two years! They walked some one thousand miles, often finding their way under cover of darkness. In one section they walked day and night for three or four days without rest. Of course there were times when it was safe to stop and in some places they spent weeks and maybe months. On some such occasions William Band taught behind the lines in improvised schoolrooms (he had been a professor of physics at Yenching); at times they found Yenching students who also had fled from the Japanese into guerrilla (Communist) territory. Everybody thinks it rather marvelous that they got through without being taken captive at some point.

**Son of eldest brother, Arthur R. Timberlake, later shot down over Germany.*

***Our earlier feeling of horror and dread of the Communists had changed when University colleagues had given us, after visiting Yenan, glowing accounts of Communist achievements--illiterate peasants learning to read and write, to work together in cooperatives, to govern their own affairs.*

...I wish we could get home in time for Dorothy's high school graduation. In some ways the high school graduation seems the most important of all.

March 8, 1944 *Friends International Centre*
Chungking, China

Dear All,

This morning we got nine people off, eight for India and one for Fuling down the Yangtze. We have had a very full house and now a breathing spell is very welcome....With all the exodus of missionaries one would think we would come to the end soon but perhaps it will go on for some months still. The high cost of living is the chief reason for the removal of missionaries but other factors enter. Mission boards want some people to take furlough now so that they will be ready to come back at the close of the war and release other people.

We have had some interesting meetings at our Centre international discussion group sessions. Last week a Korean gentleman, whom we used to know in Chengtu, spoke on Korea's hopes and aspirations for independence. He made a good deal (somewhat bitterly) of Churchill's comment at Cairo that the allies were determined that Korea should have her independence *in due course*. He argued that she should have her independence as soon as Japan can be driven out. This week Canon Allen is going to tell us about the churches in occupied Europe and their attitude toward their Quislings and the treatment of the enemy at the close of the war.

Another job I have taken over is ''instructing'' the Czechoslovak Minister Plenipotentiary. His English is very good but he likes someone to go over his English letters to see that he has not ''written nonsense.'' He says he will occasionally bring along English speeches for correction.

April 10, 1944 *Friends International Centre*
Chungking, Free China

Dear All,

Many of the Chengtu people whom we had expected to come through here on their way to India have flown by army planes to Kunming. The Bucks, I believe, are later coming to Chungking. We hope to get Dr. Buck* (former husband of Pearl Buck) to speak to our Friday afternoon international discussion group. He is an authority on

---

**J. Lossing Buck, agricultural economist, University of Nanking.*

economic problems here in China. I am sorry to miss our other Chengtu friends but we do not seem to lack for guests. We are expecting Ronald Rees this week. He is on the National Christian Council and is just now returning from furlough. We first met him when he visited Chengtu some years ago and stayed in our home. Another interesting person, whom we *may* have here if we can squeeze him in, is Mr. Bentz, a young Swede. He does work with the Japanese and other enemy war prisoners here in China. He represents the International Y.M.C.A. War Prisoners Work Committee....

April 20, 1944 — *Friends International Centre*
Chungking, China

Dear Ones at Home,

...Last Tuesday evening while we were eating dinner I heard a rap at the door (here people usually walk right in) and when I went to the door I found Shirley Tomkinson. The postal truck on which she was travelling had met with trouble and she had to come on ahead alone. Her mother was hurt. Coming down the hills from Go Lo San with the truck going at a good rate and swinging around a bend the cab door flew open throwing Janet* out. She struck her head but was not unconscious when they picked her up. They wrapped her up in blankets and laid her flat in the bottom of the truck and came on in slowly to the city where her head was dressed at the M.E.M. Hospital. She was brought on a stretcher from there to the house. She is still suffering from severe concussion but is improving somewhat. It is these frequent accidents to bus and truck travellers that make me glad to think we shall probably not have to resort to that kind of travel in China again. Of course all this is going to delay the Tomkinsons in getting off for their furlough. But we can only be thankful that Janet was not killed outright....

June 13, 1944 — *Friends International Centre*
Chungking, Free China

Dear Folks at Home,

...Four people who started off this morning by plane to Calcutta reappeared at tea time. They were up in the air about fifteen minutes but had to come down (on a military field) because of engine trouble. They walked a long distance in the heat to get some lunch, had a long

---

**Shirley's new mother. Hilda Tomkinson had died in England while on furlough.*

truck ride of two hours back to the city, and arrived here looking decidedly fagged, hot and disappointed....

...Nearly every evening we see a couple of boats out on the river filled with men rowing frantically to the beating of a drum. They are practicing for the boat races which come at the time of the Dragon Boat Festival celebrated Chinese Fifth Month Fifth, which this year is June 25. That evening little lights are sent floating down the stream. Myriads of them make a pretty sight.

The war has not been going so well for China, but there has been great excitement (and hope) aroused by the opening of the second front in Europe. Listening over the radio here in our living room those first few nights reminded me of how the passengers on the President boat used to gather around the loud speaker for news at the outbreak of the Pacific war.

We occasionally get a bit of news of the Sewells. They are allowed to receive two brief messages per month, one from England, usually limited to immediate relatives, and one from China. Friends send in quite a few but I fear they receive only a small part of them. Still the only thing one can do is keep on trying. They say they are well. How long will it be before this ghastly business is over? We anxiously wait news from home about the nephews....

Robert writes about some special Friends.

June 16, 1944 *Chungking*

Dear Home Folks,

James G. Vail of the AFSC, Philadelphia, arrived last night, so we shall be unusually busy for the short time he is here, as we want him to see as many people as possible. Unfortunately he thinks he hasn't time to go to Chengtu. He will not get a well rounded picture of Friends work in China if he sees only the small part of it which is in Chungking. A few days ago Evelyn Mary Chen Herman who was in charge of the Receiving Home at the Shanghai Friends Centre arrived, having made her way through the lines from Shanghai into Free China. Her husband, Ted Herman, was repatriated from Shanghai on the *Gripsholm* after ten and one-half months in internment camp and may soon be on his way back to China to rejoin his wife. Evelyn Mary was very successful in managing the Receiving Home until the Japanese made it impossible for her to continue. Finally the YWCA took responsibility so that she could get away. We hope it may be possible for James Vail to meet her....

A.C.Koo, a former student* at Earlham, who has been teaching in a university across the river from Chungking, recently has been ill with tuberculosis and has been unable to continue his teaching. The Centre has been able to help him a little and now that he is so much better we hope he will be able to teach again in the autumn.

Alice Kiang, daughter of our long friend, S.C. Yang, married Dr. David Kiang and is living in Chungking. She comes occasionally to the Centre Committee meetings, but as she has two very small children she cannot come very regularly to the meetings for worship. Her older girl who is now nearly three years old was the tenth grandchild on each side of the family and was born tenth month tenth day at ten o'clock! October 10 (the "double tenth") has special significance in China because it is regarded as the birthday of the Republic.

The Friends Ambulance Unit (F.A.U.) is building a small house on one of the sites near the center of the city which Friends own, and at the end of the war this house will revert to the Friends Mission. The buildings which were on this site were totally destroyed by bombing several years ago. The Canadian Mission is negotiating for the sale of the Home in which we now are living, as the cost of living is so very high that it is difficult for missions to maintain their staffs. The Canadians have two other houses in the city which can be used somewhat as this Home is now used, though on a smaller scale, so if a sale is made this Home will be discontinued. As soon as a sale is made and subsequent arrangements complèted--and about the end of November, if a sale is not made, when our agreement with the Canadians comes to an end--the F.A.U. boys will move to their new dormitory and Margaret and I will be free to return to the U.S.A. It will almost certainly be by air as far as India.

Robert L. Simkin

June 23, 1944

Friends International Centre
Chungking, Free China

Dear Folks at Home,

One of the F.A.U. boys has just come in to report on tonight's radio news--pretty bad for China. As one thoughtful Chinese has said, this is the most serious and trying time that China has faced. Morale is low, people are war-weary, and many are seeking to get what they can for themselves out of the mess. Elsewhere in the world, affairs seem to be going well for the Allies. Folk here are greatly excited over the naval

---

**A.C. Koo also was a classmate of Margaret's.*

conflict between the American and Japanese navies in the Pacific between the Phillipines and the Marianas.

But of even greater interest locally is the visit of Vice-President Wallace in Chungking....

James Vail stayed only until Tuesday morning. His chief concern was with the F.A.U., but he also had an interest in the Centre on behalf of the Service Committee. It certainly was good to have such a person here to see things firsthand. On Monday we had a Centre Committee meeting to discuss among other things the future of this work. Evelyn Mary Chen Herman came to our meeting and was welcomed. In the evening she talked to us about conditions in Shanghai, about her work in the Receiving Home for Children, and about Friends work among the European refugees. I think Evelyn Mary has few equals anywhere. She also brought news of Bishop Ward, Imogene Sargent's father. A friend is able to take him parcels of food. He is in a hospital because he has beri-beri. The friend is not allowed to see him but the bishop can send him requisition slips telling of his needs. I have written notes of what Evelyn Mary has said to send to Imogene....

Robert tells of the congestion here.

June 26, 1944 *Chungking*

Dear Folks at Home,

For the past month we have had an almost continually full house. Many refugees from Honan and a few from Hunan have overtaxed the plane accommodation to Calcutta, and therefore it is taking longer for each party to get through Chungking. Some stay with us for a month or even more. One man, who is the leader of a party of six and who experienced many difficulties overland and by river in reaching Chungking, told me last night that he was so happy on arriving to learn that we could accommodate his party that he could hardly sleep the first night. He had been sleeping on the baggage in the open courts along the way and had hardly had a good night's rest for a week past. The best we have been able to give him and his party are beds in big rooms where four or five share the room. I suppose it is this background of Chinese inns and other inconveniences of travel which causes our guests to be very appreciative and to overlook our deficiencies.

Since I started this sentence I have been called to the telephone *three* times, each time having to go upstairs to find a guest or to learn to whom a certain piece of baggage, which has arrived in another section of the city, belongs and whether it should be unloaded there or sent on to some other place. Fortunately I was able to unearth the desired information. Very often something goes wrong with the electric iron or switches or plumbing. We are always getting SOS calls of one kind or another.

...Liao Hung-Ying, a member of our Friends Meeting in Chengtu, has been in Chungking for over a year. Formerly she taught in the W.C.U.U. She has now married Derek Bryan, a British Vice-Consul who is at present in Chengtu. They were married by Friends ceremony at the Friends College....

Robert L. Simkin

July 16, 1944

Friends International Centre
Chungking, Free China

Dear Ones at Home,

...This week I am hoping to get up to the hills across the river, where the Vaughts lived, for a few days. Harold Morrison is now living in the house, which is kept for Friends workers in the city. I mean that Harold Morrison, an architect, who is a sort of associate worker of Friends, has the house with the understanding that any Friends mission personnel in Chungking city have the privilege of going there for a holiday. At any rate he came to see us this past week and invited both Robert and me to the hills. I do wish we could go together but it is difficult for us both to be away at the same time. I am trying to persuade Robert to go up and spend at least a day and a night at the end of my visit....

July 26, 1944

Friends International Centre
Chungking

Dear Ones at Home,

Here I am back at the Centre and in the harness again after a good holiday and rest on the hills of five days. I came back last evening to find Dorothy's letters. And Dad had a special surprise for me--Margaret's photo mailed many months ago for our 1942 Christmas! Am I pleased to have it! It got a bit crushed but came through remarkably well.

Dad actually has started on our plane reservation to India.

August 6, 1944

Friends International Centre
Chungking

Dear Ones at Home,

We have a plane booking for the 28th of September, which is seven weeks away. Of course if some military officials come along and want our seats on September 28th we shall be put off, but having our names in *early* we stand a very good chance of being included in the passenger list. It looks as if we might not have to fly over "the Hump" now that Myitkyina has fallen to the Allies. We hear that India is crowded with foreigners waiting for passage home. There were some fifteen hundred Westerners, mostly missionaries, hoping to sail from Bombay in early July, but only fifteen men actually were taken on. I trust that most of these folk will be out of the way before we come along, but we shall have to be prepared for certain waits along the way.

On Monday we had a terrific storm here, a regular typhoon. I have never before experienced a typhoon although they are common on the coast of China, but the storm on Monday behaved as I have been told the great coastal storms do. The wind came with terrible force and in swirls. We could scarcely close the windows against its force and even with the windows closed the rain swept in about the cracks and crevices until on one side of the house we were almost flooded. Two windows blew out. We were busy running about trying to close up the house and then mopping up the water which poured in. The rain was running in a stream along the window ledges of my study and down onto the floor. Some beds got soaked and it was a business getting mattresses fit to sleep on. (The next day the sun was out bright and hot and it was not long before they were thoroughly dry again.) A section of our compound wall blew down, but fortunately nobody was injured. In the city as a whole there was some loss of life from falling buildings, and there was considerable property damage. Later in the week there was another big wind storm but no rain with it....

Robert writes of war and its effects.

August 15, 1944 *Chungking*

Dear Folks at Home,

This afternoon I secured a visa for us to pass through India. There is much congestion in India and it may take us a long time to secure satisfactory steamer accommodations.

We have decided to close the house to guests about September 15 which will give us the remaining two weeks to turn over the property to the Canadians and sell out the Centre effects and our personal effects before we take off.

Today I walked about six miles to buy some sugar (which I am not yet sure of getting), to arrange for getting two parcels of dental supplies from the airport (also not sure of success), and to get the visa for India, as well as to transact some other kinds of business. China has been an apt pupil of the western nations in adopting red tape procedure, and there is much passing the buck, referring the applicant to another office in a distant part of the city and (as happened today) referring back again to the same office which directed one to go to the present place. Each small official is afraid he will be rapped over the knuckles by his superior officer, so he has to play safe, whether this is the efficient way to get things done or not. (The above mentioned parcels contain dental supplies for the W.C.U.U.) Just now I was called to the radio by the report of a new allied landing on the southern coast of France. It begins to look as if Germany might capitulate before the end of 1944. We certainly hope so. We also seem to see the end of the Pacific war as a possibility within the next two years or so, possibly earlier than we at one time thought likely. However, neither of the two great wars will close without a lot of heartbreaking. We hope that this time America will have learned her lesson and see that she cannot pull out again when the peace is to be made, as she did in 1919....

Robert L. Simkin

August 23, 1944 *Friends International Centre*
Chungking, China

Dear Folks at Home,

A letter from Edith posted August 5, 1943 took a little over a year to reach us!

...On Sunday afternoon we went to the other end of the city to listen to a recorded concert of fine music. Each week such a concert is given at the rooms of the American Information Service, for the American armed forces and other guests. The F.A.U. boys frequently go out and we took the opportunity to go too, as we had another engagement in that part of the city. There must have been sixty or eighty people there, largely Chinese with a sprinkling of westerners. The music was well recorded and came out clearly through the amplifier. During the second part of the concert I sat next to a boy in uniform who said he was from Fresno, California. He has been away from home only eight months, and only in Chungking for a short while, and has spent time in India, also at Lido and Kunming. When I told him that we were going home next month he heaved a great sigh. I realized how he longed to be going home too. These boys know practically no Chinese and, of course, it is strange and difficult for them to get about or to understand what is going on.

Our other engagement was with Mrs. Herman Liu, whose husband, the president of Shanghai Baptist College, I have written about before while we were in Chengtu. Mrs. Liu is a very able woman and is active in all sorts of good enterprises. We first found her at an orphanage which she runs under the auspices of the W.C.T.U. In connection with this orphanage she has a nursery school, where mothers doing war work leave their little children all week or practically all the time. We saw the little tots eating their supper, had "tea" (bean curd milk and steamed bread and peanuts) with some of the orphans, and then saw the little ones at play. This orphanage is in an old Chinese home of the better type and is really a very lovely place with rockery, moon gate, pool with overhanging trees, and extensive buildings. Just before dark, Mrs. Liu took us to her own home where we had supper. Mrs. Liu is a member of the People's Political Council and she had some extremely valuable things to tell us of present movements in the government. I came away feeling more hopeful about China than I have for some time.

I have stopped to listen to the radio news. The announcer tells us that the French patriots have freed Paris completely. The Allies are less than two hundred miles from the German border. It does seem as if the European war could not last much longer.

September 7, 1944 *Friends International Centre*
Chungking, Free China

Dear Ones at Home,

We still have a houseful of guests. Instead of decreasing they seem to be increasing. But everybody understands that we want the house cleared by the sixteenth so we hope they all are out by then.

...The news from Europe is good, isn't it? Wouldn't it be fine if the war were over by the time we take passage from India?

Robert has something to add:

The F.A.U. boys are still with us, but their new building is nearly ready and they soon will be moving. They have a garage-workshop, across the river about two miles from the city where they service their trucks and a few of them eat and sleep. They are going to move their headquarters from a small city in Yunnan to the new premises here in Chungking. While out on the road they rough it, eating in all sorts of places and sleeping in the cab, on the baggage or on the ground under the truck, so they like to get into the city for a few days with us....

September 30,1944 *1 Upper Wood St.*
Calcutta, India

Dear Ones at Home,

After ten very busy days settling affairs and closing up at Chungking we got off by plane on the 28th as planned. Those last days in China were very hot, sticky ones, and we were almost run ragged by the mountains of work to be done, but we got through it all, somehow, finally. A number of friends, Chinese and western, were at the airfield to see us off. The plane left about six a.m., I suppose, and it was good to settle down in the comfortable seats with *nothing to do*. After the first half-hour all nervousness was gone and I had perfect confidence in the bird carrying us swiftly through the air....The terraced rice fields were a wonderful sight and one area with its vivid coloring was most remarkable. I would not have believed there could be such brilliance if I had not seen it with my own eyes--irregular patches fitted in together like a patchwork quilt--crescents, half circles, and other odd shapes--in deep raspberry red, bright brick red, greens from a pale spring green to deep blue-green, browns and yellows and grays. It was fascinating and lovely.

The trip was broken by a stop at Kunming, Yunnan, where the air was fresh and bracing. On our way once again we were intent on catching our last sight of China. We were quiet as we looked below us and then settled back into our seats. Finally Robert spoke with firm conviction and evident pride, "The world will see great things from this land and its great people."

POSTSCRIPT

At 1 Upper Wood Street in Calcutta, the F.A.U. India headquarters, we were warmly welcomed and introduced to Indian life.

We had a full month before passage from Bombay was possible, weeks we thoroughly enjoyed, delighting in the architectural wonders of the ancient Mogul Empire including the Taj Mahal, "that dream in marble." We also were happy to be with Friends like Ranjit and Doris Chet Singh in New Delhi and to visit the Friends (English) mission at Itarsi. In Bombay we were interested in the Parses and their customs.

The voyage home was on a crowded troop ship and again by a circuitous route southward around Australia into the Pacific. Avoiding the war area we saw coral reefs and islands unknown to the usual tourist.

Disembarking at Los Angeles we visited California relatives and also learned of a new interracial project which the American Friends Service Committee was promoting. We were asked to be the directors. But first we needed to see our New York and New England families and especially our children, Dorothy happy at William Penn College in Iowa (she had been drawn there upon hearing the college's dynamic president, Cecil Hinshaw) and Margaret Ruth at Lincoln School in Providence, R.I.

Returning in the spring of 1945 to Los Angeles and to Friends House, the AFSC interracial project, we thought it wise for our two girls to remain where they were to complete the school year. Since Friends House was a home for male students at the University of Southern California, Robert and I the following year established Woolman House, an interracial and international cooperative home for women students. To this home our two girls finally came, Dorothy a student at Whittier College and Margaret Ruth at a Los Angeles public high school.

And what of our Chinese friends left behind? War restrictions and the Communist control of all China in 1949 made correspondence difficult, then undesirable. We could not have our friends risk receiving letters from "hated Americans." Gradually through bits of secondhand information we learned that some teachers at our University were reduced to menial labor and that some friends like Yang Fang Lin in Chungking had been cruelly harassed. But we also learned that for many Chinese life was less bitter and much happier. We could think of Du Swen De, Stephen Yang, Robert and Anna Yang, Pu Chuen Hwa and all the others like them still using the skills and knowledge acquired at the University and helping their people. The will to serve would not be lost.